THE REMAINDER OF THEIR DAYS

ISSUES IN AGING
(VOL. 1)

GARLAND REFERENCE LIBRARY
OF SOCIAL SCIENCE
(VOL. 795)

ISSUES IN AGING

Diana K. Harris
General Editor

THE REMAINDER OF THEIR DAYS
Domestic Policy and Older Families in the United States and Canada

edited by
Jon Hendricks
and
Carolyn J. Rosenthal

GARLAND PUBLISHING, INC. • NEW YORK & LONDON
1993

Library of Congress Cataloging-in-Publication Data

The Remainder of their days : domestic policy and older families in the United
States and Canada / edited by Jon Hendricks and Carolyn J. Rosenthal.
  p. cm. — (Garland reference library of social science ; v. 795. Issues
in aging ; v. 1)
  Includes bibliographical references and index.
  ISBN 0-8153-0483-8
  1. Aged—Care—Government policy—United States. 2. Aged—Care—
Government policy—Canada. 3. Aged—Health and hygiene—Government
policy—United States. 4. Aged—Health and hygiene—Government policy—
Canada. 5. Aged—Family relationships—United States. 6. Aged—Family
relationships—Canada. I. Hendricks, Jon, 1943–   . II. Rosenthal, Carolyn
J. III. Series: Garland reference library of social science ; v. 795. IV. Series:
Garland reference library of social science. Issues in aging ; v. 1.
HV1461.R46 1993
362.6'0973—dc20   92-44317
                                                                CIP

Printed on acid-free, 250-year-life paper
Manufactured in the United States of America

SERIES EDITOR'S FOREWORD

This series attempts to address the topic of aging from a wide variety of perspectives and to make available some of the best gerontological thought and writings to researchers, professional practitioners, and students in the field as well as in other related areas. All the volumes in the series are written and/or edited by outstanding scholars and leading specialists on current issues of interest.

This present volume, co-edited by two sociologists, Jon Hendricks of the United States and Carolyn Rosenthal of Canada, focuses on a comparative, cross-national discussion of social policies of the United States and Canada, especially those related to health care. The uniqueness of this work lies in the fact that it views family experiences from both a Canadian and an American perspective. In addition, this book not only fills a gap in our knowledge of social policies, but contributes to our understanding of how these policies shape and effect the lives of older families in both countries.

Diana K. Harris
University of Tennessee

CONTENTS

ACKNOWLEDGEMENTS

Any book is the product of the efforts of a great number of people; it would be inappropriate to credit the authors or editors exclusively. To begin with, our colleagues in the Canadian Association of Gerontology and the Gerontological Society of America provided critical feedback to the twin symposia out of which this book took root. Without their input, the accompanying chapters would have been revised far less.

Each of the chapters was originally prepared in its author's office and the clerical staffs there are each deserving of recognition. The Canadian chapters were coordinated through the good efforts of Wendy Armstrong at the Centre for Studies of Aging at the University of Toronto. Carol Peck, at Oregon State University, did an extraordinary job and deserves the special thanks of all concerned as she deciphered guidelines and labored through demonstrations of iconoclasm in which authors take pride as indications of individuality. Having shouldered the Herculean task of putting the entire manuscript together she is ready to unravel the mysteries of the Sphinx or the Dead Sea Scrolls.

Family Life and the Public Sphere
Jon Hendricks and Carolyn J. Rosenthal

There can be little doubt domestic programs and policies establish the legal and social conditions under which people live. The same is true whether a person is young, old, or in between. Entitlement legislation touches our lives on a daily basis and oftentimes in ways we do not immediately recognize. For good or ill, domestic policies with their mandate-laden stipulations define the arena within which older persons live out the remainder of their days. To make sense of what happens to older people, and their families, we must consider the role played by policies formulated well beyond the purview of individuals.

While we have traditionally thought of family life as somehow set apart from the public sphere, the lives of families are in fact shaped to their very marrow by the way domestic policies are written. From prenatal health care to old age pensions, domestic policies structure the financial, physical and social well-being of families. It has only been in recent years, however, that gerontologists have openly recognized that some of the dependencies associated with old age are to a greater or lesser extent socially created (Clark, 1989).

To speak of those programs aimed at individuals in any particular cohort it is necessarily to include reference to their lives as members of families. Even for those older persons who are without one or another type of family tie, the nature of domestic programs is in many cases predicated on the presence of family members first and alternative formalized surrogates later. Legal codes, entitlement legislation, even living wills and regulations surrounding terminal care specify rights and obligations of family members.

An important orienting assumption of this volume is that distinctions between individual recipients and their families are oftentimes arbitrary but always relevant for access to resources. All too frequently, the focus in explaining the well-being of older persons revolves around the attributes of individuals *per se,* without reference to the context within which their lives unfold. It is at least partially through policy formation that structural constraints are imposed on our life worlds. The theme running throughout the contributions in this volume is that meaningful explanations must incorporate attention to the effects of domestic policies on families.

The origins of this volume stem from two symposia organized for the annual meetings of the Gerontological Society of America and the Canadian Association on Gerontology. At the time, Hendricks was chair of the Behavioral and Social Sciences Section of the Gerontological Society of America and Rosenthal was chair of the Social Sciences Division of Canadian Association on Gerontology. The objective was to juxtapose United States and Canadian domestic policies as a vehicle for understanding the situation faced by older persons and their families. Since there are fundamental policy differences between Canada and the United States, we assumed these might be reflected most obviously in their very different health care systems and their relative impact on families.

Our over-riding assumption is that a structural level perspective is necessary to understand how life worlds are created. We see considerable merit in adopting what is frequently labelled a political economic perspective. The intent of such an orientation is to tie individual experiences to macrolevel structural factors. In a nutshell: old people age the way they do in part because of the way in which material and social resources are allocated (Hendricks & Leedham, 1992). In the United States for example, the ideology of the labor market is replicated in the administration of all social welfare policies. So thoroughly has this perspective been ingrained in the way we view policy regulations that it is seldom questioned. In the chapters to follow, domestic policies are therefore discussed in terms of their political and economic underpinnings and how they circumscribe family connections. This is not to say such policies are manipulative in either their intent or their outcome, merely to assert that to understand their role in the daily lives of those who come under their sway they have to be seen as a component of the political environment. As Estes (1991) points out, a critical examination of the role of policies and services in segregating old people from the mainstream is essential if we are to understand how aging is perceived.

Passuth and Bengtson (1988) have criticized political economy models for their failure to attend to individual-level interpretation and meaning. They are correct; regardless of structural constraints, people imbue their worlds with meaning according to their own criteria. Accordingly, a subtheme of the volume is that while social structure may limit possibilities, daily lives must be seen in terms of individual intentionality. The goal is an understanding of how individual actors create the connections between individual and structural facets of their identity. We adhere to what Marshall (1987) has termed an "interpretive" perspective, building on symbolic interactionism and phenomenology, and emphasizing control and meaning. Human beings, in this view, are seen as voluntaristic, strategic actors, seeking control, constructing meanings, and exercising choice within whatever constraints are imposed by social structure. Conflict, rather than consensus, is seen as inherent in human interaction. Such a view contends that "the personal is political" (Hendricks & Leedham, 1992). While much work done within the interpretive perspective has confined itself to the microlevel of analysis, an interpretive perspective is consistent with a conflict or political economy perspective at the macrolevel (Marshall, 1987). Furthermore, the lives of families are experienced at the level of interpersonal interaction but are constrained and affected by policies that exist at a macrolevel.

The cumulative effect of this volume will be to underscore the fact that aged individuals and their families make choices, but choices informed by the society in which they live. By highlighting the linkages between domestic policy as a structural component of our lives and individual life worlds we hope the reader will come to appreciate the taken-for-granted assumptions permeating economic activity, domestic policies and politics, and what it means to grow old on either side of the North American border. One impact of the chapters to follow is that the reader will be able to evaluate the extent to which a utilitarian approach to the public good (House, 1980) characterizes Canada and the United States.

In Canada, as in the United States, the impact of health and social policy on aging families is a grossly neglected area of research or even of public discussion. In part, this may be because domestic policies are typically targeted at individuals rather than at families. That does not mean there is no effect or involvement of families, however, only that legislation is taken at face value and seldom subjected to the type of meta-analysis that would bring to the fore its ramifications for families. One of the predominant fallacies of much policy analysis is the tendency to view the rhetoric of domestic policies as insulated from family life. When it comes to the level at which life is lived, they are neither distinct nor separate spheres.

Interestingly, the situation in Canada is changing rapidly. One current concern has to do with the increased emphasis on community care and the role of the family in the new arrangements that will emerge in long-term care. It is true, Canada's high rate of institutionalization, relative to other countries, suggests that some currently institutionalized elderly Canadians may be capable of being maintained in the community. Yet the current debate over rationing such services (Clark, 1989b) comes about in part because of increasing financial constraints facing Canadians. What is not yet clear is whether adequate community supports will be put in place. As is the case in the United States, the issue turns on what the role of the family—more realistically, women in the family—should and will be. Should long-term care be a right of citizenship, in the same way that acute medical care is in Canada? Should families or women be obligated to play a role in providing care to chronically ill or disabled elderly, or should social arrangements facilitate their playing a role should they wish to do so? Long-term care policy, as it is evolving in at least one Canadian province (Ontario), assumes the involvement of families. Indeed, it seems to be predicated on increased involvement of families in all components of care for the elderly (see Chapter 6). A consensus exists in gerontological research that women are highly involved in providing care to elderly family members, yet to make this a cornerstone of policy seems ill advised on several counts. Some women are already stretched to the limit in terms of the amount of help they can provide. Some women may not be willing or able to provide care. Do Canadians want a public policy that, in effect, constrains or coerces women in their life choices and life chances and implies their roles in the world of work are less valuable than those of their male counterparts? The community care philosophy is premised on a wide range of available and affordable community services. It is difficult not to be skeptical, especially when severe budget cuts within the health care system are being made daily. What if these services are not put in place, or not extensive enough? Long-term care beds are being shut down before proper community support can be put in place. Who will be left to fill in the gaps in care?

When talking about the impact of domestic policies on families, the importance of gender is paramount. It is women who, in the great majority of cases, are caregivers to the frail elderly. And it is women, to a much greater extent than men, who experience poverty in late life. To ask them to give up their paid employment during their most productive working years is to sentence them to even greater financial hardship when they themselves become elderly. It also deprives families of second incomes at a time when two earners are necessary just for families to stay afloat or to have any discretionary income at all.

In both Canada and the United States, the language of crisis is used regularly in discussing health care costs and future directions. The aging population is continually used to explain the origins of the current crisis and, since the population is expected to age even more, to create a vision of future catastrophes unless drastic measures are taken and taken quickly. Needless to say, the debate has been vigorous. In such a climate, policies premised on families shouldering an increasing share of the responsibility for the care of the elderly can be made to seem not only reasonable but necessary. Our view is quite the reverse. In both countries families are viewed as a way to save money in national budgets. While policies having that effect may shift the burden, they will not save money.

As Clark so eloquently argues (Chapter 1), Canada and the United States are quite disparate in their approaches to domestic policy. Canada has a much more developed social welfare system provided as a right of citizenship as most strongly exemplified by its system of national health insurance. Despite the current public debate on how to control the rising costs of health care expenditures, Canada's universal health care remains one of the country's most popular domestic programs. The cost issue is equally vexing in the United States, where health care expenditures have increased in recent years even more than in Canada. In 1990 the per capita costs in the two countries worked out to be $2,566 in the United States and $1,991 in Canada. Furthermore, there is universal coverage for all Canadians while in the United States approximately one in six people cannot obtain health care because they have no insurance.

Although Canada might look positively utopian to some northward-looking Americans, the Canadian situation is not without its faults or its cutbacks. One concern has to do with the erosion of current entitlements, whether in health care, income, pensions, or other domains. Canada, like the United States, faces a situation where any erosion of existing support has the potential of increasing the responsibility that will be shifted to families.

As this book developed, we recognized that to attempt an explicit or direct comparison between the United States and Canada would pose difficulties. Doing so would only provide an opportunity for distraction as each country could serve as a red herring for the other. We opted, therefore, to ask scholars from each country to address issues they regard as important within their own country and to permit the readers to draw their own comparisons. By grouping the American papers and the Canadian papers, we hope the reader will be able to develop a sense of policy issues and their effects on families in each country. Within each "national grouping," some chapters focus primarily on the macrolevel and others on the microlevel. Within all, however, the authors heeded the mandate to provide a critical analysis of how the issues have emerged and what their effects are likely to be. The introductory chapter by Clark and the editors' conclusions, are intended to provide a context for the individual contributions and place them in a broader perspective.

As should be clear from what has been said, some of the issues we wanted to cover in this book include gender, i. e., the differential impact of public policy on women versus men; community care; long-term care; the interface between community care and institutional care; family involvement and emerging issues in the decision to terminate life. Each issue is couched in terms of its place in overall domestic policy and its consequences for the families of those who come under its sway.

Chapter 1 (Clark) frames the relevant issues on both sides of the border by drawing a broad comparison of the philosophical underpinnings of domestic policies in the two countries. Clark asserts that differences between the two countries are made readily apparent by comparing two founding documents upon which the edifice of each country has been built. In the United States the Declaration of Independence emphasizes "life, liberty and the pursuit of happiness," while in Canada the British North America Act stresses "peace, order, and good government. " These two phrases capture, in Clark's view, the contrasting domestic policy perspectives, the first underscoring personal goals and aspirations and the second a sense of community and the overall goals of society. Clark examines the facts behind "apocalyptic demography" (Robertson, 1991), arguing that policy in the United States has been shaped to a greater extent by a "culture of crisis" than has been the case in Canada. While there are fundamental differences between the two countries, Clark makes the point that in some respects what is most evident is a difference of degree. An ideology of familism, for example, enters into policy formation in both countries, but more so in the United States.

Hendricks and Hatch (Chapter 2) review the principal legislation affecting the elderly in the United States and how family involvements are circumscribed by the terms of that legislation. They utilize a political economic analysis to underscore the logic of entitlement legislation and how it reflects fundamental predispositions. From the time of the initial enabling legislation, the United States has adopted a strategy in which families play a key role either by inclusion or, in some cases, by omission. As they point out, nowhere is this pattern made more clear than in the public health acts that provide for health and long-term care of the elderly.

High and Turner (Chapter 3) consider decision-making issues at the end of life, a topic attracting increasing and often sensational media attention. The question of advanced directives has gained such currency that all fifty states have implemented laws pertaining to some kind of advanced directive. High and Turner argue that policy in the area of advance directives emphasizes independence and individualism, threatening to undermine the traditional role of families as surrogate health care decision makers for elderly relatives who can no longer make decisions for themselves. This despite the finding that the vast majority of elderly people would prefer family members to serve as surrogate health care decision makers, rather than have formal regulatory solutions.

Matthews (Chapter 4) addresses the relationship between policy and the myth that old age inevitably means disease and ill health. She argues that scholars who have tried to expose this stereotype as a myth have been unsuccessful because, at the macrolevel where most arguments are made, there is an undeniable relationship between old age and poor health. She advocates a microlevel perspective to supplement macrolevel analyses. Specifically, she examines how adult children talk about their old parents to determine how important the image of disease is to their perceptions of their parents. Matthews reminds us that policies are implemented by people and they can be changed by people. In her research, children responded to their parents as unique individuals, not in terms of biomedical stereotypes of old age. As she points out, there may be a lesson there.

In the first of the Canadian chapters McDaniel (Chapter 5) links demographic aging, family and public policy. While using Canadian demographic data primarily, the chapter's points apply more generally. McDaniel acknowledges the "inexorable pull" demography has for policy-makers and the way it is taken as an imperative. A view of "demography as destiny" leads policymakers to underestimate other aspects of human life and behavior and to sidestep explanations and solutions which do not revolve around the politics of demography. McDaniel probes the issue of family *versus* state responsibility, and discusses several myths about the family which underlie policy. At the top of her list is the myth of the

caring, extended family of the past and the myth of the family as a
"private" institution insulated from the public sphere. Neither gender nor
social class differences are included in the demographic view of aging,
much to McDaniel's chagrin.

Neysmith (Chapter 6) takes to task a sector of the Canadian health
care system that is not covered by the country's national medical care
program. She argues that the categories of services covered under the
Canada Health Act, primarily hospital costs and physician fees, are not
those that are increasingly seen as essential to promoting good health.
Neysmith examines the issue of what services old people and their families
should be guaranteed, and makes explicit the nature and consequences of
defining families as a social safety net. She avows that taking the ability of
families to provide for their elderly members for granted is foolhardy. She
also asserts that families should never be forced to substitute informal for
formal care. Of course the converse is predicated on a full range of support
services being available. Neysmith contends that care of the elderly is no
longer strictly viewed as a "private trouble" but it has not yet been
redefined as a public responsibility. She concludes that social policy in
Canada has encouraged older people to remain in the community, but the
emphasis has been on individual rather than social responsibility for
maintaining independence. She argues that there has been a shift in the
locus and nature or dependency, such that older people are now more
dependent on private sources of support. Foremost among these is informal
care by women, buttressed by familial involvements.

Rosenthal, Marshall, and Sulman (Chapter 7) focus on the formal
institutional system, examining a phenomenon that is widespread in Canada,
the United States and other industrialized countries. Specifically, their
interest is in the families of patients in acute care hospitals who have been
recommended for discharge to long-term care facilities but who remain in
acute care settings for extended periods. They examine how the way the
system is structured causes protracted hospital stays, concluding that it is
not so much a lack of policy but rather a lack of implementation of policy
that is at fault. Families experience some ill effects related to the protracted
stay of their relatives in acute care hospitals, although this may be
somewhat offset by the unhappy reality that long-term care facilities do not
necessarily live up to their mandate to provide appropriate and high quality
care. One of the interesting points to emerge from their analysis is to
remind the reader that family caregiving is not restricted to community
contexts, but also continues after older family members enter institutions.

Meslin and Sutherland (Chapter 8) provide a Canadian counterpart to the High and Turner discussion. They examine advance directives as a facet of Canadian domestic policy and their impact on older people and their families. This is one area where Canada has lagged behind the United States. As the authors point out, medical ethics and legal precedents have yet to establish guidelines. Like High and Turner, Meslin and Sutherland note that in the past families have almost always been asked to speak for patients not capable of speaking for themselves.

Finally, Rosenthal and Hendricks, as the volume's editors, summarize several of the main themes running through all the chapters. As will be evident by the time one reaches the Conclusion, Canada and the United States demonstrate considerable overlap but a marked difference in emphasis. When speaking of domestic policy and the family life of older persons, it is clear that the one has an inexorable impact on the other.

REFERENCES

Clark, P. G. (1989). The philosophical foundation of empowerment. *Journal of Aging and Health*, 1, 267-285.

———. (1989b). Canadian health-care policy and the elderly: Will rationing rhetoric become reality in an aging society? *Canadian Journal of Community Mental Health*, 8, 123-140.

Estes, C. (1991). The new political economy of aging: Introduction and critique. In M. Minkler and C. Estes (Eds.) Critical Perspectives on Aging, (pp. 19-36). Amityville, NY: Baywood Publishing Company Inc.

Hendricks, J. & Leedham, C. A. (1992). Toward a Political and Moral Economy of Aging: An Alternative Perspective. *International Journal of Health Services*, 22, 125-137.

House, E. R. (1980). *Evaluating with validity*, Beverly Hills: Sage Publications, Inc.

Marshall, V. W. (1987). Social perspectives on aging: Theoretical notes. In V. W. Marshall (Ed.) *Aging in Canada: Social perspectives*, Second Edition (pp. 39-59). Markham, Ontario: Fitzhenry and Whiteside.

Passuth, P. M. & Bengtson, V. L. (1988). Sociological theories of aging: Current perspectives and future directions. In J. E. Birren and V. L. Bengtson (Eds.) *Emergent Theories of Aging*, (pp. 333-355). New York: Springer.

Robertson, A. (1991). The politics of alzheimer's disease: A case study in apocalyptic demography. In M. Minker and C. L. Estes (Eds.) *Critical perspectives on aging: The political and moral economy of growing old*, (pp. 135-150). Amityville, NY: Baywood Publishing Company, Inc.

PART I

Domestic Policy in the United States

Public Policy in the United States and Canada: Individualism, Familial Obligation, and Collective Responsibility in the Care of the Elderly

Phillip G. Clark

INTRODUCTION

Public policy can be conceptualized as the attempt to balance competing notions of the responsibility of individuals, families, and the state in developing programs to meet human needs. A comparison of the United States and Canada as contexts for public policy development can be summarized simply by contrasting two phrases that capture the essence of how these two societies view the major ends of their "social orders": the Declaration of Independence's "life, liberty, and the pursuit of happiness" and the British North America Act's (the document that created the Canadian federation) "peace, order, and good government." In the former, the emphasis is on the individual, whose personal goals and aspirations take center stage; in the latter attention is clearly on the community and the overall goals of society. At the risk of oversimplification, these two constitutional phrases capture the essence of the differences between the two societies. However, just as in any selective comparison, we may also choose to emphasize the considerable number of dimensions along which

Canada and the United States are remarkably similar. The advantage of a cross-national comparative approach in policy analysis is its ability to bring into sharp relief the underlying forces that create the policy processes and outcomes we observe. Although these factors are in many ways very similar between the two societies, they are also extraordinarily different in other respects.

Particularly important in this comparison are families: the interface between the larger society—its history, economic and social institutions, and values and priorities—and the individual. Although neither the United States nor Canada may be said to have a specific familial policy, both societies nevertheless have an array of social and health-related policies and programs that affect both individuals and their families. More importantly, these policies and programs grow out of important perceptions, assumptions, ideologies, and values concerning the process of aging, the role of families, and the appropriate mission of government. It is precisely at the familial level of analysis that these forces become most apparent and readily subject to analysis. The exploration of these themes within the context of the aging experience brings the major policy elements into sharp relief, as the aging of individuals, families, and societies creates an unprecedented social revolution affecting all levels of a community.

To provide a structure for this discussion, it is useful to examine in more detail four particular factors that have a major bearing on the ways in which the public policy process identifies social "problems" and seeks "solutions" to them. Indeed, it is precisely in analyzing how problems are defined and subsequently addressed that we can see more clearly the central forces driving public policy deliberation and development. Following Potter (1969), these factors are: facts, loyalties, assumptions, and values. Briefly, *facts* encompass the empirical definitions of the situation or "problem"; *loyalties* include sources of commitment or identity, including ideologies; *behavioral assumptions* involve questions about human nature, about how individuals or families act under certain conditions; and *values* regard underlying sets of moral principles that give direction to our individual and collective lives. Taken together, analysis of these factors reveals the underlying moral and political economy of aging (Minkler & Estes, 1991). The definition of the policy "problem" of aging and the development of a range of "solutions" to it are heavily influenced by ideological and cultural forces differentially revealing or obscuring important underlying facts, assumptions, and values. A comparative approach can bring these factors into relief for further exploration and analysis.

"JUST THE FACTS": EMPIRICAL ANALYSES OF AGING'S EFFECTS ON SOCIETY

The public policy process is inevitably tied to numbers. Empirical data are the *sine qua non* of policy deliberation, and the advent of modern computer technology enabling the policy analyst to manage and manipulate large masses of quantifiable information has given even more power to numerical studies. Nowhere are these data more compelling than in studies of population aging, where elaborate forecasts of demographic doom are routinely issued by analysts who project age composition, dependency ratios, disability rates, and the economic impact of population structure into the future. Our obsession with numerical calculations is partly due to the perception that numbers alone will release us from making any of the difficult choices normally associated with defining and solving compelling social problems. Indeed, the numbers themselves are usually seen as sufficient justification for describing a looming social "crisis," rather than simply suggesting the potential for its existence.

A critical perspective must be taken on this increasing power of numbers to command dominance in the policy process. As Evans (1985) has suggested, however interesting future demographic projections may be, their pattern of use in the present is more revealing of their true impact. Data may simply be used to cloak an appeal for increased resources to respond to an impending "health care crisis" or to veil important facts or alternative options that should be considered by the policymaker. Numbers can be manipulated and "massaged" to generate quite different conclusions and interpretations. Even recent demographic research (Easterlin, 1991) suggests that concerns over the negative impact of population aging on rates of economic growth may have been greatly exaggerated. In short, as Potter (1969) suggests, there is no "purely quantitative" approach to significant policy issues that are free from human interpretation, bias, assumptions, and values.

In this same vein, McDaniel reminds us that "ideas, research and policy thinking about aging can never be divorced from the socioeconomic context in which the phenomenon occurs" (McDaniel, 1987:330). The emergence of population aging as a "problem paradigm," a model of shared social reality, can be traced to the interaction between researchers, policymakers, and program developers and funders. In this view, demographic change becomes the engine driving a number of emerging crises, all of which are tied in some way to the growing numbers of the elderly—not to the underlying social and economic relationships that characterize a society. This power of numbers to create the conditions under which social policies are developed and implemented is important to our understanding of the impacts which these policies have on individuals and their families. Indeed, the use of empirical studies reveals a considerable amount about the underlying social assumptions that govern relationships among the state, individuals, and families. (See the chapters by Matthews and McDaniel in this book for a further elaboration of this point). In this regard, a comparison between: the United States and Canada reveals some marked differences.

THE FOUR HORSEMEN OF APOCALYPTIC AGING IN THE UNITED STATES

        Policy analysts and observers in the United States seem positively to embrace quantitative studies as a validation of "worst case" fears and concerns about aging. This unquestioned reliance on numerical characterizations of the gerontological "population problem" is tied to the emergence of the biomedical paradigm of aging (Estes & Binney, 1991). Just as the United States has in the past reduced complex international population problems such as high fertility and rapid population growth to biomedical explanations (Clark, 1979; Warwick, 1982), so too has it now simplified complex domestic population issues to explanations relying heavily on "scientific" models of causation and explanation. Taken together, these forces have created "apocalyptic demography" as the major force driving policy considerations in the United States (Robertson, 1991). This theme has been shaped more by a "culture of crisis" than by distinct, individual governmental or academic studies over time, as will be discussed later in the case of Canada. This overall characterization of a crisis has four subdivisions, "gray riders of the geriatric apocalypse": demographic, epidemiologic, economic, and technologic.

Horseman 1: Demographic Forces. It has now become almost trite to talk about the "graying of America" in terms of absolute numbers and proportions of the elderly. Any student in an introductory gerontology course can recite the facts with equal facility: to cite a recent study (Schneider & Guralnick, 1990), "middle series projections" predict that the number of persons over age 65 will increase to 52 million by the year 2020 and to 68 million by the year 2040. By the year 2030 the elderly will constitute roughly 21 percent of the United States population. Projections of the "aged dependency ratio," i.e. the number of aged persons per working population aged 19 to 64, show similar "alarming" trends: set at 20 percent in the mid 1980s, it is expected to increase to 33 percent by the year 2025 and to 38 percent by 2050 (Etheredge, 1984). Moreover, the fastest growing population group is persons 85 and older: it is predicted that by the year 2020 there will be 7 million individuals in this group, or approximately 2.5 percent of the total population, up from roughly 1.4 percent at present (Rabin & Stockton, 1987).

Horseman 2: Epidemiological Trends. Usually cited in the same breath as the demographic "facts" are epidemiological trends, representing projections of the disease burden which the growing "hordes" of the elderly will represent. Following the concept of the "failures of success" introduced earlier by Gruenberg (1977) to explain the growing prevalence of chronic illness due to the successful conquest of acute diseases, epidemiologists point to the growing specter of a "pandemic of chronic diseases and associated disabling conditions" (Kramer, 1981:1). Although more optimistic projections of declining duration of chronic illness—the "compression of morbidity" at the end of life—have been made by Fries (1983), many analysts have suggested that there is little, if any, evidence for this trend as of yet (e.g., Meyers & Manton, 1984; Schneider & Brody, 1983). At least until more concrete indications emerge, most projections "assume the worst" with regard to the combined effects of aging and chronic disease. As Rice summarized these trends, "[T]he number of very old people is increasing rapidly; the average period of diminished vigor will probably rise; chronic diseases will probably occupy a larger proportion of our life span; and the needs for medical care in later life are likely to increase substantially" (Rice, 1986:46).

The impact of this increased burden of chronic illness will be felt most directly by the institutional long-term care system, with a recent United States General Accounting Office (1991) report projecting that costs will nearly triple in the next 27 years and then nearly triple again by the middle of the next century. In constant 1987 dollars, costs are expected to rise from $42 billion in 1988 to $120 billion in 2018 and $350 billion by 2048. The number of elderly persons using a nursing home during the course of a year is projected to increase 76 percent over the next 30 years, from roughly 2.3 million in 1988 to about 4 million in 2018. The report also suggests that shifting dependency ratios will place a greater burden on the working population in paying for these increased costs.

Horseman 3: Economic Forces. Concerns about the growing numbers of the elderly with chronic illness invariably lead to concern about the costs, especially for medical care, that this group represents. Although the elderly currently represent over 12 percent of the American population, they use roughly a third of the total United States expenditures on health care. In 1981, Medicare paid over 45 percent of the per capita health care costs of elderly persons, and in 1984 this figure reached $387 billion (Callahan, 1987). A recent study of future Medicare expenses concludes that "the projected total cost...rises impressively during the upcoming decades, nearly doubling by the year 2020....By 2040, the average age of a baby boomer will be 85 years, and the level of Medicare spending...could range from $147 to $212 billion" (Schneider & Guralnick, 1990:2337).

American anxiety over the increased health care costs associated with an aging population also finds an outlet in growing discussion of how scarce economic resources should be distributed between different age groups in our society. The emergence of concern about intergenerational competition for scarce social resources and the concept of "generational equity" has been due at least in part to perceptions of demographic "facts." For example, while well over half of the money spent by the federal government on personal health care goes for persons aged 65 and older—a group representing about 12 percent of the population—less than 10 percent is directed toward children and youth, who make up roughly a third of our country's citizens (Clark, 1985). In an influential statement about the relative economic well-being of the young and the old, Preston (1984a,b) analyzed retrospectively the demographic and economic bases for the "divergent paths" of these two population groups. For example, between 1960 and 1982 declining fertility and old age mortality simultaneously increased the proportion of elderly persons in the United States by 28.4 percent, while it reduced the under-15 population by 28 percent. During roughly this same time period, poverty among the elderly fell substantially, while it increased dramatically in children by 25 percent. Simultaneously, public spending on the elderly has increased, while programs benefitting children have been curtailed or dropped. Projecting this same theme into the future, Americans for Generational Equity (AGE) has suggested that as a society we are mortgaging our children's future by continuing a Social Security program to be financed "out of the pockets" of the next generation, our children, and kept in place by a society fearful of dismantling benefits for an elderly group increasingly not in need of them (Longman, 1985, 1987).

Horseman 4: Technology. Medical technological progress, at ever-increasing cost to the health care system, has been seen by many observers as inevitable. As a result, concerns have been raised about whether our society will be able to continue funding unlimited access to this technology. As ever more sophisticated and expensive diagnostic procedures and interventions become available to treat the causes and symptoms of chronic illness, and as more and more members of our aging society have at least one chronic illness, it is clear that the United States will be increasingly likely to be caught in a medical Malthusian dilemma: the demographic-epidemiologic demand has far outstripped the "carrying capacity" of our society to meet it. The widening gap will inevitably result in the need for explicit rationing of health care services (Evans, 1983). This projection of inevitable conflict assumes, of course, that our society continues to treat conditions with whatever technology is available that may have the likelihood of some therapeutic effect, regardless of its cost. That some American observers, such as Callahan (1987, 1990), are beginning to challenge this assumption is hardly surprising and a point having important implications for the ethical issues to be discussed later.

CANADIAN DEMOGRAPHIC FACTS: LOOKING BEYOND THE NUMBERS

The empirical study of population aging has a relatively long tradition in Canada, with a history that stretches back at least as far as the mid-1970s. In contrast to the United States, however, Canadian observers have traditionally been more skeptical and reluctant to embrace unequivocally a unidimensional quantitative approach to the "problem" of a graying population. Early studies focused on more general issues and trends dealing with a changing age structure (e.g., Auerbach & Gerber, 1976) or more specifically with concerns about its impacts on health care services (e.g., Rombout, 1975a,b). Concerns were raised from the very beginning about the "problem" of population aging, however, particularly with regard to its impact on pensions and health care services (Legare & Desjardins, 1976).

Although there were some alarmist overtones to these early studies, nevertheless almost from the very beginning they tended to downplay the "problem" of demographic aging and to avoid the more strident tones that we have seen characterized such research south of the border. For example, in their study on health care impact, Boulet and Grenier (1978) used utilization and cost data on hospital and medical care services to project the effects of an aging Canadian population to the year 2031. Although the graying of Canada would have a significant impact, the authors concluded that it would not be unmanageable in its effects on per capita growth of medical and hospital costs. Similarly, Ridler (1979) accurately characterized the perception of a growing Canadian concern with questions about the country's ability to continue supporting pension programs and health care services in the face of a graying population, but he quickly dismissed these anxieties as overstated for three reasons: (1) the proportion and absolute numbers of young Canadians would decrease, yielding savings in the costs associated with education and family allowance payments; (2) the proportion and absolute number of taxpayers could be expected to increase, offering a broader base to fund public programs; and (3) the age structure of the Canadian population was not inevitable: it was subject to conscious manipulation through economic policies affecting fertility and immigration.

What is significant in these early studies is the emerging sense that the "problems" potentially associated with an aging population are overblown and can be manipulated through appropriate governmental policies and social action. There is sufficient time to prepare for the issues which population aging pose: "crisis" is defused, and the rhetoric of "problem" is transformed into the language of a socioeconomic and political "challenge." As Evans concluded in his review of the Boulet and Grenier (1978) study: "This information is most important. It suggests that present attempts to justify major increases in health system capacity to cope with impending demographic shifts are...fallacious....Whatever drove or will drive increases, it is not population structure" (Evans, 1980:132).

This theme of skepticism toward the demographic Cassandras was carried into the decade of the 1980s. Asserting its professional stake in the health care issues posed by an aging society, in 1984 the Canadian Medical Association (CMA) released its report by the Task Force on the Allocation of Health Care Resources, "Health: A Need for Redirection" (Canadian Medical Association, 1984a). This study devoted an entire section to the health care needs of the elderly and, in particular, their impact on future health care costs. The research was based largely on a separate report, "Investigation of the Impact of Demographic Change on the Health Care System in Canada," commissioned by the CMA and written by the management consulting firm of Woods Gordon (Canadian Medical Association, 1984b). Exploring the impacts of population aging over a forty year period, the study did not answer the question of whether projected increases in health care service utilization would be economically manageable. Rather, it determined the impact of alternate forms of care; for example, of substituting less costly community-based services for institutional ones. Because the effect of such resource diversion was found to be considerable savings to the health care system, the report concluded that the overall impact of the graying of Canadian society could be greatly reduced by appropriately chosen policies. Once again, the solution to the "problem" of population aging was found in the careful and deliberate choice of governmental policies and programs, not in overreaction and crisis rhetoric.

Following a series of earlier studies (e.g., Denton & Spencer, 1975, 1979) investigating the socioeconomic impacts of a changing demographic structure, Denton, Li, and Spencer (1987) concluded that a significant proportion of elderly Canadians need not pose a crisis for two reasons. First, rising health care costs in the future will at least be partially offset by increases in gross national product. Secondly, important reductions may occur in the cost of health care services; for example, advancements in technology and the use of less expensive forms and settings of care and health care professionals could generate substantial overall savings. Similarly, a major study by Canada's Chief Statistician (Fellegi, 1988) examined trends in fertility, labor-force participation, and income and explored their impacts on dependency ratios and the future costs of health care, pensions, and educational programs. Once again, the author concluded that although population aging represents a significant challenge, more powerful than demographic forces are the kinds of social and economic policies developed by the government in response to them. Public policy approaches to promoting healthier lifestyles among the elderly, improved housing, and stronger informal support systems were all seen as sufficient measures to respond to the challenge of an aging society. In a traditional

Canadian sense, strong government emerges as more than a match for these forces of the demographic apocalypse.

That such policy choices may not be easy ones is a point made by Denton and Spencer (1988), whose major conclusion is that rather than a question of insufficient levels of social resources to support the increased impact of the elderly, population aging's greatest challenge is to deal with shifting dependency ratios. Government will have to decide whether and how to redirect social resources and public spending for education, pension, and health care programs. This point underscores the importance of making social choices and suggests that such choice depends less on numbers and data than on shared societal consensus and collective decision making—distinctive Canadian themes to be discussed later.

The culmination of this series of studies and reports seems to be the emergence, at least in the academic sector, of a healthy skepticism toward the simple use of numbers to portray impending social crises based on population aging. Attempting once more to defuse the looming "crisis" created by the perceived impact of the elderly on health care service utilization, Barer et al. (1987) distinguish simple population aging from the ways in which the health care system responds to the needs of the elderly and how these needs may be changing. Developing a political economy of aging, the authors conclude that the "problem" of the elderly has been created by vested interests who perceive a new "growth industry" in the aged and who seek to divert more resources into the health care sector. Alternatively, they suggest that government might simply be using this "crisis" as a lever to pry greater efficiency from the health care system. It is not the numbers themselves, but rather the way in which they are used, that is important. In a similar vein, Evans argues that challenges to the Canadian universal health care system based on the pressures of an aging population are factually and analytically wrong. Rather, they are simply thinly veiled professional or political agendas intended to use demographic cloaks to hide other objectives. More importantly, the author suggests that the real challenge for an aging society is how to understand health itself and to delineate the appropriate boundaries of health care services, set into a collective social decisionmaking context: "...[T]he way ahead involves the development not only of programs and policies, but of new intellectual and conceptual frameworks for thinking about health in a broader social context, and about the nature of the interrelationships and obligations among the individual, the family...and the wider society" (Evans, 1980:177). In this view, the "problem" of aging is simply a challenge to the community and the government to develop a considered response to the needs of the elderly based on a shared dialogue on the appropriate objectives of health care and how individuals, families, and the community as a whole can meet them. For example, some critics of the current Canadian health care system suggest that it is too medically oriented and should instead provide more support for long-term care services (especially community-based programs) that better serve the needs of the elderly and their families. (See the chapters by Neysmith and Rosenthal, Marshall, and Sulman for further discussion of these points.)

CONCLUSION: THE SOCIAL CONSTRUCTION OF THE "CRISIS OF AGING"

Differences in approaches between the United States and Canada with regard to the factual basis of population aging and its impact on social programs and resources suggest that the generation and use of different quantitative data are influenced by forces that are far from empirical or "objective." Indeed, how the need for data is defined and how information is collected, analyzed, and presented reveal the presence of other social, economic, political, and moral agendas. As Estes and her colleagues suggest, "[E]ach of the crises making their way into the public consciousness is socially 'produced,' or constructed by what politicians, economists, experts, and the media have to say about or impute to the issues they address" (Estes et al., 1984:92). In this regard, a comparison of the United States and Canada reveals quite different approaches to the "crisis of aging," to how the "problem" of the elderly and their impact on the public purse is defined. Kane and Kane conclude with respect to long-term care:

> The difference between the Canadian and American responses to essentially the same demographic pressures is instructive. The aging of the United States population has been looked upon as a fiscal crisis. The effectiveness of programs is measured by their ability to control

costs....[I]t appears that Canadians are more likely than we are to approach long-term care primarily as a question of how to meet the service needs of the functionally impaired. Some service is assumed to be needed for the elderly population; the issue is how to provide it decently and efficiently. Public and scientific statements in Canada are calmer than the crisis-oriented pronouncements in the United States. On both sides of the border, the projected growth of the "old-old" population is recognized; but Canadian analysts make frequent reference to offsetting reductions in the numbers of other dependent groups, especially children, when they write about the needs of the elderly over the next decades. (Kane & Kane, 1985:256)

In summary, it appears that more is at stake in defining the demographic "problem" of the elderly than simply numbers. Accordingly, we turn to an examination of the second of our four factors at work in shaping the different responses of Canada and the United States to population aging, including its familial impact. This is the element of loyalties, especially ideological factors.

LOYALTIES IN SHAPING THE SOCIAL RESPONSE TO AGING: THE IDEOLOGY OF FAMILISM

Whether expressed in "official statements" or not, loyalties are a second factor affecting the development of public policies in response to an aging population. According to Potter, they constitute "expressive symbols which represent a center of value, locus of commitment, or source of identity" (Potter, 1969:23). An ideology, for example, may represent a powerful sense of identification or a locus of loyalty, embodying certain assumptions about proper guiding principles limiting the role of government in its relationships with other social institutions, such as families. This is the case in the care of the elderly, in which ideological elements arise from considerations of the proper role of government vis-a-vis families in caring for their frail members. The dilemma of "whose responsibility is it" for providing assistance has been nicely captured by Linsk and colleagues:

> In few areas do the resources of government and the moral obligations of families conflict so much as with respect to the proper roles of family and of government in support of elderly people. Government programs are faced with increasingly distasteful choices among competing needs and objectives in serving the frailest and poorest elderly population. The dilemma is to sustain informal caregiving and simultaneously contain the use of expensive institutional care and increasingly scarce health care resources. (Linsk, Keigher, & Osterbusch, 1988:204)

How the state strikes a balance between the competing perspectives of governmental versus familial responsibility in caring for frail elderly persons becomes the important issue. In comparing the United States and Canada there emerges a difference with respect to the ideology of *familism*. Based on the assumption of the "primacy of families" in meeting the care needs of their frail members, this ideology supports non-intervention by government until the familial situation becomes so overwhelming that the state has to intervene as a last resort. "This approach has been based on the principle that family life is and should be a private matter, an area that the State should not encroach upon" (Moroney, 1986:10). Moreover, as Walker points out, by viewing this private domain of families as "natural" or "normal," the government is able to create the impression that non-intervention is justified and acceptable. This myth of the privacy of the familial domain serves the interests of the state and reinforces a conservative, traditional view of relationships and gender role expectations within families.

> ...[This] ideological construction of a particular form of individualistic western family organization...underlies all contemporary forms of organization of everyday life. This ideology and particularly its prescriptive normative beliefs concerning responsibility for the care of older relatives...are internalized by family members...Today social policies, such as community care, reflect and

reinforce the ideology of familism by assuming that the
family is necessarily the right location for the care of
older relatives and that, within it, female kin are the most
appropriate carers. (Walker, 1991:104-105).

Indeed, feminists are increasingly questioning the ideology of
familism and its role in public policy formation within the context of
women's traditional role as caregiver in aging families (e.g., Faulkner &
Micchelli, 1989; and Sheila Neysmith's chapter in the current volume).
Additionally, there appears to be a paradox in government policy, which on
the one hand sees this familial domain as beyond government intervention,
while at the same time it supports health care decisionmaking
initiatives—such as living wills and durable powers of attorney—that attempt
to undermine the involvement of families in important matters about the
provision of care at the end of life. (For a further discussion of this theme,
see the chapters by Meslin & Sutherland and High & Turner in this
volume.)

Familism in the United States: Mythology in the Service of Cost Containment

In spite of the steady stream of calls for a more family-centered
public policy in the United States (e.g., Cantor & Hirshorn, 1989; Palley
& Oktay, 1990; Smyer, 1984; Zimmerman, 1978), some of which come
from policymakers themselves (e.g., Biaggi, 1981), the United States has
steadfastly refused to develop what may be considered a coherent policy on
families or even to recognize how the changing structure of American
families will affect the functions traditionally seen as their domain. Indeed,
what familial legislation has existed is primarily within the area of family
responsibility laws, which simply reinforce traditional expectations of
government for families and may even threaten their solidarity (Callahan,
1985; Lammers & Klingman, 1986; Schorr, 1980).
    Generally United States policymakers have been reluctant to
recognize the service needs of older persons as embedded within a familial
matrix, preferring to treat them instead as individual problems conveniently
disengaged from families. Feminist commentators suggest that because

women provide the major amount of care to the frail elderly, government tends to overlook, discount, or ignore these important contributions out of a traditional myopia based on sexism and the devaluation of women's contributions to society (Faulkner & Micchelli, 1989). The ideology of familism reinforces the belief that families must "spend down" their economic, psychological, and social resources before publicly funded programs will step in to offer assistance (Kermis, Bellos, & Schmidtke, 1986). This "residual approach" suggests that formal services are justifiable only when families have used up their own resources and are on the verge of total collapse.

This residualism also serves the goal of cost containment, increasingly important in the United States as federal deficits dictate the direction of major public policy decisions. In the interest of limiting public expenditures on health care for the elderly as much as possible, familism offers a convenient justification to cloak the real reasons for withholding support. Indeed, limiting access to publicly funded long-term care programs remains a major objective of government policymakers, whose concerns center on the specter of skyrocketing demand on a shrinking resource base. The implications of this mindset have been summarized by Boise:

> [F]irst, there will be pressure to continue long-term care as a means-tested rather than as a social entitlement program. Second, budget deficit reduction will continue to drive Medicare policy. This means that criteria to ensure that the costs to the Federal government remain below costs previously borne at the federal level will continue in force. Costs to family members will receive low priority and programs to address caregivers' needs will receive minimal attention. Third, it is likely that the issue of filial responsibility will be at the forefront of the debate in the coming months as Congress seeks ways to avoid further programmatic commitments. (Boise, 1990:120)

In spite of demographic projections indicating an expanding need for services to assist caregiving families, the likely outcome for the foreseeable future will be a diminution in the commitment to familial support (Zones, Estes, & Binney, 1987). In spite of calls for a closer integration of formal and informal supportive services—to develop a "holistic model of social care" (Cantor, 1991), to increase the "caring capacity of the community" (Walker, 1987), and to develop an intergenerational family policy (Faulkner & Micchelli, 1989) or a "national caregivers policy" (Pilisuk & Parks, 1988)—it seems unlikely that the United States will respond to this challenge. All these proposals and initiatives depend fundamentally on an ideology and a set of values that run counter to the dominant forces of familism and individualism in the United States—a theme to be contrasted with greater Canadian emphasis on collectivism later in this chapter. The prevailing belief in the pre-eminence of: families in caregiving matters, emphasis on individuals rather than on families as the basic unit of service needs, self-help as an increasingly justifiable mechanism for meeting those needs, and the value of individualism as the moral basis for distrust in government programs and initiatives—all these forces conspire against a rapid and effective development of the kinds of community care policies that research indicates are badly needed. In contrast to this state of affairs, Canada offers some guidance on how familial caregiving efforts can be supported and enhanced.

Familial Caregiving and Policy in Canada: Familism Tempered (but not Replaced) by Collectivism

Recent concerns have been raised in Canada as well about families and demographic change, especially in the context of economic and cultural forces (e.g., Beaujot, 1990). This has included a specific call for the recognition by policymakers of the service needs of familial caregivers for the elderly (see Connidis, 1985, as well as the chapters by Neysmith & Rosenthal, Marshall, and Sulman in this book). The ideological forces of familism also play an historically important and currently symbolic role in Canadian public policy—as evidenced by research on filial responsibility laws (Snell, 1990)—although their power has been partially blunted by such other widely held social values as collectivism. In particular, the considerably stronger history of social welfare policies, belief in the role of government, and the guiding principle of universalism—all these create a situation rather different from the United States This point is not to suggest, however, that there are no problems with adequate governmental support for long-term (and especially community-based) care across Canada.

Historically and in general, Canada represents a significantly broader social welfare state than the United States, as evidenced in its enactment of universal health care, familial allowances, and a more extensive system of unemployment insurance (Pierson & Smith, 1991). In the area of long-term care, stronger reliance on governmentally funded services tempers the ideology of familism, particularly in the four western-most provinces of Canada—which have quite well developed long-term care systems. Kane and Kane (1985, 1991) are perhaps among the most sanguine observers of the Canadian long-term care system, in which they see government as the primary payer of services. They contrast the Canadian situation to the United States as both a difference in philosophy with respect to the role of government and a different understanding of the nature of health and disability:

> [T]he United States approach places a strong reliance on the individual's ability to meet the challenge of [long-term care] with the government playing a role only after the individual has tried and failed. The government thus becomes the last dollar payer. The Canadian philosophy is just the reverse: disability is seen as a misfortune, the burden of which should not be enhanced by poverty. Society has a responsibility to share the burden by providing support for needed services. Persons with more resources can purchase or arrange for additional care beyond that minimum but the government is the first payer. (Kane & Kane, 1991:7)

Other Canadian observers are more critical of the government's role (or lack of it) in funding long-term care services, especially home and community-based programs. Some (for example, Sheila Neysmith in this volume) decry the lack of federal support and national standard-setting for home-care services, especially while traditional incentives for institutionally based medical services remain in effect. Others (see Rosenthal, Marshall, & Sulman's chapter) suggest that there remain major problems with the coordination and funding of long-term care services in some Canadian provinces, notably Ontario, Canada's wealthiest and most populated. The political will to bring about substantial and substantive change seems to be weak or absent. This problem is apparent in the recently circulated "public consultation paper" sponsored by three different Ontario ministries, titled "Redirection of Long-Term Care and Support Services in Ontario"

(Ministries of Community and Social Services, Health, and Citizenship, Province of Ontario, 1991). In spite of reasserting the principle of service accessibility by refusing no one health and personal support services at home or in long-term care facilities due to the inability to pay, the provincial government nevertheless states that it will seek "user fees" from those who can afford to pay for community support services. In addition, residents in a home for the aged or a nursing home will be asked to pay approximately $35 per day for accommodation costs, though exceptions for some residents may have to be made. Such fees are not uniformly consistent with a strong government commitment to a universally accessible long-term care system. Importantly, though, the government of Ontario will shift some (though limited) financial resources away from the acute care sector and into the long-term care field, signalling a growing recognition at least of the need for supportive home and community care.

Thus, although Canada may be seen as less supportive of long-term care in general than it is of acute care in the medical model, there is at least growing recognition in many provinces of the critical importance of doing more to assure adequate funding for supportive services at home and in the community. The fact that there is considerable provincial variation in the level and scope of support for such services is perceived by many to be a problem. However, in contrast to the United States, the support that does exist in the most progressive provinces is substantially more complete than that typically seen south of the border.

POLICYMAKERS AND THEIR ASSUMPTIONS ABOUT HUMAN BEHAVIOR

As Potter (1969) suggests, public policies are also shaped by assumptions about the nature of the human species and how individuals and their families will act under varied conditions and circumstances. In particular, assumptions about how various policies or programs will affect human behavior to increase demand for services raises particular concern, as this has a direct effect on service costs. In the area of family-related policies, the issue of service displacement or substitution is especially important. In other words, will formally provided services, paid for by government funding, replace "free" services currently being provided by family members? The specter of substitution looms large over the thinking of policymakers in the United States and (perhaps to a somewhat lesser extent) Canada, and it bolsters the ideology of familism previously discussed. Policymakers are reluctant to "threaten" familial ties and the "traditional" role of families by providing care and services that may be seen as undermining this important responsibility.

That this is an assumption about how people behave is apparent from the research literature, which tends not to support the policymakers' fears. Considerable research has shown that families continue to be extensively involved in caregiving responsibilities even when formal services are utilized (Brody, Poulshock, & Masciocchi, 1978; Cantor, 1980; Cicirelli, 1981; Hooyman, Gonyea, & Montgomery, 1985). Moreover, substitution effects are difficult to define and measure (Doty, 1986). And as Walker points out:

> [T]he assumption that state intervention would undermine family care has little support in contemporary research, indeed there are indications that non-intervention is more likely to put caring relationships under strain. It is assumed by policymakers and service providers that state help, once offered, would inevitably be preferred (at least by those giving help). But in practice, those older people receiving services from their families are *not* anxious to apply for state help instead....[R]esearch [has] also demonstrated that seeking formal help is only the final stage of a dynamic process in which the available resources of informal assistance have all been considered, and the costs associated with them evaluated, *before* any approach is made to statutory services for assistance. (Walker, 1991:103) [Emphasis in original]

Indeed, some research on the effects of paid services on informally provided care tends to substantiate the claim that they are complementary. In a Norwegian study, Daatland concluded:

> This study suggests that in Norway, at least, the family will become to an increasing extent a resource to obtain

public home services. This does not necessarily mean that the family will withdraw from care provision. In the case of heavy care needs, home help and home nursing will only be supplements to the family's own efforts. The complementarity of public and family efforts is often overlooked by policymakers, resulting in dysfunctional suggestions that have the intention of reducing public expenditures for care and the consequence of also reducing the family's possibilities and willingness to contribute care. (Daatland, 1983:655)

Although there is some evidence for substitution effects in the United States (e.g., Greene, 1983), most analysts are quick to point out that in some cases such effects may be desirable, as in the case of respite care. The precise goals of publicly funded programs must be carefully delineated. For example, is the objective to provide only care that families themselves would not provide? Is it to delay institutionalization by supporting families' caregiving efforts so their work is continued? Or is it to relieve families of some responsibilities (such as burdensome physical caregiving) so they can specialize in others that they consider more important, such as offering emotional support?

In the United States at least, fears of substitution and displacement—as well as the "woodwork" effect (rapid rate of growth in demand for services)—play an important role in how policies are designed and implemented. As Linsk and colleagues suggest, "[c]ommunity care appears focused on government providing only what it cannot get families to do for free, which represents a more passive model than a pro-active, entitlement policy" (Linsk, Keigher, & Osterbusch, 1988:211). Driven by the ideology of familism and haunted by fears of a formal care system swamped by hordes of families abandoning their loved ones to care by the state, policymakers in the United States are extremely cautious in how quickly and how far they turn on the "spigot" of publicly funded community-based programs. In Canada as well, governments are concerned about these issues, though such anxieties about substitution and woodwork effects are arguably less dominant than in the United States A stronger ethic of community care allays some of the fears of government about paying for community- and home-based services, particularly in those provinces that have more completely developed and funded long-term care systems.

VALUE CONTRASTS IN THE CARE SYSTEM: INDIVIDUALISM VS. COLLECTIVISM

Finally, and perhaps most importantly, we must consider the fourth factor in our analysis of policy perspectives: values. Ethical principles guide our development and implementation of policies and programs, and they serve as themes that set the context for how societies structure problems and how solutions to them are sought. The task of "public ethics" (Jonsen & Butler, 1975) is to tease out these various value threads so they can be examined, debated, and perhaps even changed. Moreover, as Potter (1969) suggests, the moral dimension of public policy significantly affects the roles played by the other factors we have already discussed; in other words, it has more "leverage" to influence our perception of the facts, our loyalties, and our assumptions about human nature. In addition, to understand the foundations for the development of these values, we must adopt a moral and political economy approach, which draws attention to the underlying political, economic, and moral forces shaping public policy (Hendricks & Leedham, 1991; Minkler & Cole, 1991). As Pifer (1986) suggests, the public policy approach to aging is characterized by two sets of conflicting values: individualism and collectivism. The United States and Canada each exemplify a society in which one of these values is dominant.

"Life, Liberty, and the Pursuit of Happiness": Individualism in the United States

The central importance of individualism as a constituent value in the ideology of familism has already been discussed, but its influence in setting the policy tone and agenda in the United States is far more pervasive. The individual serves both as the unit of need and service, and as the core organizing principle around which government policy is formulated and developed. As the political economic critique of public policy makes clear, the United States tends to define problems as individual rather than as social, political, or economic—thereby "stacking the deck" against more far-reaching social reforms (Estes, 1991). The preeminence of the individual in the United States is ingrained into our "national identity" and is championed in the notion of individual rights. The preamble to the Declaration of Independence set the tone even before the country was officially founded: "life, liberty, and the pursuit of happiness" have a distinctly individualistic ring to them. From such early observers of the Republic as Tocqueville to more recent social critics as Bellah et al. (1985) and Lipset (1963, 1990), individualism has been readily apparent as *the* American quality that more than any other characteristic defines who we are and how we organize our relationships and lives.

There are profound implications of this value for how United States public policy in general and aging-related familial policy in particular is formulated. First, as already mentioned, the individual is seen as bearing the main responsibility for meeting his or her primary needs. Only when the individual fails in doing this will the government step in as a last resort to guarantee some minimal level of social assistance. Within the domain of health care, for example, services are allocated based on individual need and the ability to pay, in other words by a market-based mechanism. Individual rights have become the basic currency in most medical transactions, to the point that family and other significant persons are excluded from discussions of how to improve communication and decisionmaking involving the patient and the physician (e.g., Burt, 1979; Katz, 1984). Even in theories of social justice that could underlie an expanded health care system, a strong bias toward individualism discourages dialogue and discussion leading to a more universalistic and less market-driven system (Churchill, 1987).

At a social level, the growing perceived public policy polarization between the young and the old, "kids versus canes," in the generational equity debate further exemplifies the fragmentation and group-based nature of United States politics. Originally presented as a demographic and economic argument, the generational "war" has been correctly revealed to be an ideological struggle between competing forces over the future of the welfare state (Quadagno, 1989; Walker, 1990), the nature of social inequities (Minkler, 1991), and differing interpretations of the relationship between the state and families (Binney & Estes, 1988). Unlike other nations, the United States particularizes and compartmentalizes social policies along lines of individual or static group-based need, rather than seeing public programs as responding to changing life course needs across the entire society (Heclo, 1988; Quadagno, 1989). In this view, the United States has spawned the generational equity debate *precisely because* we do not have adequate social programs to meet the needs of families over the entire life course. In spite of calls for recognizing the inextricably related needs of families across the generations (e.g., Kingson, Hirshorn, & Cornman, 1986) and for a new intergenerational politics to forge a common agenda uniting people of all ages in expanding social welfare policies (Kingson, 1988; Wisensale, 1988), it remains unclear how successful such efforts will be. At heart, the United States remains a society based on individualism, not joint efforts uniting people of different ages, cultures, socioeconomic statuses, or political ideologies.

In summary, emphasis on individualism makes the development of more universalistic policies difficult, if not impossible. If concern is directed mainly toward the self, rather than to the welfare of others, then there is little chance that a sense of community responsibility will evolve to underwrite a significantly broadened social policy base, such as universal health insurance. Indeed, little sense of identification with the broader societal interest precludes the kind of social discussion and debate that is needed to forge a moral consensus on new social priorities, especially in the health care field. Increasing emphasis on cost-cutting measures and the blind pursuit of the "perfect" technology cannot substitute for social discussion to reach agreement on health care policies and priorities (Daniels, 1986). Even though the Community Health Decisions movement—which represents a democratic process of citizen education and involvement in health care policy matters—has gained widespread recognition, it remains to be seen whether this "pilot" phase will be translated into long-term, meaningful involvement of citizens in community discussion and decisionmaking (Jennings, 1988).

"Peace, Order, and Good Government": A Contrasting Canadian Collectivism

In contrast to the United States emphasis on "life, liberty, and the pursuit of happiness," the British North America Act that created the Canadian federation sets forth the equivalent constitutional principle of "peace, order, and good government." Canadians traditionally emphasize shared collectivist ideals, a sense of community, and respect for government. Some authors trace these principles to historical patterns, such as the lack of a revolution and the patterns of settlement in Canada (Hartz, 1955; Horowitz, 1966; Lipset, 1963, 1990; McRae, 1964), although other observers question the extent to which such events were deterministic in establishing the differences between the United States and Canada (Brym & Fox, 1989; Cook et al., 1991). Still others (e.g., Conway, 1988) assert that the Canadian sense of community is based on a different set of political and religious histories, and a much smaller separation between church and state in Canada than the United States.

Particularly in the field of health care, a universalistic policy providing equal access to all Canadian citizens is based explicitly on collectivistic principles embodying community responsibility for the welfare of all members (Taylor, 1978; Tuohy, 1986; Weller & Manga, 1983). Although some critics suggest that a major weakness of the system is its emphasis on a narrow medical model of health, nevertheless the universal medical care system is the most popular social program in Canada. This fact that has enabled it to withstand various challenges to its basic tenets—equality, collectivism, and respect for government—although current challenges (to be discussed below) have cast some doubts on the program's integrity in the future. Evans (1988) argues that the health care system, more so than other social programs, may serve as a mirror or lens through which a society's dominant value orientation may be clearly discerned. It is clear that collectivistic ideals differentiate Canada from the United States in defining the very nature of the problems in geriatric health care (Clark, 1991a) and in determining relevant dimensions of quality of life and health for older persons (Clark, 1991b). Moreover, this universalistic approach to welfare policy has short-circuited any development of generational equity rhetoric in Canada by addressing the health care needs of all persons across the entire family life cycle (Cook et al., 1991).

The implications of this collectivistic value extend beyond the structure of policies currently in place and encompass the very process of public policy formation. In Canada, debate, discussion, and disagreement on health care matters are very much a public process, with annual fee negotiations between the government and physician groups but one example. The very open debate over resource allocation on health care in Canada contrasts sharply with the only implicitly political process south of the border (Evans et al., 1989). The outcome is a clearer expression of political will to achieve meaningful programmatic objectives, not simply empty posturing and rhetoric or the consideration of yet another "demonstration project" to see what works. In Canada, an overtly public process, in which citizens are involved in very direct ways, leads to a consensus on important social values and objectives which can then be implemented in concrete policies and programs.

The strong history of a universal health care system may be threatened currently, however, by recent developments in Canada. Although issues such as rationing by queuing draw substantial public concern (see, for example, Naylor, 1991), the real crisis lies "behind the scenes" in the increasing economic pressures on the health care system. Decreasing federal contributions to the provinces for the medical care system, as carried out by the Established Program Financing (EPF) arrangements, has greatly reduced the level of federal support for a universal system and has raised the concern of an array of professional groups and associations about the future (Thomson, 1991). Cost escalation pressures on the system have led to increasing alarm by the provinces, who are caught between declining federal support and growing demands generated by new technology and patterns of service utilization (Craig, 1991). These economic pressures, combined with the current constitutional crisis affecting the very fabric of the Canadian federation, has raised questions about the continuation of the medical care system along its historically universalistic lines. One possible outcome of this situation is a set of increasingly "provincialized" systems freed from federal monies and the powerful incentives accompanying these funds, but which continue to embody the basic principles of the system as it is currently structured.

SUMMARY AND CONCLUSIONS

One implication of this United States and Canadian comparative analysis is that policy issues and debates consist of several complex and interacting forces and factors. The autonomy of the individual, the obligation of families, and the responsibility of government are all interrelated against a backdrop of social, economic, political, and moral forces. A comparative approach to understanding the different empirical, ideological, behavioral, and normative factors that together make up the ways in which societies address the multi-faceted needs of the elderly and their families is essential. As increasing attention is devoted to aging in an international context, and to its varied expression in culturally diverse societies, we must acknowledge all these issues if we are truly to understand the ways in which policy and the aging society are interrelated.

Essential to an understanding of these interrelationships is a perspective based on the moral and political economy of growing old (Minkler & Estes, 1991). For example, in spite of what governmental policymakers frequently like to think, simple quantitative studies do not permit us to understand fully the nature of a social "problem." Empirical data can be used as an instrument to advance agendas based on social ideology and embodying values rooted in historical social and political assumptions about the nature of the state, individuals, and families. Thus, the "problem" of aging is a social construct and bears the marks of all these forces. Because the person or group defining the problem has power over the range of solutions to it, such definitional control is extremely important.

Cultural values play a particularly pivotal role in influencing the interrelationships among all these factors. As Potter states:

> The elements of policy thought are systematically interrelated. If...one brings about a significant change in one sector, the entire pattern will be modified. The ethical element is a particularly potent source of change, for it largely determines the logical structure of a chain of policy argument and the weight to be assigned to the considerations deemed pertinent. (Potter, 1969:28)

In the dynamic policymaking process, values exert an influence that can shift the equilibrium in one direction or another: toward or away from an emphasis on the individual or the social context as the basis for defining or solving a social problem.

For example, the highly individualistic nature of the United States promotes an apocalyptic view of the nature of population aging: conflict between individuals and age groups against a backdrop of shrinking social resources is seen as nearly inevitable. Rationing and intergenerational warfare loom as the specters of demographic doom. Empirical data are presented in such a way as to reinforce this construction, and assumptions about the proper primacy of the traditional familial model and the secondary responsibility of the government in addressing social problems are unquestioned. Aging is transformed into an individual process, biomedically defined, and one over which social policies and programs have little or no control or responsibility. The ideology of familism is cast as an ally of cost containment, thereby sealing the fate of any suggestions that government should increase assistance to the informal care network.

In Canada, by contrast, aging tends to be a more social issue, with the government response embodying collectivist principles set forth in such policies as universal health insurance. Greater reliance on social solutions defuses the apocalyptic aura of aging, with government responding to perceived needs of individuals throughout their lives. The definition and solution to the "aging problem" is perceived within this collectivistic framework, undercutting the social polarization and "zero sum" thinking common south of the border. In spite of a social history of familism, the collectivistic value in Canada tends to deflect the dichotomous thinking of family versus government in designing long-term care systems that truly do increase the social "caring capacity" for frail elderly persons and their families. Variation among the provinces remains, however, and economic pressures and political problems stand in the way of Canada adopting national long-term care policies that are as universalistic as the medical care system has been historically.

The central importance of social values in shaping our thinking about societal problems and their solutions needs to be recognized more in the development of gerontological policies that are fair, sensitive, and just. How we respond to the challenges created by the successes we have had in maintaining and extending human life will be accurate indicators of the importance we attach to that life and its quality. Instead of seeing the elderly as a burden and a problem, as the "enemy," we must come to see them as embodying needs like any other social group. As the cartoon character, Pogo, has observed, "we have met the enemy, and he is us." The "problems" of the elderly belong to each of us as we age collectively as a society. The question for the future is: will we meet this challenge with collective resolve and political will, or with individual uncertainty and social fragmentation?

REFERENCES

Auerbach, L., & Gerber, A. (1976). *Implications of the changing age structure of the Canadian population.* Science Council of Canada Pub. No. SS21-3/2-1976. Ottawa, Ontario Ministry of Supply and Services.

Barer, M. L., Evans, R. B., Hertzman, C., & Lomas, J. (1987). Aging and health care utilization: New evidence on old fallacies. *Social Science and Medicine,* 24, 851-862.

Beaujot, R. (1990). The family and demographic change in Canada: Economic and cultural interpretations and solutions. *Journal of Comparative Family Studies,* 21, 25-38.

Bellah, R. N., Madsen, R., Sullivan, W. M., Swidler, A., & Tipton, S. M. (1985). *Habits of the heart: Individualism and commitment in American life.* Berkeley: University of California Press.

Biaggi, M. (1981). Family care of the elderly: Implications for public policy. *New England Journal of Human Services,* 1, 28-32.

Binney, E. A., & Estes, C. L. (1988). The retreat of the state and its transfer of responsibility: The intergenerational war. *International Journal of Health Services,* 18, 83-96.

Boise, L. (1990). The demise of the Catastrophic Coverage Act: A reflection of the inability of Congress to respond to changing needs of the elderly and their families. *Journal of Sociology and Social Welfare,* 17, 107-123.

Boulet, J. A., & Grenier, G. (1978). *Health expenditures in Canada and the impact of demographic changes on future government health insurance program expenditures* (Discussion Paper No. 123). Ottawa, Ontario Economic Council of Canada.

Brody, S. J., Poulshock, S. W., & Masciocchi, C. F. (1978). The family caring unit: A major consideration in the long-term support system. *The Gerontologist,* 18, 556-561.

Brym, R. J., & Fox, B. J. (1989). *From culture to power: The sociology of English Canada.* Toronto: Oxford University Press.

Burt, R. A. (1979). *Taking care of strangers: The rule of law in doctor-patient relations.* New York: Free Press.

Callahan, D. (1985). What do children owe elderly parents? *Hastings Center Report,* 15, 32-37.

_____. (1987). *Setting limits: Medical goals in an aging society*. New York: Simon and Schuster.

_____. (1990). *What kind of life*. New York: Simon and Schuster.

Canadian Medical Association. (1984a). *Health: A need for redirection* (Report of the Task Force on the Allocation of Health Care Resources). Ottawa, Ontario Author.

_____. (1984b). *Investigation of the impact of demographic change on the health care system in Canada* (Report of the Task Force on the Allocation of Health Care Resources, prepared by Woods Gordon Management Consultants). Ottawa, Ontario Author.

Cantor, M. H. (1980, November). *Caring for the frail elderly: Impact on family, friends, and neighbors*. Paper presented at the 33rd Annual Scientific Meeting of the Gerontological Society of America, San Diego, CA

_____. (1991). Family and community: Changing roles in an aging society. *The Gerontologist*, 31, 337-346.

_____, & Hirshorn, B. (1989). Intergenerational transfers within the family context: Motivating factors and their implications for caregiving. *Women and Health*, 14, 39-51.

Churchill, L. R. (1987). *Rationing health care in America: Perceptions and principles of justice*. Notre Dame, IN: University of Notre Dame Press.

Cicirelli, V. G. (1981). *Helping elderly parents: The role of adult children*. Boston: Auburn House.

Clark, P. G. (1979). *Selected moral dilemmas in population program design and implementation: Kenya and the Philippines*. Unpublished doctoral dissertation. Boston, MA: Harvard School of Public Health.

_____. (1985). The social allocation of health care resources: Ethical dilemmas in age-group competition. *The Gerontologist*, 25, 119-125.

_____. (1991a). Geriatric health care policy in the United States and Canada: A comparison of facts and values in defining the problems. *Journal of Aging Studies*, 5, 265-281.

_____. (1991b). Ethical dimensions of quality of life in aging: Autonomy vs. collectivism in the United States and Canada. *The Gerontologist*, 31, 631-639.

Connidis, I. (1985). The service needs of older people: Implications for public policy. *Canadian Journal on Aging*, 4, 3-10.

Conway, J. (1988). An "adapted organic tradition." *Daedalus: Proceedings of the American Academy of Arts and Sciences*, 117, 381-196.

Cook, F. L., Marshall, V. W., Marshall, J. G., & Kaufman, J. E. (1991, May). Intergenerational equity and the politics of income security for the old. In T. Marmor (Chair), *A North American Look at Economic Security for the Elderly*. Symposium conducted at Yale University, New Haven, CT.

Craig, L. A. (1991). *Health of nations: An international perspective on U.S. health care reform*. Washington, D. C.: The Wyatt Company.

Daatland, S. O. (1983). Use of public services for the aged and the role of the family. *The Gerontologist*, 23, 650-656.

Daniels, N. (1986). Why saying no to patients in the United States is so hard: Cost containment, justice, and provider autonomy. *New England Journal of Medicine*, 314, 1380-1383.

Denton, F. T., Li, S. N., & Spencer, B. G. (1987). How will population aging affect the future costs of maintaining health-care standards? In V. W. Marshall (Ed.), *Aging in Canada: Social perspectives*, 2nd. ed., (pp. 553-568). Markham, Ontario: Fitzhenry & Whiteside.

_____, & Spencer, B. G. (1975). Health-care costs when the population changes. *Canadian Journal of Economics*, 13, 34-48.

_____. (1979). Some economic and demographic implications of future population change. *Journal of Canadian Studies*, 14, 81-93.

_____. (1988). Population aging and the economy: Some issues in resource allocation. In J. E. Thornton & E. R. Winkler (Eds.), *Ethics and aging: The right to live, the right to die*, (pp. 98-123). Vancouver, BC: University of British Columbia Press.

Doty, P. (1986). Family care of the elderly: The role of public policy. *Milbank Memorial Fund Quarterly*, 64, 34-75.

Easterlin, R. A. (1991). The economic impact of prospective population changes in advanced industrial countries: An historical perspective. *Journal of Gerontology: Social Sciences*, 46, S299-309.

Estes, C. L. (1991). The new political economy of aging: Introduction and critique. In M. Minkler & C. L. Estes (Eds.), *Critical perspectives on aging: The political and moral economy of growing old*, (pp. 19-36). Amityville, NY: Baywood.

_____, & Binney, E. A. (1991). The biomedicalization of aging: Dangers and dilemmas. In M. Minkler & C. L. Estes (Eds.), *Critical perspectives on aging: The political and moral economy of growing old* (pp. 117-134). Amityville, NY: Baywood.

_____, Gerard, L. E., Zones, J. S., & Swan, J. H. (1984). *Political economy, health, and aging.* Boston: Little Brown.

Etheredge, L. (1984). An aging society and the federal deficit. *Milbank Memorial Fund Quarterly*, 62, 521-543.

Evans, R. G. (1980). Review of health care expenditures in Canada and the impact of demographic changes on future government health insurance program expenditures. *Canadian Public Policy*, 6, 132-133.

_____. (1985). Illusions of necessity: Evading responsibility for choice in health care. *Journal of Health Politics, Policy, and Law*, 10, 439-467.

_____. (1988). "We'll take care of it for you": Health care in the Canadian community. *Daedalus: Proceedings of the American Academy of Arts and Sciences*, 117, 155-189.

_____, Lomas, J., Barer, M., Labelle, R. J., Fooks, C., Stoddart, G. L., Anderson, G. M., Feeny, D., Gafni, A., Torrance, G. W., & Tholl, W. G. (1989). Controlling health expeditures: The Canadian reality. *New England Journal of Medicine*, 320, 571-577.

Evans, R. W. (1983). Health care technology and the inevitability of resource allocation and rationing decisions. *Journal of the American Medical Association*, 249, 2047-2052, 2208-2219.

Faulkner, A. O., & Micchelli, M. (1989). The aging, the aged, and the very old: Women the policymakers forgot. *Women and Health*, 14, 5-19.

Fellegi, I. P. (1988, October). Can we afford an aging society? *Canadian Economic Observer*, 4, 1-4, 34.

Fries, J. F. (1983). The compression of morbidity. *Milbank Memorial Fund Quarterly*, 61, 397-419.

Greene, V. L. (1983). Substitution between formally and informally provided care for the impaired elderly in the community. *Medical Care*, 21, 609-619.

Gruenberg, E. M. (1977). The failures of success. *Milbank Memorial Fund Quarterly*, 55, 3-24.

Hartz, L. (1955). *The liberal tradition in America.* Toronto: Longmans.

Heclo, H. (1988). Generational politics. In J. L. Palmer, T. Smeeding, & B. B. Torrey (Eds.), *The vulnerable*, (pp. 381-411). Washington, D. C.: The Urban Institute Press.

Hendricks, J., & Leedham, C. A. (1991). Dependency or empowerment? Toward a moral and political economy of aging. In M. Minkler & C. L. Estes (Eds.), *Critical perspectives on aging: The political and moral economy of growing old*, (pp. 51-64). Amityville, NY: Baywood.

Hooyman, N., Gonyea, J., & Montgomery, R. (1985). The impact of in-home service termination on family caregivers. *The Gerontologist*, 25, 141-145.

Horowitz, G. (1966). Conservatism, liberalism, and socialism in Canada: An interpretation. *Canadian Journal of Economic and Political Science*, 32, 143-171.

Jennings, B. (1988). A grassroots movement in bioethics. *Hastings Center Report*, 18 (Suppl.), 1-16.

Jonsen, A. R., & Butler, L. H. (1975). Public ethics and policy making. *Hastings Center Report*, 5, 19-31.

Kane, R. L., & Kane, R. A. (1985). *A will and a way: What the United States can learn from Canada about caring for the elderly*. New York: Columbia University Press.

_____, (1991, May). Long-term care in the United States and Canada: A question of wills. In T. R. Marmor (Chair), *A North American look at economic security for the elderly*. Symposium conducted at Yale University, New Haven, CT.

Katz, J. (1984). *The silent world of doctor and patient*. New York: Free Press.

Kermis, M. D., Bellos, N. S., & Schmidtke, C. R. (1986). Our parents' keepers: An analysis of values and dilemmas in home care of the frail elderly. *The Journal of Applied Gerontology*, 5, 126-138.

Kingson, E. R. (1988). Generational equity: An unexpected opportunity to broaden the politics of aging. *The Gerontologist*, 28, 765-772.

_____, Hirshorn, B. A., & Cornman, J. M. (1986). *Ties that bind: The interdependence of generations*. Washington, D. C.: Seven Locks Press.

Kramer, M. (1981, May). *The increasing prevalence of mental disorders: Implications for the future*. Paper presented at the National Conference on the Elderly Deinstitutionalized Patient in the Community, Arlington, VA.

Lammers, W. W., & Klingman, D. (1986). Family responsibility laws and state politics: Empirical patterns and policy implications. *The Journal of Applied Gerontology*, 5, 5-25.

Legare, J., & Desjardins, B. (1976). La situation des personnes agees au Canada. *Revue Canadienne de Sociologie et d'Anthropologie*, 13, 321-336.

Linsk, N. L., Keigher, S. M., & Osterbusch, S. E. (1988). States' policies regarding paid family caregiving. *The Gerontologist*, 28, 204-212.

Lipset, S. M. (1963). *The first new nation: The United States in historical and comparative perspective.* New York: Basic Books.

_____. (1990). *Continental divide: The values and institutions of the United States and Canada.* New York: Routledge, Chapman, and Hall.

Longman, P. (1985, June). Justice between generations. *The Atlantic Monthly*136, 73-81.

_____. (1987). *Born to pay: The new politics of aging in America.* Boston: Houghton Mifflin.

McDaniel, S. A. (1987). Demographic aging as a guiding paradigm in Canada's welfare state. *Canadian Public Policy*, 13, 330-336.

McRae, K. (1964). The structure of Canadian history. In L. Hartz (Ed.), *The founding of new societies*, (pp. 219-274). Toronto: Longmans.

Meyers, G. C., & Manton, K. G. (1984). Compression of mortality: Myth or reality? *The Gerontologist*, 24, 346-353.

Minkler, M. (1991). "Generational equity" and the new victim blaming. In M. Minkler & C. L. Estes (Eds.), *Critical perspectives on aging: The political and moral economy of growing old*, (pp. 67-80). Amityville, NY: Baywood.

_____, & Cole, T. R. (1991). Political and moral economy: Not such strange bedfellows. In M. Minkler & C. L. Estes (Eds.), *Critical perspectives on aging: The political and moral economy of growing old* (pp. 37-49). Amityville, NY: Baywood.

_____, & Estes, C. L. (1991). *Critical perspectives on aging: The political and moral economy of growing old.* Amityville, NY: Baywood.

Ministries of Community and Social Services, Health, and Citizenship, Province of Ontario (1991). *Redirection of long-term care and support services in Ontario.* Toronto: Queen's Printer for Ontario.

Moroney, R. M. (1986). *Shared responsibility: Families and social policy.* New York: Aldine.

Naylor, C. D. (1991). A different view of queues in Ontario. *Health Affairs*, 10, 111-128.

Palley, H. A., & Oktay, J. S. (1989). Issues in setting the agenda for a long-term care policy for the frail elderly. *Home Health Care Services Quarterly*, 10, 15-43.

Pierson, P., & Smith, M. (1991, May). Economic strain, neo-conservative governance, and welfare state retrenchment: Implications for the elderly. In T. R. Marmor (Chair), *A North American Look at Economic Security for the Elderly*. Symposium conducted at Yale University, New Haven, CT.

Pifer, A. (1986). The public policy response to population aging. *Daedalus: Proceedings of the American Academy of Arts and Sciences*, 115, 373-395.

Pilisuk, J., & Parks, S. H. (1988). Caregiving: Where families need help. *Social Work*, 33, 436-440.

Potter, R. B. (1969). *War and moral discourse*. Richmond, VA: John Knox Press.

Preston, S. H., (1984a). Children and the elderly: Divergent paths for America's dependents. *Demography*, 21, 435-457.

_____ (1984b). Children and the elderly in the United States *Scientific American*, 251, 44-49.

Quadagno, J. (1989). Generational equity and the politics of the welfare state. *Politics and Society*, 17, 353-376.

Rabin, D. L., & Stockton, P. (1987). *Long-term care for the elderly: A factbook*. New York: Oxford University Press.

Rice, D. P. (1986). The medical care system: Past trends and future projections. *New York Medical Quarterly*, 6, 39-70.

Ridler, N. B. (1979). Some economic implications of the projected age structure of Canada. *Canadian Public Policy*, 4, 533-548.

Robertson, A. (1991). The politics of Alzheimer's disease: A case study in apocalyptic demography. In M. Minkler & C. L. Estes (Eds.), *Critical perspectives on aging: The political and moral economy of growing old*, (pp. 135-150). Amityville, NY: Baywood.

Rombout, M. K. (1975a). *Hospitals and the elderly: Present and future trends*. Long Range Health Planning Staff Paper 75-2. Ottawa, Ontario Health and Welfare Canada.

_____. (1975b). *Health care institutions and Canada's elderly*. Supplement to Long Range Health Planning Staff Paper 75-2. Ottawa, Ontario Health and Welfare Canada.

Schneider, E. L., & Brody, J. A. (1983). Aging, natural death, and the compression of morbidity: Another view. *New England Journal of Medicine*, 309, 854-855.

_____, & Guralnick, J. M. (1990). The aging of America: Impact on health care costs. *Journal of the American Medical Association*, 263, 2335-2340.

Schorr, A. (1980). *"...thy father and thy mother... ": A second look at filial responsibility and family policy.* Social Security Administration Publication No. 13-11953. Washington, D. C.: U.S. Government Printing Office.

Smyer, M. A. (1984). Aging and social policy: Contrasting western Europe and the United States. *Journal of Family Issues*, 5, 239-253.

Snell, J. G. (1990). Filial responsibility laws in Canada: An historical study. *Canadian Journal on Aging*, 9, 268-277.

Taylor, M. G. (1978). *Health insurance and Canadian public policy: The seven decisions that created the Canadian health insurance system.* Montreal: McGill-Queen's University Press.

Thomson, A. (1991). *Federal support for health care: A background paper.* Ottawa: The Health Action Lobby.

Tuohy, C. (1986). Conflict and accommodation in the Canadian health care system. In R. G. Evans & G. L. Stoddart (Eds.), *Medicare at maturity: Achievements, lessons, and challenges*, (pp. 393-434). Calgary, Alberta: University of Calgary Press.

United States General Accounting Office (1991). *Long-term care: Projected needs of the aging baby boom generation.* Report No. HRD-91-86. Washington, D. C.: USGPO.

Walker, A. (1987). Enlarging the caring capacity of the community: Informal support networks and the welfare state. *International Journal of Health Services*, 17, 369-386.

_____. (1990). The economic 'burden' of ageing and the prospect of intergenerational conflict. *Ageing and Society*, 10, 377-396.

_____. (1991). The relationship between the family and the state in the care of older people. *Canadian Journal on Aging*, 10, 94-112.

Warwick, D. P. (1982). *Bitter pills: Population policies and their implementation in eight developing countries.* New York: Cambridge University Press.

Weller, G. R., & Manga, P. (1983). The development of health policy in
    Canada. In M. M. Atkinson & M. A. Chandler (Eds.). *The
    politics of Canadian public policy* (pp. 223-246). Toronto:
    University of Toronto Press.
Wisensale, S. K. (1988). Generational equity and intergenerational policies.
    The Gerontologist, 28, 773-778.
Zimmerman, S. L. (1978). Reassessing the effect of public policy on family
    functioning. *Social Casework*, 59, 451-457.
Zones, J. S., Estes, C. L., & Binney, E. A. (1987). Gender, public policy,
    and the oldest-old. *Ageing and Society*, 7, 275-302.

CHAPTER 2

Federal Policy and Family Life of Older Americans

Jon Hendricks and Laurie Russell Hatch

Family-related issues in the United States have become especially politicized in recent years. Prior to the 1991 and 1992 political whirlwind surrounding the Family and Medical Leave Act and President Bush's vetos, the most visible manifestation of the changing ideology was the Reagan administration's explicit endorsement of a single family type—the perceived traditional family structure (Pankhurst & Houseknecht, 1986). While this endorsement was clearly a direct political statement aimed at "profamily" action, many existing social policies have underlying assumptions that imply traditional notions of the family (e.g., Folbre, 1987). Values associated with the cult of domesticity (Jorgensen, 1989) underlie much social policy and hold sway today as much as at any point in the past.

Despite a seemingly fragmentary approach to service provision in the United States, a close analysis of federal health and social policies aimed at older adults highlights assumptions about the role and place of the family, and reveals the effects these policies have on not only the direct recipients, but their families as well. To examine such effects, it is important to move beyond traditional definitions of family typically used by governmental agencies and policymakers. The United States Census Bureau (1986), for example, defines as "family" those persons who are "related by birth, marriage, or adoption and residing together." For a fuller, more accurate picture of family life, we must also include extended family members, "quasi-kin," and alternative family forms including homosexual couples and heterosexual cohabitants. For all types of families, political decisions and social policies have a compelling impact. At the same time, family composition is a critical factor in determining whether economic support will be needed from sources such as Federal entitlements. Thus, not only family needs but family structure become part of the entitlement process. Our purpose in this chapter is to examine the interconnections between selected federal programs and the family structure and dynamics of older United States citizens. In particular, we are interested in exploring how Social Security, Supplemental Security Income, Medicare, and Medicaid impact the family life of older adults. Following an introductory section which provides an overview of linkages between Federal entitlements and family life, each of these programs will be discussed in terms of how they circumscribe the life worlds of older persons and their families. Because life worlds vary greatly depending upon membership in gender, marital, social class, racial and ethnic groups, it is essential to consider how older persons and families from heterogeneous backgrounds are affected by eligibility criteria and the underlying assumptions of social policies.

FAMILIES AND FEDERAL ENTITLEMENTS

Among the structural features of families that help to determine elders' need for Federal entitlements to ensure basic economic survival, the existing literature suggests that marital status and having children are paramount. At all stages of the life course, married persons are better off financially than their unmarried counterparts (Keith, 1986). There is also ample research demonstrating that being married is associated with more stable health (Bengtson, Rosenthal & Burton, 1990; Haring-Hidore et al., 1985; Zollar & Williams, 1987). Although marriage apparently exerts beneficial effects for both genders, research is needed on the effects of stable long-term relationships with same-sex companions (Lee, 1990). However, at least a few gerontologists have implied that homosexuality may facilitate adaptation to aging because gay men and lesbian women are not restricted to traditional gender roles (see Teitelman, 1987). As Teitelman notes, most gerontological research, service provision and, by extension, social policies implicitly assume that elders are exclusively heterosexual in orientation, thus neglecting a potentially powerful influence on attitudes, behavior, and lifestyle. As has occurred in some geographic locales, the federal government may face increasing pressure to recognize the existence of alternative life styles and to provide equitable treatment for those who do not fit traditional definitions.

What is sometimes called intergenerational solidarity may provide protection to elders on several key dimensions of well-being, and may, perhaps, be even more salient today than in the past (Bengtson, Rosenthal, & Burton, 1990). Though having children does not necessarily translate into a higher standard of living in later life (Keith, 1983), many studies do indicate that children are an important source of financial support (e.g., Hays, 1984; Rempel, 1985), and the absence of family involvements is clearly related to economic hardships. Those who live alone are at greatest risk for being poor (Keith, 1986). Further, although studies have shown that frequency of interaction with children does not necessarily increase elders' psychological well-being (e.g., Conner et al., 1979; Lee, 1979), it appears that well-being *is* enhanced when elders believe they see their children "frequently enough" (Ward et al., 1984).

Satisfactory social relations with family and friends may enhance physical as well as emotional health. Antonucci and Akiyama (1991) report that individuals who are socially isolated have lower immunological functions than those with more robust relationships. In addition, individuals' need for health services, their access to and use of such services, are affected by their social relationships as well as their economic resources (Antonucci & Akiyama, 1991; Herzog, 1989), which in turn are situated within a larger societal context.

In a society in which the principal value of women has traditionally been defined in terms of reproductive potential and youthful beauty, once past reproductive capacity or youthful good looks, social valuation turns harsh. But throughout life, women are at greater risk for poverty than men (Minkler & Stone, 1985). Among Americans age 65 and older, women represent fifty-nine percent of the population, but nearly seventy-two percent of those who are poor (Soldo & Agree, 1988). Family circumstances are an especially important element in women's greater risk for poverty. Due primarily to male mortality and social values, women are far less likely than men to remarry when they become widowed or divorced, and they are more likely to live alone (Soldo & Agree, 1988). Although seventy-two percent of all men aged 70 and older live with a spouse, only twenty-three percent of comparably aged women do so (Hess,

1985). These family circumstances reveal only part of the explanation for women's greater risk of being poor, however. Economic status in later life is also conditioned by lifetime work and family patterns. Such factors as discontinuous work histories, wage differentials, and the predominance of women in unpaid labor performed within the home are each implicated as significant elements in women's less favorable economic position during old age (Soldo & Agree, 1988). These and other factors (Holden, 1989) eventuate in older women's lower likelihood of receiving private pensions, and in the fact that women receive smaller pensions or Social Security benefits than men when they are eligible.

Dressel (1991) contends that income statistics buttress arguments for the "racialization" as well as for the "feminization" of poverty in later life. She cites data from Minkler and Stone (1985) to show that non-married elderly women are more likely to fall in the "near-poor" category (125 percent of the poverty level) or below the poverty line than non-married elderly men, a finding that holds across racial groups. However, unmarried African-Americans of both genders are more likely to fall below poverty than unmarried white women. Married African-Americans also are more likely to be poor than married whites. Overall, the percentage of older African-Americans who live below or very near the poverty level is roughly three times greater than among white elderly. (Aging America, 1991) Though family bonds and obligations may be based more broadly within African-American families than they are among white families (see Chatters et al., 1985; Stack, 1974), family relationships are not sufficient to overcome the economic disadvantages. Other racial and ethnic groups who are at disproportionate risk for poverty in old age—as well as earlier stages of the life course—include Mexican-Americans, Puerto Ricans, and Native Americans (AARP, 1987; Aging America, 1991).

It should come as little surprise that older women who are members of racial and ethnic minority groups are most likely to be poor. Though current cohorts of older minority women are more likely than white women to have participated in paid labor throughout their lives, they remain less likely to draw income from a private pension (Soldo & Agree, 1988), and also less likely to draw income from Social Security because the jobs these women held were less likely to be covered by Social Security or, in the case of domestic service, often were not reported even when legally required (Grambs, 1989). Higher rates of widowhood exacerbate the risk of poverty for African-American women: Among women aged 65 to 74, over half of African-American women were widows in 1983, compared to 38 percent of white women. Among women 75 years and older, 72 percent of the African-American women and 67 percent of the white women were widows (Grambs, 1989).

Thus, the heterogeneity of the older population must be stressed when considering their economic position. While it is true that the relative economic status of older Americans has risen in recent decades, with one result being that elderly households are no more likely to be classified as poor than households headed by a non-elderly individual (Holden, 1989), economic problems are still exacerbated in old age. Elders in the oldest-old categories have the lowest incomes, yet are also saddled with health care costs greater than any other adult age group (Arendell & Estes, 1991). Paradoxically, the poverty level for older persons is set lower than for the population in general, apparently based on an assumption that an individual's needs decrease with age. The formula for establishing poverty levels for the general population is based on a subsistence diet; the lower poverty level established for the elderly population assumes that their dietary needs are even lower than general subsistence levels (Margolis, 1990).

In 1991, forty-five percent of all full-time employees in the United States were not covered by any private pension plan. For these persons, Social Security and their own accumulated assets will be all the financial resources they may claim as their own upon retirement. Among those whose incomes place them in the poorest one-fifth of the population, Social Security accounts for between eighty and eighty-five percent of their annual family incomes. However, among the richest one-fifth, Social Security totals only twenty-four percent of their adjusted family income (Social Security, 1989).

It may be argued that the availability of retirement income—whether from private or public sources—exerts a positive influence on the quality of family interaction. Pension income helps to provide economic autonomy to elders who might otherwise require support from their adult children or other family members. Thus, economic independence can help promote more satisfactory emotional relationships than would be possible when interaction is shaped by the elder's need for support. Of course, resources may flow in either direction, but most conceptual models suggest that interaction will work best when a reasonably balanced exchange system exists (Cook, 1991).

But the notion of "economic independence" may be misleading when income derives from Federal entitlements. Most entitlement legislation specifies certain eligibility conditions, which are real and have clear effects on family life. For example, some Federal payments are available only to elders who do not reside with financially responsible others. Constraints on living arrangements mean also that certain kinds of family interaction are likely to be restricted. Ultimately, such legislation may work to isolate older persons in single person households who might otherwise choose to live with other family members. Other Federal entitlements require that older persons (and if married, their spouses as well) expend virtually (Hatch & Thompson, 1992) all financial resources before assistance, thus placing them at or below established poverty levels. Those very programs and policies directed at older persons to insure health and social welfare, create not only strengths for individuals and their families but dependencies as well.

SOCIAL SECURITY

Financial hardships facing the elderly were painted in bold relief during the 1930s. With the New Deal came what was arguably the first full-fledged effort to formulate real national social welfare policies. True, there were many local and state programs targeted at various problem areas—workman's compensation and mothers's pensions being excellent cases in point—but the Great Depression brought Federal legislation online for the first time (Amenta & Carruthers, 1988). This period marked the beginnings of Federal intervention in the lives of older persons, circumscribing what those receiving Social Security benefits could and could not do. Interestingly, from the time of the initial enabling legislation, wage income has been prohibited while dividends from stocks, bonds and savings have been entirely permissible.

Social Security benefits and family life are intertwined in many ways for the over 40 million people who received them as we entered the 1990s. Regulations under the Social Security "earnings test" prohibit earnings above a specified threshold between the ages of 65 and 70 if full benefits are to be retained. In 1991 that level was $10,440 with proportionate reductions up to $20,000 of earned income; after that point benefits cease until income drops or the individual reaches age 70. Those who choose to or who must work are thereby penalized while those with incomes from "unearned" sources are not. Working therefore becomes an endeavor for which penalties may be levied. Dependencies upon Social Security as well as on family members are thereby created by virtue of the way the enabling legislation is written.

Formal governmental policies are implicated as especially significant in the lives of minority elders and unmarried older women. Compared to non-Hispanic white men, women and minorities receive lower Social Security payments but are more reliant on Social Security as their primary or sole source of income. As was alluded to above, Social Security becomes increasingly important to those who have always had lower incomes by virtue of their occupations or by virtue of a lifetime's employment in peripheral occupations and in marginal labor pools (Hendricks, forthcoming). One in three unmarried older women receiving Social Security depends on it for more than 90 percent of her income (Arendell & Estes, 1991) and it is safe to say that as a rule of thumb, over eighty percent of the income for minority elderly derives exclusively from Social Security (Social Security, 1989).

Direct effects of Social Security regulations in creating dependencies within the family can easily be seen when divorce or widowhood occur. In marriages that endure less than ten years, the spouse is not assured of Social Security coverage. In most cases when death is responsible for marital disruption, the surviving spouse typically is a woman, due to gender differences in life expectancies and societal norms that promote women's marriage to men slightly older than themselves. Also, current cohorts of older women are likely to have limited and discontinuous labor force histories and therefore unlikely to have accumulated Social Security benefits deriving from their own work experience.

The "widow's gap" in Social Security benefits is a serious concern for women who have worked within the home most of their adult lives: In 1990 the Older Women's League issued a report pointing out that despite its intent to be "gender neutral," Social Security did, in fact, favor men on the basis of their continuous work histories. Displaced homemakers do not qualify for unemployment since their labors in the home were unpaid throughout their lives or they moved into and out of the paid labor force depending on family and caretaking demands. Adding to the difficulties these women face is the fact that Federal monies have been cut for employment and training programs that could be available to prepare these women to enter or re-enter the paid labor force (Arendell & Estes, 1991).

Dependencies are created in intact marriages as well. Employed wives can earn their own Social Security benefits, but because women typically earn less than men and have less continuous labor force histories, these benefits usually are lower than the husband's. To date, Federal social policy has not recognized that years spent working within the home contribute to the economic and social functioning of the larger society—and more specifically, help to maintain capitalism (e.g., Cowan, 1987; DeVault, 1987; Glazer, 1987). Homemakers care for adult family members who participate in paid labor, and also care for and socialize future generations of workers. There can be little debate that replacement costs would be significant indeed if such services were purchased in the marketplace (Vanek, 1984), yet they are not considered in the Social Security calculations for the individuals who perform them. In addition to childbearing and childrearing, many women's paid work history is interrupted—or terminated by—the health care needs of older family members (Arendell & Estes, 1991; Hatch & Thompson, 1992). Similarly, no market value is ascribed to family care of dependent elderly either. As Aronson (1985) notes, since it does not appear on any balance sheet it is viewed as being "free"—entailing no costs. But incomes forgone, Social Security credits unearned, careers curtailed are not cost free, and may in fact be that "prelude to poverty" (Finch & Groves, 1980) of which Aronson writes.

The Social Security program was established at a time when the so-called "traditional family," with one (male) breadwinner and a non-employed spouse predominated among the middle and upper classes. Though Social Security provisions continue to reflect traditional assumptions about gender roles within the family, and the meaning of "productive" versus "nonproductive" (i.e., paid vs. unpaid) labor, some changes favorable to women have been enacted in recent years. For marriages that last at least ten years, divorced spouses can now claim some portion of the beneficiary spouse's Social Security income. Further, a husband (or wife) cannot sign away dependent benefits in order to receive a higher Social Security payment during his (or her) lifetime without written approval from the other spouse (Grambs, 1989).

SUPPLEMENTAL SECURITY INCOME

Poor elderly who are ineligible for Social Security benefits, or otherwise fit eligibility criteria, can receive assistance from the Supplementary Security Income program. Established in 1974, this program provides subsistence income to persons over 65 and those who are blind or disabled, all of whom must meet stringent means tests for assets and income. As of 1991, monthly income could not exceed $407 for individuals or $610 for couples. Under the guidelines, income is defined to be not only earnings, cash, checks, but also "in-kind" items, such as food or shelter provided by others. Those with assets greater than $2000 for individuals or $3000 for couples must "spend down" in order to be eligible for the program. If an SSI recipient lives with an ineligible spouse, the spouse's income has to be taken into account when calculating eligibility. Once eligible, recipients remain below the poverty level despite receipt of benefits since Federal SSI guidelines stipulate incomes of approximately ninety percent of the poverty level and state supplements to the Federal benefits averaged only $36 per month in 1991.

The potential for SSI to circumscribe the life world of elders is obvious, since in addition to the means test, SSI recipients are penalized if they live with others or receive in-kind contributions from them. There are certain exclusions, such as the first $20 of monthly income from any source, the first $65 of earned income, one-half of any remaining income, and medical care payments made by third parties. A certain value for personal effects and cars are also excluded, as is the recipient's home and household goods. However, the cash value of life insurance policies is included, minus a $1500 exclusion. The primary point is that benefits are automatically reduced by one-third if recipients should live with anyone who provides any amount of support or maintenance. (U.S. Senate, 1991:123)

MEDICARE/MEDICAID

As a nation, the United States spent something on the order of $540 billion for health care in 1991. This figure represents approximately thirteen percent of the GNP, and will likely rise to fifteen percent by the turn of the century. While few social controversies are ever acknowledged in the debate over health care (Navarro, 1987), the impact of Federal health care policies on families, social classes, or the elderly is mentioned even less. Though the elderly, as a group, are healthier than their predecessors apparently were in the past, the share of health spending attributable to the elderly is growing larger relative to their own past history and to other age groups. In 1991, per capita costs for health care for older persons came to $5,360, for an aggregated total of $162 billion, or about one-third of the total health care spending in the United States With extensions in life expectancy and growth in the number of persons falling into the "oldest-old" category, the pressures are sure to mount—especially on the further reaches of life expectancy. It is important to note, however, that while the focus too frequently isolates specific age groups within the population, that focus masks the fact that a person's health profile derives from a lifetime's experiences. Those who become ill or incapacitated at any particular point reflect all their past experience. Claims on the health system occur at a particular point in time, but the underlying etiology has been a long time coming.

Overall, per capita health spending in the United States is somewhat less at $926 than in Canada ($1,031), but more than in Britain ($711). Yet, in both Canada and Britain, the government's share of the total health dollar is substantially greater than in the United States--40.8 percent in the United States versus 76.0 in Canada and 86.2 percent in Britain. With total health care spending in the United States running at about 13 percent of the GNP, compared to 6.2 percent in Britain and 8.5 percent in Canada, an apparently impending crisis will no doubt affect us all. The elderly are likely to be harder hit, however, since, as we have said, approximately one-third of all government expenditures are ear-marked for their health care.

In an effort to control the elderly's portion of the cost of national health care, the Federal government undertook sweeping changes in 1983 with the establishment of a prospective payment system. Medicaid and other third-party payers quickly followed suit, adopting prospective payment and

capitation guidelines. Despite widespread recognition of hardships and
inequality, nothing resembling a national health agenda has materialized to
date. Whether this picture will change in the latter 1990s is a difficult
question to answer, despite the hue and cry of those persons and their
families who find themselves driven to destitution by the burden they
encounter in the medical marketplace.

A slightly longer view may help bring the need for medical
coverage for older persons into sharper focus. Despite the many changes in
health provisions for all types of workers in the United States, the number
of two-worker families who have no health insurance of any type has risen
in the past decade. In 1987, approximately 26.5 million households
composed of married couples had both spouses employed, yet about forty-
five percent had health insurance through only one working spouse, while
another forty-two percent had coverage provided by both spouses' jobs. The
residual had no health insurance at all. That means that for thirteen percent
of these families, it took two wage earners to make ends meet, but in doing
so they were not accorded what many citizens of the United States take for
granted as a life necessity. Even worse, among the lowest income
categories, the percentage without employer-provided health insurance rose
from thirty percent in 1977 to forty percent ten years later (Shur & Taylor,
1991). It should   not be surprising that upon entering old age, the
previously uninsured may make significant demands of Medicare or
Medicaid.

Unfortunately, while attempting to control costs—giving the system
what the Special Committee on Aging of the United States Senate referred
to as a "new lean and mean look" (U.S. Senate, 1987)—the reforms have
done little to alter the picture of chronic illness. Throughout the 1980s,
administrations in Washington, D.C. advocated greater reliance on informal
care mechanisms as a way to control costs. Consequently, the burden
shifted from the governmental agencies to individuals and their families. As
the 1980s came to a close, AARP president Robert Maxwell termed the
absence of comprehensive health insurance a "national family crisis" (quoted
in *Dollars and Sense*, 1988). Not only are older persons expending their life
savings to cope with chronic illnesses, but middle-aged children are being
asked to surrender part of their own financial security to care for aged
parents. The costs of chronic illness are themselves catastrophic—for
individuals, third-party payers, and the families of those who are ill. The
average 65+ year old household in the United States faced actual cash

expenditures for health care, including insurance premiums, of some $2,670 in 1986 (out of a total of $8,340) (U.S. Senate, 1987).

As the United States continues to age as a society, monies for health care financed by the Federal government are bound to increase. In 1988, the last year for which figures are available, approximately 29.2 percent of all health expenditures in the United States came from governmental sources. Third party payments for health benefits provided by industry are also risky; the plaint heard repeatedly as United States industry tries to re-establish itself is that the onus and responsibility of health insurance are impediments to economic growth. In the mid-1980s, some seven million United States retirees receive health benefits from their former employers. Faced with rising costs, industry has taken to cutting back existing benefit agreements. Sometimes, as in the well-known case of LTV Corporation, companies have declared bankruptcy to void commitments made to labor at various points in time to provide life-long health care. Questions of how to finance retirement benefits and health insurance have traditionally been addressed by treating them as deferred wages which accrue to workers and are payable at a later date. Now, however, time has caught up and these deferred benefits must be honored. The choice often taken is to shift older workers onto public health insurance programs even while retaining them in the work force. Workers, not knowing whether this is legal or not, often do not exercise their options and thus find themselves with less coverage than they would be due. At the same time, a number of cost-conscious public figures are beginning to speak of rationing health care during times of economic crisis (Moody, 1991; Murray, 1991). There is little doubt that as the population has aged, the percentage of public resources devoted to the elderly's support has also increased. True as that may be, and as intractable as the problem may seem, it is not directly our topic here. What is instead at issue is the extent to which participation in the health benefits program has consequences for other areas of life—especially family life.

One change proposed by the administration of then President Reagan illustrates the point. Instead of beginning Medicare protection on the first day of the month in which a person turns 65, the administration proposed delaying coverage until the beginning of the following month. The outgrowth would be that either employer health insurance or individuals themselves would be responsible for expenses incurred during that one-month period. Since families provide approximately eighty percent of the care provided older persons (Horowitz, 1985), any attempt to ration health resources would only result in families—when they are available—having to assume an even greater share of the responsibility. The point becomes all the more relevant when it is recalled that when institutionalization in a nursing facility does occur, it may reflect destabilizing changes in available informal or family support as much as it does a sudden change in physical health status. At a time when families have been asked to shoulder ever more responsibility it seems ill-advised to assume that such cost-saving proposals can have any salutary effect at all.

For those on Medicare, post-retirement out-of-pocket medical expenses typically account for fifteen percent or more of their annual income. Those with lower incomes expend an even greater proportion on medical expenses. Persons beset by catastrophic illnesses face even greater expenses still. In 1990 the average cost of daily care in a nursing home amounted to well over $100.00, with annual costs totalling between $30,000 and $40,000 (U.S. Senate, 1991). Medicare is intended to provide limited coverage for acute conditions; it offers no protection against long-term conditions or the care they may necessitate. Nor does Medicare protect against high co-payments billed by physicians over and above the ceilings set by Medicare. Further, Medicare does not pay for nursing home care after the first one hundred days. If an older person remains in the nursing home, costs must be borne by the individual, the family or by private insurance until virtually all assets are expended. At this point Medicaid will become available, provided the facility is willing to accept Medicaid reimbursement. The alternative is to go without formal medical attention and to rely instead on informal care providers or seek reclassification to qualify for Medicaid. Even then, Medicaid, admittedly the single largest payer of long-term care, provides only 80-85 percent of daily charges (U. S. Senate, 1991).

In 1988, about seven million disabled older persons in the United States required some type of health-related assistance (U. S. Senate, 1991:216). As has been said, that help was supplied by family and friends for the most part. For those lucky enough to be in areas where home health care is available, the onus is somewhat lighter. Home care is far from universally available at this time, however. For some conditions, such as Alzheimer's disease, the long-term burden is extraordinary even for those families able to utilize some home health care. Yet Medicare and Medicaid insist on labelling the condition a mental illness, and thus ineligible for substantive insurance coverage.

Home health care, an alternative of choice for many elderly, has been a small and relatively stable category of outlay for Medicaid, amounting to no more than $2.9 billion annually or about 2.7 percent of the Medicaid budget (U. S. Senate, 1991). However, this type of funded care represents a confusing kaleidoscope of differing eligibilities among an array of agencies. As the United States Senate Special Committee on Aging (1991:188) reports, the Health Care Financing Administration's welter of unwritten and unpublished guidelines imposes serious constraints on the use of paid home health services. The rate of growth of utilization of services has actually slowed since 1983, while administrative denials of reimbursement requests have tripled. It is clear that public health care policy is weighted toward institution-based care in nearly all states. The outgrowth is the great majority, over three-quarters, of home health care is provided by non-governmental sources—principally family members.

The importance of family in the care of older persons is well-documented (Montgomery, Hatch, Pullum, Stull & Borgatta, 1987). As has been noted, families typically provide three-quarters of all home health care for older persons (U.S. Senate, 1991), but that statistic does not tell the full story. A closer look makes clear the primary care provider is most commonly a spouse, with children coming second in the hierarchy of care providers. Other relatives, including siblings, grandchildren, nieces, nephews and cousins provide care when a spouse or child is unavailable, but at lower levels of intensity and for shorter durations of time. Friends and neighbors are less likely than any category of family member to be primary caregivers, and then to provide support at far lower levels of intensity (e.g. Horowitz, 1985). Availability and types of caregivers will depend upon gender, marital status, sexual preference, and whether or not elders have children. In addition, caregiving hierarchies differ by race and ethnicity. In particular, friends may come to be viewed and treated as kin among African-Americans (Chatters et al, 1985), especially among those who are poor (e.g. Stack, 1974). Further, although women are more likely than men to be primary caregivers when looking at the general population (Horowitz, 1985), this gendered pattern is apparently even stronger among Latin Americans. In his study of Latinos, Henderson (1990) reported the ranked hierarchy of caregivers as 1) wife, 2) sister or other adult female "blood relative," 3) female nonkin, 4) male "blood relatives," and 5) male in-laws.

Suggestions for shifting an even greater portion of the responsibility for care of the elderly to their families—typically identified in traditional terms—will in effect shift the burden to women (e.g., Brody, 1981; Lang & Brody, 1983). Care of the sick, the very young, and the frail elderly are consequences, at least in part, of women's traditional gender roles and their longer lives. With greater numbers of women entering and remaining in the labor force, women's continuing responsibility for household tasks and family care is seen by many as becoming increasingly onerous (e.g., Cowan, 1987; DeVault, 1987; Glazer, 1987). Already critical, this issue will become even more pressing in future, when the "oldest-old" comprise a larger proportion of the population than presently. The demographics are themselves predictive of the types of issues likely to be of concern tomorrow and the day after.

Cost containment is of undeniable importance, yet shifting the load to "the family" is hardly a way to make the problem go away nor will it be without cost. Under the Reagan administration, preliminary steps were taken to develop a voucher system wherein individuals would receive a set cash amount to spend in the private medical marketplace any way they saw fit. But this too, it was argued, aimed more at cost-shifting than cost-containment. Needless to say, the plan never got off the drawing board. Yet, with each successive reform, beneficiaries and their families have been forced to shoulder an increasingly larger share of the total health bill.

Medicaid: A Safety Net?

Since 1965 Medicaid has been providing health insurance for the indigent and those who require long-term care. While government sources maintain that one-seventh of the United States population is medically indigent, that hardly tells the whole story. The eligibility criteria are clear enough, but it is not particularly revealing simply to say that recipients must be in dire circumstances. Today, Medicaid provides protection for fewer than half of all United States citizens falling below the poverty level; the remainder, as they say, fall between the cracks. Among the elderly, slightly more than one-third, 36 percent, receive Medicaid. In 1987, 23.1 million persons received Medicaid benefits from the $45 billion contributed by Federal and state governments. Interestingly that number represents some seven million fewer persons than just four years previously.

As these statistics imply, Federally sponsored health programs have been in for surgery in the political amphitheater. In order to qualify for Medicaid, an individual must have a monthly income $111 below Federally established poverty levels ($336 a month), and married couples must live on $200 less than the poverty level set for this family category ($504). In 1991, Medicaid paid 42 percent of the national long-term care bill, and 48 percent of all nursing home residents received Medicaid. Such care accounted for almost 45 percent of the total Medicaid budget and some 90 percent of the public monies spent on nursing home care. The tab for the Federal government's outlay for long-term care in 1991 came to approximately $20.6 billion or roughly 45 percent of the nation's total expenditures for long-term care. The remaining 55 percent is financed largely out-of-pocket by the elderly or their families. It remains for the individual or the family—however "family" is defined and meaningful for that individual—to bear the brunt of the costs involved. Accordingly, it has been said that long-term care may pose the single greatest threat to individuals over the age of 65 and their families (U.S. Senate, 1987). The specified requirements differ depending on family status and income, but as a rule of thumb, elderly who receive Supplemental Security Income are generally eligible for Medicaid. Under the prospective payment system of Medicare, hospitals are discharging persons back into the community or into long-term care situations "quicker and sicker" than had previously been the case. The most typical pattern is that those who return to their homes require prosthetic services from an informal network for an additional period prior to returning to a full range of activities of daily living. But ironically, under then President Reagan, payments for home health and nursing benefits were reduced by $2.4 billion below what Congress had mandated for the four years ending in 1988.

For those who are institutionalized, there are dramatic personal and family consequences. "Spend down" requirements for Medicaid have recently been rewritten so that among married couples, the non-institutionalized spouse may retain the family home plus certain other assets yielding monthly incomes up to $1500. While this in itself is undoubtedly a positive step, Medicaid provisions still impose real constraints on spousal and family financial well-being. As costs of long-term care escalate, the financial burden will become even more crushing for patients and their families. Financing care is probably not even the half of it. For every person who lives in an institution, there are twice as many living in the community who also require some type of supportive care in order to remain in the community (U.S. Senate, 1991:216).

In fact, adequate long-term care for those with chronic conditions is a distant goal at best. Estimates are that twenty percent of persons over age 65 require assistance in performing daily living functions such as bathing, eating, dressing, shopping, and so on. According to the United States Senate Special Committee on Aging (1987), three-quarters of the 4.6 million physically disabled older people in the United States received non-paid assistance to help them cope and thereby forestall institutionalization. Some of this care was provided free of charge by community health agencies, but the largest share was provided through an informal care network comprised primarily of family and friends. As the United States Senate Special Committee on Aging notes: "These figures illustrate the extent to which informal, family caregiving provide for the long-term care needs of the disabled elderly population....The majority of unpaid caregivers are women, usually wives, daughters, or daughters-in-law (1991:217)."

There is a side to the available statistics that is indeed disquieting. So significant has the problem become that in 1991 an unprecedented joint agency taskforce, comprised of representatives from the United States Department of Health and Human Services, the Administration on Aging, Health Care Financing Administration, Social Security Administration, and the National Institute on Aging, was convened to develop a comprehensive plan to address the causes of elder abuse. Further, the 1992 reauthorization of the Older Americans Act incorporated a national center on elder abuse. In a summary contribution, Johnson (1991) identified dependency, stress, absence of alternatives to care, isolation, unanticipated change as among the nine most significant risk factors implicated in elder abuse. Contrast that with Canada, where health and long-term coverage is universal and where intergenerational tension over the provision of care is not problematic as sufficient alternatives are provided. This is not to suggest no older Canadians are abused, only that when viable alternatives to family care exist, the incidence of abuse may be far lower. Actually, the documented incidence of elder abuse and neglect in Canada is said to be between two and four percent (National Advisory Council on Aging, 1991).

Then too, death rates are fifty percent higher for the poor elderly on Medicaid than for other aged persons (U.S. Senate, 1987). This most needy group makes fewer visits to physicians, about 33 percent fewer trips, receives 29 percent fewer drugs, and are 18 percent less likely to be hospitalized. Many elders in poverty either do not receive necessary medical care or rely on informal care provided by their families. Thus, current Medicaid requirements increase the need among recipients to rely on family care, a need that may be exacerbated in future. Further, to qualify for Medicaid, elders living with offspring cannot claim certain benefits, nor can

Medicaid be paid if spouses retain significant assets. These are both clear examples of how Federal policies shape the social world of family interaction, and circumscribe certain aspects of the family life of older persons.

CONCLUSIONS

Had there been no change in life expectancy over the course of the century, the context of family life for today's older persons might be far different. Years ago Hareven (1981) called for a demythologizing of our view of family relations in industrial societies. She challenged the notion that the aged were embedded in a complex caring and loving family network. Whatever the changes, the realities of old age today are changing more rapidly than the cultural norms specifying appropriate behavior, resulting in a real lag between current levels of need and available options. As Hagestad (1986) notes, there is no historical precedent for the types of interaction facing families with older members. Neither is there precedent for family interaction molded by governmental payments which stipulate types of support, living relationships and financial interdependence among older persons and their families. Whether the family life of older persons grows stronger or is sundered will depend in part on the nature of public policy decisions.

Some policymakers are calling for increased family participation in the economic and physical care of dependent elders. Such policies are based on several assumptions that are not valid for many elders today, and for even fewer tomorrow. First, these policies presuppose an unchanging and isolated gendered division of labor (Hess, 1985). Such a presupposition brings with it potential conflicts for those women who are faced with major life decisions when "choosing" between personal careers and caregiving demands. Women are more likely than men to assume a caregiving role, and to perform tasks that keep them "on call" twenty-four hours a day. In addition, female caregivers of the frail elderly are less likely to receive formal services than their male counterparts (see Abel, 1990). Hess (1985) has argued that calls for greater reliance on family care for the frail elderly assume that women *should* provide such care. She also submits that recommendations to provide renumeration for family caregiving assume that women would prefer to earn money by caring for an infirm elder than by pursuing jobs they might otherwise hold in the labor market. Further analysis of the political economy of gender and aging is needed, including the long-term implications of "the hidden gendered agenda" implicit in aging policies (Hess, 1985).

Second, these policy recommendations assume that family members—typically spouses or children—are available to elders. Due to a number of factors—personal choice, lack of availability of appropriate partners and so on—many elders are not married (59 percent of women aged 65 and over and 22 percent of men), and one in five does not have living children (AARP, 1989). The trends indicate that a larger proportion of the older population in the future will be composed of unmarried persons, due in large part to increases in divorce (Uhlenberg & Myers, 1981), and a growing proportion of older Americans will be childless (Sweet & Bumpass, 1987). Thus, for a significant proportion of older persons, the family members who are assumed to provide assistance are not available in the first place. Furthermore, even when family members are available, not all will take on a caregiving role (Montgomery & Hirshorn, 1991).

Aronson (1985) refers to the tendency to see families in terms of ephemeral idealized norms, as examples of what Eichler (1983) calls a monolithic bias, and she points out in no uncertain terms that the realities of family life are seldom uniform. The dearth of family resources available to older women in future cohorts will be offset in part by women's increased participation in the labor force, thereby providing them with greater access to Social Security and private pensions. For most older persons of both genders, however, personal resources will not be sufficient to provide for all financial and health care needs. On average, the lifetime savings of most Americans will not finance four months in a nursing home (U.S. Senate, 1991). It is time that policymakers recognize that family support—however such support is defined—will be sorely stressed when such support is required; family resources cannot expand infinitely to fill the gap between the needs and the personal resources of the older population and what the government provides.

What has to be acknowledged is that the same ideology that undergirds the social stratification of the United States is also part and parcel of the country's social policies. For good or for ill these entitlement policies circumscribe life chances, occupational involvements, socially defined identities, and the nature of family involvements for all who come under their sway (Hendricks, forthcoming). Social policies and statutes affect the texture of old age just as surely as dimensions of gender, race, ethnicity, sexual preference, income, or patterns of mortality. Neither in Canada nor in most industrialized countries, do personal or familial destitution go hand-in-hand with institutionalization and the ills of old age (Sheppard, 1990). Only in the United States does a person risk bankruptcy to secure medical care or shelter in their old age. We routinely refer to the GNP as an index for reducing current old age expenditures but we might well ask: What is wrong with the GNP? Why is GNP in the United States growing more slowly than that of other industrialized nations? The public ferment is real, no doubt about it, but it may also result from misperception. To point a finger at the families of older persons, to demand that they do more by shouldering a greater responsibility for daily care or by simply being there for older people is to either ignore some obvious realities about family life or to promulgate what may well amount to a false argument.

REFERENCES

Abel, E.K. (1990). Family care of the frail elderly. In E. K. Able & M. K. Nelson (Eds.), *Circles of care: Work and identity in women's lives.* (pp. 65-91) Albany, NY: State University of New York Press.

Aging America (1991). *Aging America: Trends and projections.* Washington, D. C.: Cooperative Publication of United States Senate Special Committee on Aging, American Association of Retired Persons, Federal Council on the Aging and United States Administration on Aging.

American Association of Retired Persons. (1987). *A Portrait of older minorities.* Washington, DC: AARP Fulfillment.

_____. (1989). *A Profile of older Americans.* Washington, DC: AARP Fulfillment.

Amenta, E. & Carruthers, B. G. (1988). The formative years of United States social spending policies: Theories of the welfare state and the American states during the great depression. *American Sociological Review* 53, 661-678.

Antonucci, T., & Akiyama, H. (1991). Social relationships and aging well. *Generations* (Winter), 39-44.

Arendell, T. & Estes, C. L. (1991). Older women in the post-Reagan era. In M. Minkler & C. L. Estes (Eds.), *Critical perspectives on aging: The political and moral economy of growing old*, (pp. 209-226). Amityville, NY: Baywood.

Aronson, J. (1985). Family care of the elderly: Underlying assumptions and their consequences. *Canadian Journal of Aging* 4, 115-125.

Bengtson, V. L., Rosenthal, C. & Burton, L. (1990). Families and aging: Diversity and heterogeneity. R. H. Binstock & George, L. K. (Eds.), In *Handbook of aging and the social sciences*. (pp. 263-287). San Diego: Academic Press.

Brody, E. M. (1981). Women in the middle and family help to older people. *The Gerontologist*, 21, 471-480.

Chatters, L. M., Taylor, R. J., & Jackson, J. S. (1985). Size and composition of the informal helper networks of elderly blacks. *Journal of Gerontology,* 40, 605-614.

Conner, K. A., Powers, E. A., & Bultena, G. L. (1979). Social interaction and life satisfaction: an empirical assessment of late-life patterns. *Journal of Gerontology*, 34, 116-21.

Cook, K. (1991). *Social Exchange Theory*. Newbury Park, CA: Sage.

Cowan, R. S. (1987). Women's work, housework, and history: The historical roots of inequality in work-force participation. In N. Gerstel & H. E. Gross (Eds.), *Families and Work*. (pp. 164-177). Philadelphia, PA: Temple University Press.

DeVault, M. L. (1987). Doing housework: Feeding and family life. In. N. Gertstel & H. E. Gross (Eds.), *Families and work.* (pp. 178-191). Philadelphia, PA: Temple University Press.

Dollars and Sense. (1988). Who cares for our elders? No. 133, 16-17.

Dressel, P. L. (1991). Gender, race and class: Beyond the feminization of poverty in later life. In M. Minkler and C. L. Estes, (Eds.), *Critical perspectives on aging: The political and moral economy of growing old* (pp. 245-252). Amityville, NY: Baywood.

Eichler, M. (1983). *Families in Canada today: Recent changes and their policy consequences.* Toronto: Gage.

Finch, J. & Groves, D. (1980). Community care and the family: A case for equal opportunities? *Journal of Social Policy*, 9, 487-514.

Folbre, N. (1987). Families and work. In N. Gerstel & H. E. Gross (Eds.), *The pauperization of motherhood: Patriarchy and public policy in the United States*. (pp. 491-511). Philadelphia, PA: Temple University Press.

Gove, W. (1972). The relationship between sex roles, mental illness, and marital status. *Social Forces*, 51, 34-44.

Glazer, N. Y. (1987). Servants to capital: Unpaid domestic labor and paid work. In N. Gerstel & H. E. Gross (Eds.), *Families and work* (pp. 236-255). Philadelphia, PA: Temple University Press.

Grambs, J. D. (1989). *Women Over Forty: Visions and Realities* (Revised Ed.). New York: Springer.

Hagestad, G. O. (1986). The aging society as a context for family life. *Daedalus*, 115, 119-139.

Hareven, T. (1981). Historical changes in the timing of family transitions: Their impact on generational relations. In R. W. Fogel, E. Hatfield, S. Keister & E. Shanas (Eds.), *Aging: Stability and change in the family*,(pp. 143-165). New York: Academic Press.

Haring-Hidore, M., Stock, W. A., Okun, M. A., & Witter, R. A. (1985). Marital status and subjective well-being: A research synthesis. *Journal of Marriage and the Family*, 47, 947-953.

Hatch, L. R. & Thompson, A. (1992). Family Responsibilities and Women's Retirement. In M. Szinovacz, Ekerdt, D., & Vinick, B. (Eds.), *Families and retirement*. (pp. 99-113). Newbury Park, CA: Sage.

Hays, J. A. (1984). Aging and family resources: Availability and proximity of kin. *The Gerontologist*, 24, 149-153.

Henderson, J. N. (1990). Alzheimer's disease in cultural context. In J. Sokolovsky (Ed.), *The cultural context of aging*, (pp. 315-330). New York: Bergin & Garvey.

Hendricks, J. (Forthcoming). Governmental responsibility: Adequacy or dependency for the aged. In S. Ingman & D. Gill (Eds.), *Distributive justice and geriatric care*, Albany: SUNY University Press.

Herzog, A. R. (1989). Physical and mental health in older women: Selected research issues and data sources. In A. R. Herzog, K.C. Holden & M. M. Seltzer (Eds.), *Health & economic status of older women*, (pp. 35-91). Amityville, NY: Baywood.

Hess, B. B. (1985). Aging policies and old women: The hidden agenda. In A. S. Rossi (Ed.) *Gender and the life course.* (pp. 319-331). New York: Aldine.

Holden, K. C. (1989). Economic status of older women: A summary of selected research issues. In A. R. Herzog, K. C. Holden & M. M. Seltzer (Eds.) *Health and economic status of older women.* (pp. 92-130). Amityville, NY: Baywood.

Horowitz, A. (1985). Family caregiving to the frail elderly. In M. P. Lawton & G. L. Maddox (Eds.), *Annual review of gerontology and geriatrics.* (pp. 194-246). New York: Springer.

Johnson, T. J. (1991). *Elder mistreatment: Deciding who is at risk.* Westport, CT: Greenwood Press.

Jorgensen, L. A. B. (1989). Women and aging: Perspectives on public and social policy. In J. D. Garner & S. O. Mercer (Eds.) *Women as they age* (pp. 291-315). New York: Haworth Press.

Keith, P. M. (1983). A comparison of the resources of parents and childless men and women in very old age. *Family Relations*, 32, 403-409.

_____. (1986). The social context and resources of the unmarried in old age. *International journal of aging and human development*, 23, 81-96.

Lang, A. M. & Brody, E. M. (1983). Characteristics of middle-aged daughters and help to their elderly mothers. *Journal of Marriage and the Family*, 45, 193-202.

Lee, G. R. (1979). Children and the Elderly: Interaction and morale. *Research on Aging*, 1, 335-360.

Lee, J. A. (1990). Foreword. *Journal of Homosexuality*, 20, xiii-xix.

Margolis, R. J. (1990). *Risking old age in America.* Boulder: Westview.

Minkler, M. & Stone, R. (1985). "The feminization of poverty and older women." *The Gerontologist*, 25, 351-357.

Montgomery, Rhonda J. V., Hatch, L. R., Pullum, T., Stull, D. E., & Borgatta, E. F. (1987). Dependency, family extension, and long-term care policy. In E. F. Borgatta, & Montgomery, R. J. V, (Eds.), *Critical issues in aging policy: Linking research and values.* (pp. 162-177). Newbury Park, CA: Sage.

_____, & Hishorn, B. A. (1991). Current and future family help with long-term care needs of the elderly. *Research on Aging*, 13, 171-204.

Moody, H. R. (1991). Allocation, yes; age-based rationing, no. In R. H. Binstock & S. G. Post, (Eds.), *Too old for health care? Controversies in medicine, law, economics and ethics.* (pp. 180-203). Baltimore: Johns Hopkins.

Murray, T. H. (1991). Meaning, aging and public policy. In R. H. Binstock & S. G. Post, (Eds.) *Too old for health care? Controversies in medicine, law economics and ethics.* (pp. 164-179). Baltimore: Johns Hopkins.

National Advisory Council on Aging (1991). *Elder abuse: Major issues from a national perspective.* Ottawa Government of Canada, Minister of Supply and Service, (#71-2/3-2-1991).

Navarro, V. (1987). Federal Health Policies in the United States. *Milbank Memorial Fund Quarterly,* 65, 81-111.

Pankhurst, J. G. & Houseknech, S. K. (1986). The family, politics, and religion in the 1980s: In fear of the new individualism. In A. S. Skolnick & J. H. Skolnick (Eds.), *Family in transition,* (pp. 576-598). Boston, MA: Little, Brown.

Rempel, J. (1985). Childless elderly: What are they missing?" *Journal of Marriage and the Family,* 47, 343-348.

Sheppard, H. L. (1990). We have met the elderly and they are us. *New York Times Book Review,.* January 21, 1990, 36-37.

Shur, C. L. & Taylor, A. K. (1991). Choice of health insurance and the two-worker household. *Health Affairs,* 10, 155-163.

Social Security. (1989). Income and assets of social security beneficiaries by type of benefit. *Social Security Bulletin* 52, 6.

Soldo, B. J. & Agree, E. M. (1988). America's elderly. *Population Bulletin,* 43, Special Issue.

Stack, C. (1974). *All our kin: Strategies for survival in a black community.* New York: Harper and Row.

Sweet, J. A. & Bumpass, L. L. (1987). *American households and families.* New York: Russell Sage Foundation.

Teitelman, J. L. (1987). Homosexuality. In G. L. Maddox (Ed.), *The encyclopedia of aging.* (pp. 329-330). New York: Springer.

Uhlenberg, P. & Myers, M. A. P. (1981). Divorce and the elderly. *The Gerontologist,* 21, 276-282.

United States Census Bureau. (1986). *Current population reports, series p-20,* No. 411. Washington, D. C., United States Government Printing Office.

United States Senate, Special Committee on Aging. 1987. Developments in Aging, 1986: Volume 1. Washington, D. C. USGPO.

_____. 1991. Developments in Aging, 1990: Volume 1. Washington, D. C. USGPO.

Vanek, J. (1984). Housewives as workers. In P. Voydanoff, P. (Ed.) *Work and family: Changing roles of men and women*, (pp. 89-110). Palo Alto, CA: Mayfield

Voydanoff, P. (1984). *Work and family: Changing roles of men and women.* Palo Alto, CA: Mayfield.

Ward, R. A., Sherman, S. R. & LaGory, M. (1984). Subjective network assessments and subjective well-being. *Journal of Gerontology*, 39, 93-101.

Zollar, A. C. & Williams, J. S. (1987). The contribution of marriage to the life satisfaction of black adults. *Journal of Marriage and the Family*, 49, 87-92.

CHAPTER 3
Advance Directives, Surrogate Health Care and Decision Making and Older Families
Dallas M. High and Howard B. Turner

Dramatic advances in health care technology during the twentieth century have had a profound effect on our capability to prolong life, shaking the foundations of our understanding of life, dying and death. Technologies ranging from the development of sanitary, disease-free environments and an increased role of drug and immunization therapies for control of communicable diseases to advanced surgical techniques, artificial life support and vital organ replacement have dramatically increased survival beyond the high risk periods of infancy and childhood and added years for persons over 65. Yet, these same technologies can threaten the values of autonomy and freedom at the end of life. Older Americans are especially at risk as serious illness and incapacity often prevent them from making personal decisions about health care.

The national challenge in health care decision making is to protect the rights and autonomy of older people while providing the best medical technology possible to preserve life. To meet this challenge State legislative bodies, together with legal and medical professionals and advocates for the elderly, have devised mechanisms for making choices in advance about health care, including rebuttal of the use of life-sustaining technologies. Emerging public policy in the United States in the final two decades of the twentieth century could be characterized as a love affair with advance directives for health care. Such policies also impact significantly on the families of older people. The emerging emphasis on independence and individualism threatens the tradition of familial interdependence in surrogate health care decision making for elderly members who can no longer make decisions for themselves.

In this chapter we discuss the unprecedented public policy interest in living wills and durable powers of attorney for health care as mechanisms of decision making for those elderly persons diagnosed as decisionally incapacitated. We examine the standards of surrogate decision making, substituted judgment and best interests. Contrary to the policy trend, we report results from empirical studies showing that over 90 percent of elderly people prefer that family members serve as surrogate health care decision makers without resorting to formal regulatory solutions. We argue that educational interventions and the Patient Self-Determination Act of 1990 are not likely to increase significantly the use of advance directives among the elderly. We further argue that the policy trends have unwittingly ignored the self-determinative preferences of the elderly and the empowerment of the elderly within familial interdependencies. We finally recommend alternative policies for protecting the elderly's preferences, including adoption of a rebuttable presumption in favor of family surrogates.

BACKGROUND

Life expectancy at birth in the United States has risen sharply, from 47 years in 1900 to 75 in 1987 (National Center for Health Statistics [NCHS], 1991). A parallel rise in the relative size of the older population is clearly evident: 4 percent of the total population in 1900, 12.6 percent in 1990, and predicted to reach as high as 23 percent by the year 2050 (U.S. Bureau of Census, 1989). Yet, the same technologies which have helped to extend life have contributed to marked shifts in the structure of mortality. Improvements in nutrition, sanitation and medical technology have contributed to a drastic change in the causes of death, shifting them from short-term infectious, communicable and parasitic diseases to long-term degenerative diseases —literally "body-wearing-out" diseases. In the early part of the century death was most often the result of influenza, tuberculosis, pneumonia and bronchitis. Now cardiovascular disease, malignant neoplasms and cerebrovascular diseases account for over 66 percent of all deaths (NCHS, 1990). Not only are we living longer, but our dying is taking longer too. While the dying process once would have taken days it now is extended over a period of weeks or months. This century has also seen Americans become increasingly dependent upon institutions to care for dying people. In 1900 only 5 percent of United States citizens died in hospitals while in 1980 over 60 percent did (NCHS, 1985). Surprisingly, some evidence suggests that the older one becomes the more the likelihood of dying in a hospital declines. For example, only about 50 percent of those over 85 die in hospitals (Office of Technology Assessment [OTA], 1987). More and more of the oldest-old are dying in nursing homes since they are increasingly used to care for severely debilitated and terminally ill elderly. Indeed, approximately 13.5 percent of all United States deaths occur in institutions other than hospitals (NCHS, 1985). Undoubtedly, the United States' experience with the hospice movement, which emphasizes home care, is beginning to have some impact on where people die since most people prefer to die at home. Nevertheless, the trend during the 20th century and the impact on the individual's and family's experience of death and dying are unmistakable. We have, in effect, moved dying from a moral order of dealing with one's mortality to a technological order motivated by an effort to overcome death (Cassell, 1975). By so doing we have moved the place of dying and dealing with our mortality from families and homes to hospitals and other institutions. Once presided over by the patient with family in attendance and in care, the dying process is now presided over by a paid functionary in an institution under the watchful eye of an impersonal technology.

Changes in United States demography and family structure have likely contributed to moving death and dying from the moral order to the technological order. Decreases in the size of families, an increase in life expectancy and the increasingly common experience of four and five generation families have all played a role. The drop in total fertility rates from 3.7 in 1900 to 1.9 in 1988 (Bengtson, Rosenthal & Burton, 1990; NCHS, 1977, 1990) suggests a reduced potential for familial interdependencies. Coupled with the increase in life expectancy, this has led to a significant increase in the length of time older persons live independently from families, particularly children. Similarly, the increased commonality of four and five generation families has resulted in a more vertical family structure, one which allows, or even encourages, individual family members to pursue greater privacy and independence. Additionally, geographical mobility has reduced the percentage of children and retired parents who maintain residential proximity to one another. While this does not necessarily mean a reduced frequency of interaction among kin (Troll, Miller & Atchley, 1979) it does highlight the trend of greater residential independence —intimacy at a distance —increasingly preferred by families (Chappell, 1990). Collectively these changes have moved death and dying from the environment of families to institutional settings.

The confluence of the factors of greater life expectancy, causes of death precipitating longer periods of disability and dying, removal of death and dying from the moral order of families to technological institutions and changes in family structure have produced an unprecedented need to rebut the unbridled use of life-sustaining technologies. While at any one time many thousands of elderly persons are receiving these interventions, they may not prolong a patient's life so much as prolong dying, contributing to a patient's suffering without improving the condition. Burdens may outweigh benefits. Life-sustaining interventions may sustain the life of a patient indefinitely but without hope of recovery.

The focus on the elderly and their families is especially important since death occurs more at older ages and older people are at greater risk of dementing and terminal illnesses than are younger people. As a result elderly persons are more likely to become candidates for life-sustaining treatments. Consequently, decisions about withholding or withdrawing life-sustaining treatments directly affect older people more frequently than younger people. Such decisions are likely to come at a time when cognitive impairment is present due either to a terminal illness, unconsciousness or dementia. When this occurs consent to or refusal of treatment must be made by someone other than the patient. Prior to the extensive use of life-sustaining technologies, families were typically called upon to make such decisions.

The incidence of elderly persons becoming decisionally incapacitated is significant in and of itself. Some reports concerning the prevalence of dementia among the elderly provide estimates of about 1 percent for those age 65 to 74; about 7 percent for those age 75 to 84; and about 25 percent for those over age 85 (Evans et al., 1989). Recent revised estimates of Alzheimer's disease prevalence indicate that more than 10 percent of persons over 65 are affected and that by the year 2050 as many as 10 million persons in the United States may have a probable diagnosis of Alzheimer's disease (OTA, 1987). These estimates suggest that the impact of cognitive impairment among the elderly will continue to be significant in health care and devastating to individuals who once were fully capable of making autonomous decisions. For those who once could express their own wishes and participate in the health care decision process but have become decisionally helpless, long-term institutional care is often required. Over 50 percent of all nursing home residents have significant cognitive impairment (Harper & Lebowitz, 1986).

ASSESSING DECISION MAKING CAPACITY

Assessing decision making capacity in elderly patients is one of the most difficult clinical problems confronting health care professionals in the United States. Of course, the law presumes that adults have a right of self-determination to consent to or refuse treatment, subject to some limitations and that adults are competent until evidence is presented in a court of appropriate jurisdiction to rebut the presumption. The adult is then, in effect, declared "incompetent" and a guardian or conservator is appointed. Such rulings should be distinguished from medical assessments of decisional capacity or incapacity since the latter are not formal declarations by a court and do not entail any privation of rights. Unfortunately, these matters are not always held distinct by those who care for the elderly. In addition, many health care providers and families often presume that elderly persons are decisionally incapable merely due to advanced age. Indeed, some States still use a standard of "advanced age" as sufficient ground to appoint a conservator for property. Ageism rears its head again when considerations of capacity for decision making are being made. Likewise, efforts to determine incapacity on the basis of dementia or outcomes of decisions by elderly persons must be resisted as status biased. For example, it is inappropriate to consider decisional capacity or incapacity as all or nothing categories when applied to persons with dementia of the Alzheimer's type. There are degrees of incapacity and capacity, and these may fluctuate. Further, capacities can be shown to be decision or task specific. For example, a patient may be unable to consent to renal dialysis due to temporary disorientation or confusion or intermittent dementia but at another time is able to consent to treatment for an abscess on the forearm.

While there are no uniformly agreed upon procedures for assessing decision making capacity, the President's Commission and other groups have advocated for what are termed functional criteria (President's Commission, 1982). Functionally an individual may be said to be decisionally incapacitated when unable to: 1) take in and comprehend information regarding his/her specific medical situation; 2) deliberate on accessible alternatives; and 3) make a reasoned choice. Care must be taken not to confuse apparently irrational choices with a determination of inability to reason. Likewise, it should not be presumed that unusual beliefs held by an individual are evidence of decisional incapacity. Yet, because we lack procedural explicitness regarding functional definitions, the elderly are particularly vulnerable to having their wishes ignored, dismissed, or violated. Estes (1991) reminds us of the profound link between macro and micro considerations (society and the individual) in the way one ages and that the aged tend to be labeled with a preponderant focus on physical debility and decline. No person should be considered decisionally incapable just because he or she is old. Moreover, it is advisable for health care professionals to consult with family members and others (such as friends) for valuable information in making an assessment of the elderly patient's actual abilities to function decisionally.

When it has been determined that an elderly person is unable to make decisions for him/herself, it naturally follows that someone else must make decisions for that person. The dilemma is how best to protect the rights of the elderly while providing the best possible care, including medical care. How can someone else appropriately accept or refuse life-sustaining treatment for an elderly person who, once capable, can no longer speak for him or herself? The dilemma has become particularly pressing since in the United States one of the most basic and cherished rights consists in privacy and self-determination, interpreted by the courts to include a right to make one's own health care decisions (See *Schloendorff v. Society of New York Hospitals*, 1914). Since the goal of many social and health care programs has been to maintain autonomy and independence as long as possible, the elderly person who loses a capability of making decisions risks losing all self-determination and independence, including a right to make health care decisions. To meet this challenge legal and medical professionals, ethicists, social and government agencies and advocates for the elderly, disabled and the terminally ill have urged that advance planning for health care decisions be undertaken.

Because older people are especially likely to experience impairment of ability to make and communicate choices, the United States Senate Special Committee on Aging (1986) found it important to issue a special report on planning for health care decisions. Written for policymakers and professionals who work with the elderly, the purpose of the report was twofold: 1. to encourage advance communication between the elderly and those who might make health care decisions for them in the event of incapacity; 2. to encourage the use of advance directives, such as living wills or durable powers of attorney for health care. Further, a society known as Choice in Dying, a merger of Concern for Dying and Society for the Right to Die, is devoted almost exclusively to questions concerning medical decision making at the end of life and the advocacy of advance directives. Over the past decade and a half most state legislative bodies have responded to the advocacy for decision making planning and have enacted laws for advance directives. Indeed, the United States has experienced what could be called an "advance directive fever."

ADVANCE DIRECTIVES

Although formally legislated instruments for health care decision making and rebuttal of the use of life-sustaining technologies are a late twentieth century development in the United States, there is nothing new about planning for health care and decision making. Many patients have simply discussed with their physicians how they might wish to be treated and the physician agrees to follow that course of action should the patient become decisionally incapacitated. Others have discussed treatment preferences with family members or have evoked tacit agreements (High & Turner, 1987). Still other oral communications have been shared with friends, co-workers, or clergy. Or, communications about one's own preferences may have been expressed indirectly through conversations about the experiences of others. Consider the following: "I think it is just awful the way Jane Smith died—tubes and everything. I would never want that." In addition, professionals and family members have functionally known the wishes of an individual through inferences from their known values, personal beliefs and religious practices. The commonly cited example of the religious prohibitions of blood transfusion by a devout Jehovah's Witness is germane. Because of these informal activities most case law in the United

States dealing with advance directives has been with oral directives, especially comments made to family members (Meisel, 1989). The courts have often enforced oral directives even though there are obvious legal advantages to written directives.

In addition to oral directives, informally written directives have been used by some people. These take the form of a letter written to a physician, family member, clergy, an attorney, and/or others. Prior to the extensive legislation of advance directives form letters or living will forms received strong support from advocacy groups like the Society for the Right to Die and Concern for Dying. Often printed in newspaper columns like "Dear Abby" or on billfold size cards, these model drafts have generally not been legally binding. Moreover, because these documents have been designed to be used by an indefinite number of people in vastly differing circumstances, they resulted in offering perilously vague instructions for decision making.

Due in part to the litigious atmosphere within the United States formalization by legislation of advance directives has been widely endorsed by physicians, attorneys, ethicists, courts, and public interest groups. Such legislation has been justified on the basis of protecting the rights of citizens to refuse treatment, especially life-sustaining treatment when it would only prolong the dying process, and to protect physicians and other surrogate decision makers from civil and criminal liability. The two most common approaches to formalization of advance directives have been legislation of written instruction directives and proxy decision maker appointments.

The best known example of a formal instruction directive is a living will, a generic term covering legislation of natural death acts, rights of terminally ill acts, death with dignity acts, etc. As of the end of 1992, all fifty states and the District of Columbia have living will statutes. A living will is a written document which gives instructions to health care providers and others about the particular kinds of treatment an individual would want or not want to prolong life. Typically an individual uses a living will to direct others to withhold or withdraw life-sustaining treatments in the event of a terminal illness. Living wills are executed while the individual is still capable of making decisions. They become effective as determined by the statute. Basic to all statutes is the requirement that the patient be unable to make his or her own decisions. Most statutes require that the declarant be terminally ill, but sometimes this is ambiguously defined. Many states require that a patient must be certified by physicians to be terminally ill. Some laws require that a specified form must be used to execute a living will, although more frequently a form is merely suggested. The laws also require technical procedures for executing a living will such as having it witnessed and/or notarized.

As planning instruments living wills suffer the drawback of requiring the declarant to exercise anticipatory judgment regarding future health care circumstances. The accuracy of such anticipation is at best difficult, if not impossible. If a document is written in a language general enough to cover a wide range of circumstances then it likely will be vague and ambiguous. If the document is drafted with sufficient specificity the document cannot provide guidance for those circumstances not specifically anticipated. In any event the instructions provided in a living will usually have to be interpreted by the decision makers and the health care providers. Further, since many living will statutes require that a terminal condition exist, the instruction directive may not apply to persons who suffer from persistent vegetative or permanently unconscious existence.

The second mechanism for health care decision making planning is the appointment of a proxy or agent. When a proxy directive is created an individual names and authorizes another person to make health care decisions for him or her in the event the individual becomes decisionally incapacitated. As of the end of 1992, all fifty states and the District of Columbia have established statutatory provisions for people to appoint proxies for health care decision making. Most states have extended their statutes for the durable power of attorney to include health care. A durable power of attorney differs from a common-law power of attorney in that it does not lapse once the principal becomes incapacitated. A durable power of attorney can be designed to become effective only when the principal becomes decisionally incapacitated, known as springing durable power of attorney. Some states have preferred to establish a separate Health Care Proxy Act (New York) or a Designation of a Health Care Surrogate Act (Kentucky). Several other states have court decisions, Attorney General opinions, or other statutes which indicate that their general durable power of attorney also permits the appointment of a proxy for health care decisions. The majority of the statutes empower the proxy to make a wide range of health care decisions without limitation to a terminal condition. The proxy directive need not give direct instructions to the designated proxy concerning any anticipated decisions. However, if proxy decisions are to reflect the decisions the principal would have made had the principal been capable, then instructions may be needed.

One advantage the proxy appointment has over the instruction directive is that the proxy can have knowledge of the contemporaneous medical circumstances when making the decision instead of having to anticipate those circumstances. However, the proxy decision maker may be expected to replicate the decision of the patient. Indeed, the President's Commission for the Study of Ethical Problems in Medicine and Biomedical and Behavioral Research recommended that any substitute decision maker ought to act consistently with the patient's wishes (President's Commission, 1983), and many state statutes have followed that recommendation by making it a requirement of proxy appointments. In these instances the proxy may suffer a distinct disadvantage if the wishes of the patient are not known. Much debate continues over the utility of such a requirement, known as the substituted judgment standard, distinguished from the best interests standard.

STANDARDS OF DECISION MAKING: SUBSTITUTED JUDGMENT OR BEST INTERESTS?

The most important legal limitation placed on proxy decision makers is the standard by which any decision is to be made. The two basic standards, substituted judgment and best interests, were derived from areas of law other than health care decision making. For many years, both the courts and the medical profession assumed parens patriae roles and acted according to what was best for the incapacitated person and proxies were expected to do the same. However, over the past decade the courts, acting on cases involving life-sustaining treatments, have shown a preference for acting on the basis of what the patient would want if he or she could decide for himself or herself (Meisel, 1989).

Substituted judgment calls on proxy decision makers to render decisions as the patient would have done had the patient been capable. It is a subjective test. A substituted judgment decision is founded on the patient's own values, beliefs and goals. Accordingly, substituted judgment can only be employed when the patient's own views and preferences are known. The greater the knowledge of the patient's views the greater the likelihood that the proxy decision will accurately replicate the patient's own decision. By contrast, the best interests standard holds that proxy decisions are acceptable on the grounds that they benefit the patient according to socially shared values of a hypothetical "reasonable" person. Factors such as relief of suffering, the usefulness or futility of the intervention, risks, benefits and burdens are considered to provide an objective test. Decisions reached by application of the best interests test may or may not reflect a patient's own preferences. Of course, some form of the best interests standard must be employed when the views and preferences of the patient are unknown or lack sufficient clarity to act on them.

Notwithstanding the basic differences between the two standards, the courts, state statutes, and ethical and legal commentators have developed various understandings and interpretations of each standard, most especially substituted judgment (Meisel, 1989). For example, court opinions in Missouri and New York have determined that substitute decisions must be made on the basis of "clear and convincing evidence" concerning direct expression of patient preferences (*Cruzan v. Harmon*, 1988; *In re O'Connor*, 1988; *In re Storar*, 1981). Indeed, the New York Health Care Proxy Act abides by a clear and convincing standard of evidence regarding any proxy consideration in withholding or withdrawing artificial nutrition and hydration. Other court opinions and state statutes, such as Massachusetts, permit substituted judgment decisions based on inferences and sometimes extend the substituted judgment standard to situations where the patient had never been capable of making decisions.

The courts, legal commentators and ethicists continue to wrestle with various interpretations of the substituted judgment standard and sometimes attempt to bridge best interests and substituted judgment. Others have criticized both standards. In her important work "Litigating Life and Death," Rhoden (1988) finds flaws in both standards and urges that they be abandoned in favor of a rebuttable presumption of family decision making. She argues persuasively that the subjective substituted judgment test most often requires an evidentiary level that seldom can be reached in considering the wishes of the patient given fluid medical circumstances. The objective best interests test, she contends, requires measurements of pain and suffering, risks and benefits in ways which dehumanize patients by suggesting that only their present physical sensations count. She further suggests that the two standards are not as distinct as many courts and commentators have assumed. Indeed, a few state statutes for proxy (or surrogate) decision making (e.g., Florida and Kentucky) have made it clear that the agents must consider the recommendations of the physician, the wishes and the best interests of the patient.

Despite differences of interpretation and an ongoing debate concerning the standards themselves, several recent studies have attempted to measure proxy predictions of patient's decisions or the concordance between the proxy and the elderly person's choices via medical decision making vignettes (Ouslander, Tymchuk & Rahbar,1989; Seckler et al., 1991; Tomlinson et al., 1990; Uhlmann, Pearlman & Cain, 1988; Zweibel & Cassel, 1989). These studies have involved physician proxies, physician selected proxies, patient selected proxies,such as family members, and other health care professionals. None has produced a high replication rate of the decisions made by the elderly person. However, at least two of the studies (Seckler et al.,1991; Tomlinson et al., 1990) found that family members evidenced better approximation of the elderly person's choice than others, especially when the proxy was instructed to respond as the elderly person would, even though high levels of concordance were not obtained. All of these studies have proceeded either on the presumption that a highly concordant exercise of substituted judgment is the ideal for proxy decision making or that the usefulness of the standard itself should be tested by the concordances of choices on health care decision making vignettes. Most of the studies conclude that increased discussion between proxy decision makers and elderly patients and fully specified, written directions are needed to ensure better and more accurate proxy decisions. This conclusion suggests that proxies, including family members, do not do a very good job.

Only the study by Seckler and colleagues (1991) explicitly raises doubt about the validity and utility of the substituted judgment standard itself. The authors contend that a standard of a "clear and convincing evidence," as required in Missouri and upheld by the United States Supreme Court, is unrealistic, if not impossible, to achieve. They suggest that a different standard that "reflects the generally trusting and interdependent relationship" among various people is better and more realistic. That standard could include trust of family and professional caregivers, best interests considerations which respect patient's wishes and values, and rational and sensible judgments about use of medical technology.

The suggestion by Seckler and colleagues coincides with empirical reports from elderly people when queried about health care decision making in the event of decisional incapacity. The evidence suggests that elderly persons themselves are more concerned about who will be the proxy decision maker than with the decision making standard itself (High, 1989). Elderly people prefer to rely informally on trusted surrogate decision makers without regard to whether the decision will reflect substituted judgment or best interests. Frequently elderly people believe that close family members, particularly spouses and/or trusted adult children, can make better decisions at the time of the medical crisis than they themselves could by advance deliberation (High, 1988a, 1990b; High & Turner, 1987). The elderly regularly point out that it is virtually impossible to anticipate all the potential medical circumstances in which a decision would have to be made—an inherent weakness of the living will.

The elderly person's apparent desire not to drive a wedge between the substituted judgment and best interests standards for surrogate decision making may actually be a signal that the welfare and autonomy of the elderly are not best served by the extremes of either standard. This propensity of the elderly is consistent with an often overlooked effort on the part of some courts to bridge the gap between the two standards (*In re Conroy*, 1985; *Foody v. Manchester Memorial Hospital*, 1984; *In re Torres*, 1984). In the Conroy case, for example, the court developed a middle standard, a "limited objective" test, which requires "some trustworthy" evidence of the patient's own wishes in addition to weighing the patient's best interests. Tensions between the objective and subjective tests may be relieved if personal wishes, values, beliefs and preferences form a part of the best interests considerations. And it is likely that family members are in the best position to act accordingly. Moreover, despite a growing myth (discussed more fully later) that families are inappropriate to serve as substitute decision makers for their elderly members or that they are not constitutionally authorized or that they make poor substitute decision makers by a strict substituted judgment standard, there is strong evidence the elderly, as well as persons of other age groups, prefer that family members serve (Gamble, McDonald & Lichstein, 1991; High, 1991a).

SURROGATE DECISION MAKING AND THE ELDERLY'S FAMILIAL EXPECTATIONS

The late 1960s and the 1970s marked the beginning of efforts by patients, especially the terminally ill, to free themselves from the tyranny of technology. The struggles in medical ethics during the 70s were basically seen as conflict "between the old Hippocratic paternalism (having the physician do what he or she thought was best for the patient) and a principle of autonomy" (Veatch, 1984). In the medical context paternalism had reigned for centuries and never before "had there ever been any acknowledgment of the patient as a dignified agent free to participate in and exercise self-determination over medical decisions" (Veatch, 1984). The principle of autonomy gave vent to characterizing successful aging as independence and avoidance of dependence, including avoidance of dependence on families (Rowe & Kahn, 1987). Similarly, the push for advance directives for health care decision making, together with use of substituted judgment, was seen as advancing the elderly's autonomy and independence. Indeed, it has been sometimes argued that a living will can avoid conflict with family members and can be used to contravene the wishes of family members who may wish to do everything possible to sustain the life of a relative. However, to gain some freedom from a tyranny of technology by promoting autonomy is one thing, but to regard this as rugged individualism and to characterize one's health care decision making and quality of life as solitary pursuits is another thing altogether. Indeed, the triumph of autonomy, even if temporary, may be a factor in producing another antifamily myth in the United States. Indeed, a new myth about families of older people may be emerging which holds that families are inappropriate and unfit to serve as surrogate decision makers for their relatives. Decisions, so the myth goes, are best seen as individual expressions and independent from families (High, 1991a).

Ironically, many voices promoting autonomy have failed to acknowledge the autonomous preferences of the elderly in the contexts of social care and health care decision making. Drawing on 15 years of research, Cantor (1991) notes that elderly persons themselves prefer to turn first and most frequently to an informal system of care, including families, "the cornerstone of the support system." Only then are the preferences followed by friends, neighbors and formal organizations "in a well-ordered hierarchical selection process."

Our own research indicates that Cantor's findings regarding the elderly's selection process for general social care can be extended to the process of health care decision making. Unfortunately, research regarding the elderly's preferences for surrogate health care decision making has been seriously neglected. We began to correct this by conducting in-depth interviews with 40 community dwelling persons ranging in age from 67 to 91. As part of the study the participants were asked, "Is there someone who knows you well enough that you would trust him or her to make health care decisions on your behalf in the event you could not make them for yourself?" Later in the same interview we asked, "If you were too sick to make an important decision about your health care, who would you want to make the final decision for you?" To both questions all but two of the participants who had family (N=38) indicated that they. would prefer a family member as a surrogate (High & Turner, 1987; High, 1988a). Characteristically, a hierarchical ordering pattern was present: spouse, adult children, siblings, other family, friends and others. Additional interviews were conducted two years later to allow for comparison of responses on choice of surrogates between those elderly persons who had family and those who did not. Ninety percent of the former preferred relatives as surrogates, whereas the elderly without families expressed bewilderment about who would serve as a surrogate (High, 1990a, 1990b).

Larger studies representative of all adults show similar findings. State-wide surveys conducted in 1987 (N=746) and 1989 (N=676) included the question, "If you were too sick to make an important decision about your health care, who would you want to make that decision for you?" The choices offered were family member, close friend, doctor, lawyer and other. If "family member" was given, the respondent was then asked, "Which family member?" and offered choices of spouse, adult child(ren), sibling(s), parent(s), other and combination. With less than a 4 percent margin of error, both surveys showed better than a 90 percent preference (91 percent and 94 percent respectively) for family surrogacy, including 94 percent of those aged 61-95 in the 1989 survey (High, 1991a). These findings are consistent with a nationwide poll conducted by the Times Mirror Center for the People and the Press in Washington, DC (N=1213) which revealed that 71 percent of the respondents preferred that family members make health care decisions for persons who had not completed an advance directive and who were unable to make their own health care decisions (Poll, 1990). Likewise our studies are consistent with a study conducted by Horowitz, Silverstone and Reinhardt (1991) regarding autonomy and surrogacy issues in family caregiving relationships. From explorations of four measurements the authors conclude that their findings support "policy initiatives that attempt to legitimize the role of family members as the most appropriate surrogate decision makers for incapacitated elders."

USE OF ADVANCE DIRECTIVES

While there is evidence to suggest that elderly residents of the United States want their immediate family members involved in surrogate health care decision making, information on older persons' use of formal advance directives is at best sketchy and variant. In addition, available information comes mainly from small, nonrepresentative samples or from simple surveys or polls. However, a distinction can be drawn between attitudes concerning support for the availability of advance directives and behaviors of actual use and completion of those same instruments. That is to say, there is a difference between people saying that they are interested in or support legislation for advance directives and sitting down and filling out a living will or appointing a proxy.

It is clear that in recent years professional medical associations, physicians, attorneys and ethicists have widely endorsed advance directives and the public has generally supported legislation which makes these instruments available (American Academy of Neurology, 1989; Council on Ethical and Judicial Affairs of the American Medical Association, 1989; Emanuel et al., 1991; High, 1988b; Orentlicher, 1990; President's Commission, 1982; United States Senate Special Committee on Aging, 1986). However, evidence is accumulating to indicate that only a relatively small percentage of United States citizens are completing advance directives. Studies report usage rates ranging from 4 percent to 20 percent. A frequently cited rate of 9 percent for completed living wills is based on a 1986 poll of 995 respondents conducted by SRI Gallup for Hospitals magazine (Emanuel & Emanuel, 1989; Steiber, 1987). A 1988 public opinion survey of 1500 respondents conducted by the American Medical Association showed 15 percent had completed a living will (Most MDs, 1988). Another Gallup poll conducted in November, 1990, surveying a randomly-selected national sample of 1018 adults indicates that 20 percent of Americans had written some kind of living will (Gallup & Newport, 1991). The poll further indicated that only 62 percent of older people favored living wills. That rate of use is consistent with the results, reported in 1986, of a survey of Florida physicians and nurses (Anderson et al., 1986).

Rates of advance directives use among elderly persons appear to be no higher than those for the overall population. Two studies of persons

60 years and older, with samples of 55 and 75, reported usage rates of 4 percent and 0 percent respectively, even though 52 percent of the respondents in the latter study were familiar with North Carolina's living will (Gamble, McDonald & Lichstein, 1991; Zweibel & Cassel, 1989). Our own exploratory studies conducted in 1986 involving 40 older persons drawn from a pool of research volunteers revealed that 18 percent had completed a living will and 15 percent had designated a health care surrogate. Further in-depth studies in 1988 of elderly persons without families revealed only slightly higher completion rates: 20 percent for both living wills and designation of a health care surrogate (High & Turner, 1987; High, 1988a; High,1990b). And our 1991 state-wide survey of 646 randomly selected Kentucky adults, including 135 persons 65 or older, continued to reveal low usage rates. Only 12 percent of all ages had completed some kind of living will, including 9 percent who indicated their living will was incompliance with Kentucky law. Twenty one percent of persons 65 or older indicated that they had completed a living will, although only 16 percent had executed a document in compliance with Kentucky law. Surrogate designation rates overall were at 20 percent, again with only 9 percent indicating that their designation complied with Kentucky law (High & Turner, 1991). Persons 65 or older exhibited slightly higher usage rates: 27 percent had designated a health care surrogate but only 18 percent believed that their appointment procedure complied with Kentucky law.

Any increases in advance directive usage rates in the decade of the 90s will likely be influenced by the first "right to die" decision handed down by the United States Supreme Court in 1990. Although the ruling in *Cruzan v. Director, Missouri Department of Health* (1990) did not pertain to an elderly person, its bearing on surrogate decision making by families of elderly persons is far reaching and profound (High, 1991a). Nancy Cruzan, a 32-year-old woman, had remained in a persistent vegetative state supported by gastrostomy hydration and nutrition since an automobile accident in 1983. Her parents had sought to have medical treatment terminated. In a 5-4 decision the majority of the Court upheld Missouri's requirement for "clear and convincing evidence" of the incompetent patient's own intentions to refuse treatment before allowing any termination of treatment. The Court held that the constitution did not prohibit Missouri from requiring this heightened standard of evidence, which as partial fulfillment may include a written statement of the patient's treatment refusal, expressed prospectively. Although only two states, Missouri and New York, as mentioned earlier, require a standard of "clear and convincing" evidence, it is clear that public awareness of the Court's decision precipitated increased interest in advance directives whether or not elderly persons are completing them with greater prevalence.

Nevertheless, the public usage rates of advance directives is nowhere near what advocates would like to see. Likely, multiple factors contribute to their nonuse. Intervention studies in the 1990s should assist in clarifying them. A study conducted by Hare and Nelson (1991) in Minnesota involving the distribution of a booklet and two physician-initiated discussions managed to increase the use of the living will by 15 percent, 8 out of 52, over a 5 month period. Two other groups, a control group and a group receiving only the booklet, remained constant during the period yielding no completions of a living will. The investigators had expected a much higher success rate and speculated that there is a natural plateau for clinic populations beyond which physician attempts at encouraging completions are not successful. Other intervention studies and assessment of factors contributing to the low use of advance directives are in progress (High, 1991b). Our own 1991 survey of Kentucky residents revealed that the primary reasons given by the participants consisted of procrastination, not thinking it was necessary, wishing to rely informally on family, needing more information, believing it was too early to plan for future impairments and not trusting how the document would be used (High & Turner, 1991). Other studies have either found or speculated on similar reasons, in addition to suggesting that patients are dependent on physicians to raise the issue or that patients are not sure whom to designate as a surrogate or do not have anyone to designate (Emanuel et al., 1991; Gamble, McDonald & Lichstein, 1991; High, 1988a; Roe et al., 1990).

THE PATIENT SELF-DETERMINATION ACT OF 1990

In an effort to protect individual rights of decision making in health care, especially for end of life decisions, and to encourage the public to complete advance directives, in 1990 the United States Congress passed what has become known as the Patient Self-Determination Act. The decision of the United States Supreme Court in the Cruzan case, handed down four months previously, has been credited as an impetus for passage of the Act. Specifically, the federal legislation requires hospitals, nursing homes, home health care agencies, hospice programs, and institutions and agencies that serve Medicare and Medicaid patients to do the following: 1. Provide each individual upon admission or enrollment written notice of their rights under state law to make decisions concerning medical care, including the right to accept or refuse treatment, and the right to formulate advance directives; 2. Provide individual patients with written policy of the institution or agency regarding the implementation of their rights; 3. Document the individual's medical record on whether the individual has advance directives; 4. Ensure that decisions are made freely by prohibiting conditioning medical care on whether the individual has executed an advance directive; 5. Ensure compliance with requirements of state law (whether statutory or common law) by respecting advance directives; 6. Provide education for staff and the community regarding advance directives (Public Law No 101-508,1990). By mandating these actions under Medicare Provider Agreements the legislation does not grant new rights to patients. Rather, it affirms existing rights to accept or refuse treatment within limits provided by law and to execute advance directives as provided by statutory or common law. The impact of this legislation on issues discussed in this chapter should be substantial and longitudinal studies will be required to assess both the positive and negative consequences. In the meantime, potential benefits and problems can be addressed.

Advocates for advance directives regard the Act as a useful response to the fact that so few United States citizens have advance directives. Under the Act patients will be provided information about their rights and advance directives without having to take the initiative. Further, ready availability of information may increase discussion among family members about end-of-life decisions, thereby encouraging the communication process, and may encourage more discussion between patients and health care providers than presently occurs (LaPuma, Orentlicher & Moss, 1991). Potentially physicians and other health care providers will benefit by reducing concerns over liability in treatment decisions and helping to provide good faith communication between the clinician and patient.

The Act presumes that receipt of written information about advance directives will encourage more people to complete advance directives. Although the provision of written information to patients could serve as an intervention, as noted earlier, at least one study has shown that providing patients with information does not result in increased use of advance directives (Hare & Nelson, 1991). Not only is it possible that the Act will fail to increase the use of advance directives, it could, as LaPuma and colleagues (1991) suggest, be counterproductive. Because the Act requires that patients be informed of their rights under state law, many state laws on advance directives provide fewer rights than rights guaranteed under the United States Constitution. Many states have statutes which only apply to terminally ill patients and exclude the possibility of refusing artificial nutrition and hydration. Moreover, lack of uniformity among the states on both living wills and proxy decision making instruments may confuse patients and health care providers alike. Both the lack of uniformity and the restrictiveness of some state laws create the potential for patients being incorrectly informed of their rights.

The most promising aspect of the Act is its requirement that medical staffs be educated about advance directives. Should staff become better educated not only would they be in a better position to answer questions raised by patients and their families concerning advance directives, but they may become less reluctant to initiate advance directives discussions with patients. On the other hand, the Act could serve to reduce discussion between health care providers, patients and families. Since patient rights and advance directives are being addressed on admission or enrollment clinicians may assume there is no need to initiate such discussions. In many institutions and agencies compliance with the Act will consist primarily of proforma acts of distribution of written materials and medical record notation of whether or not a patient has an advance directive. Such procedures are more likely to become ends in themselves rather than means to encouraging further discussion.

Distribution of written materials about patient rights, institutional procedures or agency policy along with advance directives at the time of admission or enrollment while signing various forms for authorization of treatment, release of information, coordination of benefits, personal property, etc. has the potential of becoming yet another aspect of a mechanical process. The written materials may become "lost" among many others or at least not read. Clearly hospitals and nursing homes are not optimal settings for first discussions of advance directives. Acutely ill patients are likely not to benefit from such discussions much less from written information simply handed to them. Indeed, it is preferable that patient choices over advance directives not be made at the time of admission or enrollment due to the possibility of fear, pain, distress, or other factors that may cause choices to be less than voluntary or well reasoned. Under the conditions of hospital admission, for example, there is the potential for the patient to be coerced. Given the roles that social structural factors like race, class, gender and age play in shaping individual experiences and outcomes, such coercion could be expected to be most directed at minorities, the poor and the elderly (Minkler, 1991).

It is clearly undesirable to advocate that all persons complete advance directives since, as we have already noted, most elderly persons prefer procedures of informal family decision making in the event of decisional incapacity. Indeed, White and Fletcher (1991), while arguing for the Act, suggest that many people, especially those with close and intact families, do not need advance directives. Not only should it be recognized that people vary in their ways of dealing with health care decision making, but also that people who do write advance directives have little interest in the instruments per se. After all, advance directives are fall-back measures and are needed only if rights are not respected and trusting relationships and communications fail. The downside of advance directives, now reinforced by the Patient Self-Determination Act, is that an emphasis on legal and regulatory solutions tends to undermine any presumptive favor of family decision making in caring for decisionally incapacitated elderly relatives.

DEVELOPING UNITED STATES PUBLIC POLICY AND A CASE FOR FAMILY DISCRETION

Enactment of the Patient Self-Determination Act and legislation either passed or pending in all states of the union on advance directives signals that the United States is rapidly establishing public policy regarding individual rights to accept or refuse life-sustaining treatment and provide health care decision making for decisionally incapacitated persons. Although we have already drawn attention to some resistance among the general public, including the elderly, to joining a large advance directives push, the social effect of the emerging policy is to emphasize individual self-determination while avoiding dependencies on other possible decision makers such as institutions, health care professionals and families. In recent years social and health care practitioners have regularly instituted programs to maximize independent living for the elderly thus avoiding the erosion of independence by long-term care. Indeed, no other notion has dominated bioethical considerations in aging and health more than an ethic of personal autonomy as an extension of the United States' penchant for a rugged individualism and defense of individual freedoms and rights.

Unfortunately, policymakers interested in protecting the autonomy of the individual elderly person have often ignored both the elderly person's preferences to trust family surrogates and the family's own interest in health care decision making (Churchill, 1989; High, 1991a; Horowitz, Silverstone & Reinhardt, 1991). Health care decisions almost always entail responsibilities to other people, including considering the interests of others (Hardwig, 1990). For many elderly persons the interests of their family members constitute part of their own interests in the decision making process. That is to say, elderly people explicitly want to take into account the impact a health care decision involving life-sustaining treatment will have on their family unit or on individual members of the family. Moreover, health care decision making construed as individualistic self-determination within atomistic occurrences equally fails to account for the necessary condition of a social context of decisions. Not only are considerations of others involved but decisions arise because we are social beings. And we are social beings due basically to the interdependencies within families. Likewise, personal autonomy is relational, and it cannot be understood apart from relationships within an individual's family as a whole (Cohler, 1983).

The emphasis on advance directives and individualistic self-determination have served to undermine the traditional role of families serving as surrogate health care decision makers for decisionally incapacitated relatives. The growing effect is to consider families neither to have authoritative rights nor to be directly responsible for surrogate decisions. Of course, family members maybe appointed to serve as surrogates under a durable power of attorney for health care or other proxy instrument, but family members are expected ethically and legally, under the principle of substituted judgment, to convey the wishes or written declaration of the individual patient. The United States Supreme Court ruling in the Cruzan case endorsed such a course of argument by ruling that families have no constitutional authority in surrogate decision making. In effect, the Court reduced the role of families to acting as couriers of clear and convincing evidence of the patient's wishes independent of the context and primary social unit in which those decisions would normally be made.

As a result, the importance of relationships among family members was markedly devalued. The reality that personal autonomy is relational in nature and must be explored in the most basic social milieu of families to be understood and appreciated was virtually ignored. Good faith actions within generational interdependencies which are often accomplished in less than formal or legal proceedings were denigrated in deference to the powerful allegiance to solitary pursuits of individual self-determination. To construe the social/familial relationships as essentially irrelevant to the decision-making process and its outcomes is to force those who are family members to act as strangers to their decisionally incapacitated relatives. The most significant impact from the Cruzan case is widespread advocacy for advance directives since the Court suggested that the best protection for any person's wishes regarding the use or refusal of life-sustaining treatment is to execute formally written declaration.

Unwittingly, current policy trends in the United States ignore the self-determinative preferences of the elderly and the empowerment of personal autonomy within familial interdependencies (Clark, 1987). Policy should protect those preferences if personal autonomy and protection of individual rights is to be advocated. Appropriately, some gerontologists remind us that the personal autonomy of elderly persons is not decreased or threatened by family interdependence but is empowered instead. For example, Clark has argued that, conceptually, personal autonomy of the elderly takes root in the web of human relationships. Therefore, personal self-determination is empowered not by isolation and independence, protected by legal solutions, but by interrelationships of caring, concern, and negotiation (Clark, 1987, 1989). It is undisputable that families are a major source of care for older people. And recent health care cost containment policies, such as the development of DRGs (diagnostically related groups), are adding significantly to the already substantial caregiving roles of families (Estes, 1988). Importantly, Horowitz and her colleagues (1991) have further shown that family caregiving relationships can enhance autonomy of older relatives rather than hinder it. Our own studies confirm that the elderly view family decision-making, when properly used, as an extension of their own autonomy. Surrogate health care decision making within families is a natural delegation via the ties and loyalties of family units themselves (High, 1988a).

CONCLUSION

Undoubtedly, any country dominated by a desire to emphasize individualism and independence and to seek formalized legal solutions to issues of forgoing life-sustaining treatment or making surrogate health care decisions for its elderly members, will find it difficult to accept the sufficiency of an appeal to the loyalties and ties within a kinship system of families. Any wholesale change from the pursuit of individualism and independence in health care decision making to a greater emphasis on interdependence and reliance on informal means of family decision making is not likely to occur in the United States. The continuing, seemingly geometric, growth of an already enormously large medical-industrial complex makes such change even more unlikely. Indeed, assault on families in the crucial areas of care and surrogate health care decision making will likely continue and very well may give birth in the 90s to another full-fledged myth about families, namely that families are inappropriate and unfit to make decisions for their incapacitated members (High, 1991a). However, some things can be done.

1. It must be acknowledged that, when possible, elderly persons prefer to rely on their families for surrogate health care decision making and this reliance is reflective of the empowerment individuals derive from families. The fact that some families abuse or otherwise fail to serve their elderly members is not sufficient reason to ignore the elderly's preferences and family empowerment. Rather, we need research not only investigating family abuse, but a significant initiative into how family involvement in surrogate decision making works without formalization and appeal to the legalistic solutions.

2. Interestingly, the accumulative effect of United States policy regarding advance directives, surrogate health care decision making, advocacy of individual autonomy and the "right to die" decision by the United States Supreme Court has been to place the burden of proof on families to show their good faith. As it stands families are accorded

little presumptive authority in the legislative or court system which could place the burden of proof on others and the state to show that the family's wishes and decisions are inconsistent with the wishes and values of the relative or do not serve the relative's best interest. To remedy the clash between the overpowering bent for formalized certainty of individual self-determination and the realism that it is not likely obtainable, a rebuttable presumption in favor of family surrogates should be adopted in the court system (Rhoden, 1988). The family can be presumed to be the best decision maker, not only regarding knowledge about and concern for the older relative, but because family members share in a social nexus of values.

3. Finally, it is likely that universalization of the advance directive process is not realistically achievable. That is to say, it is unlikely that there will be any widespread and overwhelming participation by the elderly population in the advance directive process. Moreover, it is not clear that all of life's events, especially end-of-life health care decisions, can or should be anticipated (Seckler et al., 1991). There is surely a better alternative to a rapidly developing advance directive mania and an unbridled legal and ethical advocacy of individual independence in health care decision making for the elderly. That alternative may entail reinstating the elderly's link to familial relationships in surrogate health care decision making. After all, our society's history and values lend more support to family decision making than to any other.

REFERENCES

American Academy of Neurology (1989). *Resolution on legislation regarding durable power of attorney for health care*. Minneapolis: American Academy of Neurology.

Anderson, G. C., Walker, M. A. H., Pierce, P. M., & Mills, C. M. (1986). Living wills: Do nurses and physicians have them? *American Journal of Nursing*, 86, 271-275.

Bengtson, V., Rosenthal, C., & Burton, L. (1990). Families and aging: Diversity and heterogeneity. In R. H. Binstock & L. K. George (Eds.), *Handbook of aging and the social sciences*, 3rd ed. (pp. 268-287). San Diego: Academic Press.

Cantor, M. H. (1991). Family and community: Changing roles in an aging society. *The Gerontologist*, 31, 337-346.

Cassell, E. J. (1975). Dying in a technological society. In P. Steinfels & R. M. Veatch (Eds.), *Death inside out*, (pp. 43-48). New York: Harper and Row.

Chappell, N. L. (1990). Aging and social care. In R. N. Binstock & L. K. George (Eds.), *Handbook of aging and the social sciences*, 3rd ed. (pp. 438-454). San Diego: Academic Press.

Churchill, L. R. (1989). Trust, autonomy, and advance directives. *Journal of Religion and Health*, 28, 175-183.

Clark, P. G. (1987). Individual autonomy, cooperative empowerment, and planning for long-term care decision making. *Journal of Aging Studies*, 1, 65-76.

_____. (1989). The philosophical foundations of empowerment. *Journal of Aging and Health*, 1, 267-285.

Cohler, B. J. (1983). Autonomy and interdependence in the family of adulthood: A psychological perspective. *The Gerontologist*, 23, 33-39.

Cruzan v. Director, Missouri Department of Health, 110 S.Ct. 2841 (1990).

_____. *v. Harmon*, 760 S. W. 2d 408 (1988).

Council on Ethical and Judicial Affairs of the American Medical Association. (1989). *Current opinions*. Chicago: American Medical Association.

Emanuel, L. L., Barry, M. J., Stoeckle, J. D., Ettelson, L. M., & Emanuel, E. J. (1991). Advance directives for medical care—a case for greater use. *The New England Journal of Medicine*, 324, 889-895.

Emanuel, L. L., & Emanuel, E. J. (1989). The medical directive: A new comprehensive advance care document. *Journal of the American Medical Association*, 261, 3288-3293.

Estes, C. L. (1988). Cost containment and the elderly: Conflict or challenge? *Journal of the American Geriatrics Society*, 36, 38-72.

_____. (1991). The new political economy of aging: Introduction and critique. In M. Minkler & C. L. Estes (Eds.), *Critical perspectives on aging: The political and moral economy of growing old*, (pp. 19-36). Amityville, NY: Baywood.

Evans, D. A., Funkenstein, H. H., Albert, M. S., Scherr, P. A., Cook, N. R., Chown, M. J., Hebert, L. E., Hennekens, C. H., & Taylor, J. O. (1989). Prevalence of Alzheimer's disease in a community population of older persons. *Journal of the American Medical Association*, 262, 2551-2556.

Foody v. Manchester Memorial Hospital, 40 C. S. 127, 482 A. 2d 713. (Super. Ct. 1984).

Gallup, G., & Newport, F. (1991). Mirror of America: Fear of dying. *Gallup Poll News Service*, 55, 3-5.

Gamble, E. R., McDonald, P. J., & Lichstein, P. R. (1991). Knowledge, attitudes, and behavior of elderly persons regarding living wills. *Archives of Internal Medicine*, 151, 277-280.

Hardwig, J. (1990). What about the family? *Hastings Center Report*, 20, 5-10.

Hare, J., & Nelson, C. (1991). Will outpatients complete living wills? A comparison of two interventions. *Journal of General Internal Medicine*, 6, 41-46.

Harper, M. S., & Lebowitz, B. D. (1986). *Mental illness in nursing homes: Agenda for research*. Rockville, MD: National Institute of Mental Health.

High, D. M. (1988a). All in the family: Extended autonomy and expectations in surrogate health care decision making. *The Gerontologist*, 28, 46-51.

_____. (1988b). Foregoing life-sustaining procedures: Survey and analysis of Kentuckians' opinions. *Journal of the Kentucky Medical Association*, 86, 293-295.

_____. (1989). Standards for surrogate decision making: What the elderly want. *Journal of Long-term Care Administration*, 17, 8-13.

_____. (1990a). Old and alone: Surrogate health care decision-making for elderly without families. *Journal of Aging Studies*, 4, 277-88.

_____. (1990b). Who will make health care decisions for me when I can't? *Journal of Aging and Health*, 2, 291-309.

_____. (1991a). A new myth about families of older people? *The Gerontologist*, 31, 611-618.

_____. (1991b). *Use of advance directives among the elderly:*

Development and measurement of educational dissemination and intervention strategies, Grant #90-150. The Retirement Research Foundation.

_____, & Turner, H. B. (1987). Surrogate decision-making: The elderly's familial expectations. *Theoretical Medicine*, 8, 303-320.

_____. (1991). Are Kentuckians using advance medical directives? *Journal of the Kentucky Medical Association*, 89, 547-551.

Horowitz, A., Silverstone, B. M., & Reinhardt, J. P. (1991). A conceptual and empirical exploration of personal autonomy issues within family caregiving relationships. *The Gerontologist*, 31, 23-31.

In re Conroy, 98 N. J. 321, 486 A.2d 1209 (1985).

In re O'Connor, 72 N. Y. 2d 517, 531 N.E.2d 607, 534 N.Y.S.2d 886 (1988).

In re Storar, 52 N. Y. 2d 363, 420 N.E.2d 64, 438 N.Y.2d 266, cert. denied, 454 U.S. 858 (1981).

In re Torres, 357 N. W. 2d 332 (Minn. 1984).

LaPuma, J., Orentlicher, D., & Moss, R. J. (1991). Advance directives on admission: Clinical implications and analysis of the patient self-determination act of 1990. *Journal of the American Medical Association*, 266, 402-405.

Meisel, A. (1989). *The right to die*. New York: John Wiley & Sons.

Minkler, M. (1991). Overview. In M. Minkler & C. L. Estes (Eds.), *Critical perspectives on aging: The political and moral economy of growing old*, (pp. 3-18). Amityville, NY: Baywood.

Most MDs favor withdrawal of life support: Survey. (1988). *American Medical News*, June 3, 9.

National Center for Health Statistics. (1977). *Trends in fertility in the United States*. Washington, DC: U.S. Government Printing Office.

_____. (1985). *Vital statistics of the United States*, 1980 (Vol. II). Washington, DC: U.S. Government Printing Office.

_____. (1990). *Vital statistics of the United States*, 1988 (Vol. I). Washington, DC: U.S. Government Printing Office.

_____. (1991). *Vital statistics of the United States*, 1988 (Vol. II). Washington, DC: Public Health Service.

Office of Technology Assessment. (1987). *Life-sustaining technologies and the elderly* (OTA-BA-306). Washington, DC: U.S. Government Printing Office.

Orentlicher, D. (1990). Advance medical directives. *Journal of the*

American Medical Association, 263, 2365-2367.

Ouslander, J. G., Tymchuk, A. J., & Rahbar, B. (1989). Health care decisions among elderly long-term care residents and their potential proxies. *Archives of Internal Medicine*, 149, 1367-1372.

Poll: 79% support letting terminally ill refuse treatment. (1990, June 7). *The Lexington Herald-Leader*, 3.

President's Commission for the Study of Ethical Problems in Medicine and Biomedical and Behavioral Research. (1982). *Making Health Care Decisions* (Vol. 1). Washington, DC: U.S. Government Printing Office.

_____. (1983). *Deciding to forego life-sustaining treatment*. Washington, D. C.: U.S. Government Printing Office.

Public Law No. 101-508, 104 S. 1388 (1990).

Rhoden, N. K. (1988). Litigating life and death. *Harvard Law Review*, 102, 375-446.

Roe, J. M., Goldstein, M. K., Pascoe, D., & Massey, K. (1990). Durable power of attorney for health care (DPHC): A survey of persons for use and non-use by a senior center population. *The Gerontologist*, 30 (Special Issue), 81A.

Rowe, J. W., & Kahn, R. L. (1987). Human aging: Usual and successful. *Science*, 237, 143-149.

Schloendorff v. Society of New York Hospitals 211 NY 125, 105 N. E. 94 (1914).

Seckler, A. B., Meier, D. E., Mulvihill, M., & Paris, B. E. C. (1991). Substitute judgment: How accurate are proxy predictions? *Annals of Internal Medicine*, 115, 92-98.

Steiber, S. R. (1987). Right to die: Public balks at deciding for others. *Hospitals*, 61, 72.

Tomlinson, T., Howe, K., Notman, M., & Rossmiller, D. (1990). An empirical study of proxy consent for elderly persons. *The Gerontologist*, 30, 54-64.

Troll, L. E., Miller, S. J., & Atchley, R. C. (1979). *Families in later life*. Belmont, CA: Wadsworth Publishing Co.

Uhlmann, R. F., Pearlman, R. A., & Cain, K. C. (1988). Physicians' and spouses predictions of elderly patients' resuscitation preferences. *Journal of Gerontology*, 43, M115-M121.

United States Bureau of Census. (1989). *Projections of the population of the United States, by age, sex, and race: 1988 to 2080*, by Gregory Spencer. Washington, DC: U.S. Government Printing Office.

_____. (1986). *A matter of choice: Planning ahead for health care decisions*. Washington, DC: U. S. Government Printing Office.

Veatch, R. M. (1984). *Autonomy's temporary triumph*. Hastings Center Report, 1, 38-40.

White, M. L., & Fletcher, J. C. (1991). The patient self-determination act: On balance, more help than hindrance. *Journal of the American Medical Association*, 266, 410-412.

Zweibel, N. R., & Cassel, C. K. (1989). Treatment choices at the end of life: A comparison of decisions by older patients and their physician-selected proxies. *The Gerontologist*, 29, 615-621.

CHAPTER 4
Undermining Stereotypes of the Old Through Social Policy Analysis: Tempering Macro- with Micro-Level Perspectives

Sarah H. Matthews

Challenging negative stereotypes about the old has been a goal of the field of social gerontology since its inception in the 1940s. Ethel Shanas' Robert W. Kleemeier Award Lecture (1979), for example, was in this tradition when it compared the difficulty of destroying the myth that old people are isolated and forgotten by their adult children to the legendary Hydra monster that sprouted two heads for each one that was cut off. An equally irascible myth is the widely held notion that old age means disease and poor health. At a time when the number and proportion of elders are growing and the cost of health care has escalated, that this purported relationship translates into high health care costs has attracted the attention of policymakers who are concerned about balancing budgets (Clark, 1991). Slaying this "monster" has taken on a sense of urgency.

This paper takes issue with the way that those social scientists who occupy center stage in the debate over the relationship between ill health and old age have framed their argument. It does this by reviewing the assertions that macro-level scholars have made to refute the myth. The argument is then made that this strategy is unlikely to be successful because there is an undeniable relationship between old age and declining health. As an alternative strategy, the advantage of using a micro-level perspective to supplement a macro-level analysis is then stressed. As an example, the way adult children talked about their old parents in open-ended interviews is examined to see how important this image of disease actually is to their perceptions of their elderly parents. The paper juxtaposes two bodies of gerontological literature—one on long-term-care health policy, the other on family relationships—that are rarely thought to inform one another. The destruction of a myth is facilitated when there is a more plausible view available to take its place. This chapter, then, is an effort to identify such a view.

FRAMING THE ISSUE FROM MACRO-LEVEL PERSPECTIVES

Social Construction of Old Age in American Society. In a recent book entitled *Beyond Sixty-Five: The Dilemma of Old Age in America's Past,* the historian Haber describes how the medical model of old age was socially constructed by various professionals in the nineteenth century. Focusing on their writings she examines "the creation of formal 'scientific' classifications of aging and the effect these categorizations had upon the care of the elderly" (Haber, 1983:7).

> In the nineteenth century, for the first time, writers produced a growing body of literature devoted strictly to the ills of senescence. Doctors, statisticians, welfare advocates, and business planners all formulated theories on the nature and needs of the elderly....The conception of old age uniformly emphasized its infirmities and limits. The old, they believed, by reason of their altered physiological, anatomical, and psychological state, were no longer able to play an active or necessary role in society. (Haber, 1983:4)

Superannuation--the exclusion from social life of those who on the basis of age alone were classified as old—was justified because of the biological differences that presumably distinguished those who had passed the chronological milestone of 65 from those who were younger. In an increasingly bureaucratic society, age became the single criterion for exclusion and the resulting categorical social policies. Implicit in Haber's carefully-researched treatise is that this definition is only one of the possible ways that old age might have been socially constructed in the United States.

Another example comes from the anthropologist Sankar (1988) who focuses on the oldest-old, a "'newly discovered' age grouping" (Binstock, 1985:426) "defined arbitrarily as those aged 85 and over" (Suzman & Riley, 1985:177). She identifies one of the most important elements of their cultural construction as the "imputed causal link between old age and disease."

> The assumption is that the oldest-old will be sick, frail, alone, and depressed. The stereotype of the elderly as a uniformly needy and sick population is a strong one in American culture. (Sankar, 1988:346)

Bringing Haber's view up to the late 1980s, then, Sankar argues that the cultural stereotype of the old as diseased and dependent continues to be held by policymakers and the public alike.

Estes paints a similar picture from the perspective of political economy which focuses not only on the social construction of old age but on how it is maintained and perpetuated:

> Biomedical models foster thinking about the problems of aging as individual biological inevitabilities--largely, of physiological decline and decay. It is a conceptualization of old age that has supported the "medicalization" of aging (that is, thinking of aging problems as primarily medical problems). This tendency initially directed attention to medicine for solutions, and subsequently has led to the coalescence between the aging and a growing medical-industrial complex. (Estes, 1986:244)

In this view, the social or cultural construction of old age as disease has resulted in a medical-industrial complex whose members not only benefit greatly from its continued acceptance but also have the power to see that it is perpetuated.

Countering the Stereotype. All the scholars cited above (and others could have been included) agree that there is a pervasive stereotype that when people are old, their health is very likely to be poor. Moreover, they believe that the stereotype is inappropriate. As evidence of this misconception, they point to the fact that many of the old are hardy and that many of their problems stem not from biological decline but from social arrangements that foster poverty and isolation. Neugarten and Neugarten, for example, write:

> Old age is often said to begin when a person requires special health care because of frailty or chronic disease, or when health creates a major limitation on the activities of everyday life. Yet half of all persons who are now seventy-five to eighty-four report no such health limitations. Even in the very oldest group, those above eighty-five, more than one-third report no limitations due to health; about one-third report some limitations, and one-third are unable to carry out everyday activities (Neugarten & Neugarten, 1986:34).

As another example, Sankar argues that it only *appears* that the oldest-old use a disproportionate share of health care dollars and are responsible for the rise in health care expenditures:

> It is not old age itself that accounts for increased health care utilization but nearness to death. It has been demonstrated that approximately 5 percent of the Medicare population account for 30 percent of the costs...and these 5 percent are in the last year of life (Sankar, 1988:348).

Estes and Binney provide a third example. After arguing that the "biomedical view of aging is reinforced by family, friends, and personal contact with the medical profession" (Estes & Binney, 1989:594), they suggest three groups whose presence undermines the "solid and widespread public acceptance of the biomedical paradigm": The first is the old themselves who are "entering their 'older years,' healthy, active, and with expectations of an increasing life expectancy approaching two or more decades." The second is increased awareness on the part of both old and young of "lifestyle modifications" such as exercise and better nutrition which "challenge notions of the inevitability of disease, disability and decay in old age." Last is groups such as the Gray Panthers, American Association of Retired Persons, and the Older Women's League that serve as "role models for vibrant, active and intelligent elders..." (Estes & Binney, 1989:595). These three groups, by exhibiting exemplary health and vigor, serve at least potentially as evidence that old age and ill health are not synonymous.

As a final example, Minkler writes of recent attempts "to counteract the decline and loss paradigm in geriatrics and gerontology" (Minkler, 1990:246). She cites Riley and Bond (1983) who forcefully argued that to equate aging with functional impairments to be guilty of a particularly damaging form of age prejudice that ignores the very real differences between normal aging and disease processes.

Minkler also cites psychologists who have found in longitudinal studies no evidence of decline in intellectual functioning until just before death as well as health researchers who provide evidence that many declines begin well before old age and "have little functional consequence." Minkler then, attempts "to slay the monster" by citing recent scientific research that claims to find no relationship between old age and disease or decline.

All of these authors argue that although there is some truth to there being a correlation between old age and disease, the correlation is moderate at best as psychologists, social scientists, and medical scientists attest. The implication is that once citizens and policymakers are enlightened about the error of attributing a higher magnitude to this correlation than is justified, the cultural construction of old age as disease will be undermined and a more realistic one will emerge to take its place.

It seems unlikely that this will happen. There is an undeniable relationship between old age and disease or frailty. By Haber's own analysis (1983), long before the United States became urbanized, industrialized, and bureaucratized, there were those who were defined as "too old" or "overaged" because they no longer were able to perform what was expected of adults, and evidence indicates that this is the case in most societies. No social scientific sleight of hand can make humans into "wonderful one-horse shays" regardless of how much we wish it were so.

FRAMING THE ISSUE FROM MICRO-LEVEL
PERSPECTIVES

Instead of denying that there is a correlation between old age and physical problems, acceptance of the relationship while at the same time exploring what these physical changes mean to those who experience them seems a better way to promote a more realistic cultural construction of old age. This is not simply a matter of distinguishing between disease--the manifestation of biophysiological phenomena--and illness--the "social psychological state presumably caused by the disease," (Conrad & Kern, 1986:7). Rather, from a sociological perspective, physical changes are manifest in relationships. The application and negotiation of stereotypes occurs in social interaction. Therefore, these changes affect not only elders but also those with whom they are in relationships. Can we assume that the elderly and those with whom they interact in fact allow these cultural constructions to dictate their interactions, as Estes and Binney (1989) assert? How do the elderly deal with physical changes? We cannot readily assume that we know the answers to these questions. Instead they must be investigated empirically. And this requires focusing on the everyday lives of those who are old and those who interact with them--a micro-level perspective in which individuals are assumed to be actors constructing their lives in relationships with others and, as such, testing cultural stereotypes.

Perhaps one of the great injustices that the aged suffer is the unwillingness of researchers and policymakers alike to treat them as capable actors. Although there are studies of the effects of chronic illness on everyday life, the elderly, who are most likely to be affected by them, quite simply have been overlooked (Belgrave, 1986). The only exception is Alzheimer's disease, which literally deprives its elderly victims of the ability to interact in ways that are symbolically meaningful. Instead of assuming that we know how social policies and chronic diseases affect old persons, it may behoove us to allow them to tell us.

In a recent paper on nursing homes, Diamond (1988) argues that a complete understanding of long-term-care social policy can only be ascertained if the everyday lives of the residents and staff in long-term care institutions are studied:

> The research objective here is to start with everyday
> situations and link them to social policy. I would argue
> that many social policies now do not reflect an
> understanding of their consequences for everyday life. In
> this procedure one gets to know people over time and
> studies how their lives are shaped by policies. This
> necessarily involves a redefinition of who constitutes the
> social actors in social policy to include not only those who
> make policies, but also those who live them out
> (Diamond, 1988:52-53).

To study the everyday lives of the inhabitants—residents, staff
members and visitors—of an institution is one thing. To attempt to do this
outside of one requires confronting the heterogeneity of the elderly
population and the variety of ways that social policies affect them.

Social policies by necessity treat the elderly as a category, but in
their everyday lives old people are treated by most of those around them,
especially those closest to them, as unique individuals (Townsend, 1981).
The effects of any one social policy, then, will differ depending on a variety
of contingencies that are difficult to understand without actually studying
the effects of implemented social policies on the everyday lives of those
who presumably are affected by them. In discussions of the effects of social
policies, this is often overlooked. Estes, for example, attributes a great deal
of power to:

> the bureaucracies and professions constituting this [aging]
> enterprise, particularly the medical sector, [which] have
> ensured that the aged will be dependent upon their
> services....Such an enterprise tends to foster the unilateral
> dependency of elders on bureaucratic institutions while
> isolating them from society through age-segregated
> policies (Estes, 1986:243).

Although clearly influential with respect to the options available to
the old and the definitions of their problems, social policies do not
unilaterally dictate how people will behave. Instead, people make decisions
about how to act in given situations to accomplish their ends. They interact
with other people, not with social policies.

In fact, the intentions of policymakers and implementers may be
of little consequence to the old and those linked to them who are

manipulating the existing environment to accomplish their own ends and who manage, in Spence's words (1986), "to prevail." However, social policies are easily examined and statistics describing users of services are readily available, thanks to the record keeping that takes place on a massive level in modern societies. The everyday lives of those whom policies affect are much more difficult to capture in research. That there often is a world of difference between the intent of policies and the use to which they are put is evident in studies of powerful actors. The nursing home industry, for example, according to Vladeck (1980) has been able successfully to defend itself from increased regulation at almost every turn. The idea that elderly persons themselves may be capable of the same type of defense rarely has been entertained.

APPLICATIONS OF THE STEREOTYPE IN THE CONTEXT OF FAMILIES

Earlier it was suggested that it is important to keep in mind that changes in health status derive their meaning not only from the individual elders' experiences of them but also from those with whom they are in relationships. Data collected for a research project on older families from adult children who had at least one, non-institutionalized parent aged 75 or older, is used to illustrate this assertion. If the biomedical model is as pervasive as has been claimed, its application by adult children should be evident.

Altogether 298 adult children--149 pairs of siblings--described how meeting filial responsibilities was accomplished in their families. In the written questionnaire completed before the adult child participated in a face-to-face interview, respondents were asked, among many other questions, to assess their parent's health using a four-item scale, to identify any health problems their parents might have, and to assess their functional and instrumental health status by indicating how much help the parent needed with 15 activities of daily living. Of more interest here, however, were responses to the first question in the open-ended interview in which each adult child was asked to describe the current situation of their parent(s):

> We chose the age of 75 as the minimum age for parents
> in our study because we felt that after that age people are
> likely to be dealing with some of the problems that
> accompany aging. What about your parent(s)? Would you
> tell me what (his, her, their) situation is like?

There is a great deal of variety in the types of problems these adult children described. In their responses to this question and to the others in the open-ended interview, however, it is evident that, while considered significant, health status did not define the parent for the adult children. As evidence to support this assertion, the responses to the above and other questions of two pairs of siblings are presented.

> CASE 1. One daughter explained her mother's living arrangement:
> Ever since my father died [30 years ago] we've had my
> mother living with one of us, and we have a system
> where she rotates her one-month stays among Leah,
> Marie, and me...She has various physical problems that
> are listed in the other questionnaire but nothing that has
> developed lately. They are all things she's had for quite
> some time....She's aware of everything, reads the paper
> every day, is aware of current events. One problem that
> is sometimes troublesome is her inability to go up and
> down stairs well, and at my house the only bathroom is
> upstairs and in Marie's house she has to go down the
> stairs to get to a toilet. Since she has diarrhea often she
> sometimes has accidents.

> Her sister's description of the situation is similar:
> She has physical problems only. Her mind is very keen
> and alert. She has arthritis in her knees and uses a
> walker. She has glaucoma, high blood pressure, and
> wears two hearing aids. She does have a hiatal hernia.
> She has the tender, loving care of her family and she
> can't live on her own because of her physical
> disabilities....The only problem we have is trying to get
> her to take a bath. That's our only problem. It's

maddening, but that is the only problem we have with her.

Although both of these daughters acknowledge that their mother has many physical problems, they do not define her in terms of them.

CASE 2. Another pair of sisters described their mother whose health status would be rated by most measures as very poor. The first one said:

Well, she's 97....In the last year health wise she's hard of hearing, much worse, can't hear over the telephone. She does wear a hearing aid, but it doesn't help much. She doesn't get out unless we take her. She has angina. She's a little afraid to go, even in her building. She takes medication for angina regularly. She doesn't get out of her apartment for weeks on end unless we take her. She gets around very well in the apartment. My sister and I get her groceries. She's a little afraid of going out in the last few years.

Her sister's assessment is similar:
She's very independent in her own apartment....She's had angina for forty to fifty years. Takes many pills and knows every one. She checks to be sure they are right. We never have to worry about that. She has good sense....She is a grande dame in a sense. She creates that respect in us. She's a very bright woman and knows what she's doing. She has a marvelous sense of humor....Loneliness is the biggest problem. She craves company. She has high blood pressure, takes pills for that. She had a mastectomy two years ago. Had cataracts eight years ago. Gall bladder surgery three or four years ago. She took those so well. She doesn't go under her own steam. She says she can't because her heart acts up, but it's also because she's frightened. So she won't do that much. We take her out, not as much as we used to. Her apartment is far from the elevator and so we wheel her to the car and then she walks a little. It's a chore to

take her out now. Mother is very deaf....I find I have to
find different ways to say the same thing so that she'll
hear one word and get the gist of it.

Again, this mother is severely limited in her ability to get around
and has had and currently has major health problems, but both daughters'
primary concern is with her hearing impairment because it interferes with
communication. Her other physical ailments are baggage that must be carted
along with her but do not prevent her daughters from continuing to see her
as a gifted woman.

In these two cases, the elders clearly were experiencing physical
problems. Although each continued to live in the community, each would
have been defined as in need of care--not only elderly but frail and in
declining health. However, the daughters, while recognizing that their
mothers had severe physical problems, nevertheless viewed the problems
as annoying nuisances for their mothers rather than as defining their
mother's essence. They had not allowed stereotypes to get in the way of
their seeing their mothers as persons first.

It would appear, then, that the cultural stereotypes of old age as
disease is not powerful enough to determine interpersonal relations between
those who know one another well. Although Estes and Binney (1989:594)
write that "the biomedical view of aging is reinforced by family, friends,
and personal contact with the medical profession and by one's own belief
system," very few of the adult children who participated in this research
project use this view to interpret and respond to their own elderly parents.

This is not a new observation. According to Townsend:

There is a sharp contrast between the low status in which
old people are held publicly and the regard in which they
are held privately in their families. In the family age is
of secondary importance. People are grandparents,
parents, brothers or sisters and friends or neighbors first
and foremost....The defensive and restorative mechanisms
of the family temper the dependency created by the state
(Townsend, 1981:13).

His point, however, is somewhat different from the one being made
here. Social policies that affect the elderly are not implemented
anonymously, but in relationships with professionals, friends, neighbors,
and family members, in everyday life. To depict the world as sharply

divided between public and private is to forget that social policies are implemented by people. Research that focuses on the everyday lives of the elderly and their interactions with others may provide greater understanding of the social constructions of elderly persons that in fact are in use.

CONCLUSION

This paper began with a review of the principal arguments made by social scientists attempting to put an end to the "myth" that to be old is to be in poor health. These scholars conclude that the cultural construction of aging as disease is widely held but inaccurate because most aged persons are in relatively good health. The position adopted here is that expecting successfully to counter the stereotype by touting the good health of the elderly is foolhardy because the relationship between old age and disease, frailty, and decline, is undeniable.

An alternative strategy was suggested, that is, to investigate whether this cultural construction in concrete situations actually affects the everyday lives of the old and those with whom they interact. Inclusion of cases describing the ways that adult children interpreted or assigned meaning to their old parents when their health status was in fact poor was intended to show that the adult children continued to treat their parents as people who happened to have medical problems rather than the reverse. The biomedical view of aging apparently is not as pervasive as is assumed.

Much of the current debate about health care policy for the old is at a macro-level. Stereotypes and segregating social policies are assumed to be of overriding significance. The examples given above indicate that it is a mistake to ignore the fact that the old must deal with old bodies, just as it is mistake to assume that analyses of cultural constructions and social policies are applied in whole cloth in everyday life. Minkler (1990:256) voices concern about the "new emphasis on healthy or 'successful' aging" because it may lead to "prejudice against disabled elders." She warns that "we must...accept the fact that for many elders...chronic illness and disability will be a continuing reality." Future research may reveal that those who interact with elderly persons already have accepted that frailty and disability do not get in the way of their continuing to interact with the elders in their lives foremost as people.

In *Long Lives: Chinese Elderly and the Communist Revolution*, Davis-Friedmann is awed by "The easy rapport between young and old and the general acceptance of the frailty of the old....." After witnessing a poignant scene involving a frail old woman and a young boy in Beijing, she asks:

> What explains the apparently effortless acceptance of the old and their frailties? What are the roots of this pervasive sympathy, and why does there appear to be so little variation between official ideology and private expectations? (Davis-Friedmann, 1983:9)

In everyday life for many of the old in the United States, there may in fact be much more "effortless acceptance of frailty" than is revealed when only a macro-perspective is used to analyze social policy.

REFERENCES

Belgrave, L. L. (1986). The experience of chronic disease in the everyday lives of elderly women. Paper presented at the Annual Meeting of the Gerontological Society of America, Chicago.

Binstock, R. H. (1985). The oldest-old: A fresh perspective on compassionate ageism revisited? *The Milbank Memorial Fund Quarterly*, 63, 420-451.

Clark, P. G. (1991). Geriatric health care policy in the United States and Canada: A comparison of facts and values in defining the problems. *Journal of Aging Studies*, 5, 265-281.

Conrad, P. & Kern, R. (Eds.) (1986). *The sociology of health and illness: Critical perspectives*. New York: St. Martin's Press.

Davis-Friedmann, D. (1983). *Long lives: Chinese elderly and the communist evolution*. Cambridge, Massachusetts: Harvard University Press.

Diamond, T. (1988). Social policy and everyday life in nursing homes: A critical ethnography. In A. Statham, E. M. Miller, & H. O. Mauksch (Eds.), *The worth of women's work: A qualitative synthesis*, (pp. 39-56). Albany: State University of New York Press.

Estes, C. L. (1986). The aging enterprise: In whose interest? *International Journal of Health Services*, 16, 243-251.

_____, & Binney, E. A.(1989). The biomedicalization of aging: Dangers and dilemmas. *The Gerontologist*, 29, 587-596.

Haber, C. (1983). *Beyond sixty-five: The dilemma of old age in America's past.* New York: Cambridge University Press.

Minkler, M. (1983). Blaming the aged victim: The politics of scapegoating in times of fiscal conservatism. *Journal of Health Services*, 13, 155-168.

_____. (1990). Aging and disability: Behind and beyond the stereotypes. *Journal of Aging Studies.* 4, 245-260.

Neugarten, B. & Neugarten, D. (1986). Aging in the aging society. *Daedalus*, 115, 31-49.

Riley, M. W. & Bond, K. (1983). Beyond ageism: Postponing the onset of disability. In M. W. Riley, B. B. Hess, and K. Bond (Eds.), *Aging in society: Selected reviews of recent research* (pp. 243-252), Hillsdale, NJ: Lawrence Erlbaum Associates.

Sankar, A. (1988). The living dead: Cultural construction of the oldest-old. In Philip Silverman (Ed.), *The elderly as modern pioneers*, (pp. 345-356). Bloomington: Indiana University Press.

Shanas, E. (1979). Social myth as hypothesis: The case of the family relations of old people. *The Gerontologist* 19, 3-9.

Spence, D. (1986). Some contributions of symbolic interaction to the study of growing old. In V. W. Marshall (Ed.), *Later life: The social psychology of aging*, (pp. 107-123). Beverly Hills, CA: Sage Publications.

Suzman, R. & Riley, M. W. (1985). Introducing the oldest-old. *The Milbank Memorial Fund Quarterly*, 63, 177-186.

Townsend, P. (1981). The structured dependency of the elderly. *Ageing and Society*, 1, 5-28.

Vladeck, B. (1980). *Unloving care: The nursing home tragedy.* New York: Basic Books.

PART II

Domestic Policy in Canada

CHAPTER 5

Caring and Sharing: Demographic Aging, Family and the State

Susan A. McDaniel

Attention, by both researchers and policy-makers, to the public policy challenges posed by population aging has been skewed toward the large-scale issues of labor supply, pensions, and health care. Although excellent research has been done on family aspects of aging (e.g. Connidis, 1989; Rosenthal, 1990; Statistics Canada, 1991; Stone, 1988; Walker, 1982; Wolf, Burch & Soldo, 1990), linkages among demographic aging, family and public policy challenges are seldom fully drawn. Of course, there are notable exceptions to this simple generalization, and several useful beginnings have been undertaken (Neysmith, 1989; Walker, 1991).

This chapter does not set out to provide a comprehensive review of the growing literature on families and aging in public policy context. Nor does it purport to bring the final word on the importance of families in general. Rather, it examines some of the more salient public policy issues related to demographic aging and families. As well, the chapter points toward the kinds of frameworks and issues that might be useful in future research. Since the chapter by Neysmith in this volume addresses some of the micro-macro links between families and society, the focus in this chapter will be more specifically on the macro, the political economic, or structural, level.

The chapter concentrates on Canadian data and Canadian public policy challenges. As they appear relevant, some comparative illustrations will be provided with United States data, and, to a lesser degree, with United States policy issues. Before American readers are tempted to skip quickly back to the first section of the book and its attention to questions rooted in the context of the United States, it might be added that many, if not most, of the concepts, principles and structural issues discussed here transcend national borders.

DEMOGRAPHIC AND SOCIAL POLICY

Social policy, including public and private policy, of the 1990's is often times undergirded by demographic analysis. Policy, to be effective, must be attentive to population trends and structure including age/sex composition, labor force participation, the type and size of families and households as well as the racial (in the United States) or ethnic (in Canada) composition. As well, the dynamic aspects of demographic change are important for public policy, particularly social policy development, such as trends in birth and death rates, in population aging, changing patterns of marriage and divorce, and migration, urbanization, suburbanization, and immigration trends.

While basic to policy development, demographic trends in and of themselves say nothing about which directions policy should take, although one might think otherwise to hear so much talk in both private and public sectors about "the demographics." The demographic seems to have an inexorable pull for policymakers. Once a trend is attributed to demographic patterns, they are often considered to be the driving force behind policy. This is certainly true of demographic aging, which has been argued to be the paradigm of the 1980's and 1990's, guiding public policy as paradigms of youth or economic growth did in the past (McDaniel, 1987). It is as if, on the one hand, demography is the subterrain of public policy, and on the other hand, demographic forces themselves are thought to be virtually untouchable by public policy (although not for want of trying).

In the United States, there has been remarkable public attention to intergenerational equity issues since the publication in 1984 of Preston's Presidential address to the Population Association of America (Preston, 1984), and the simultaneous emergence of the lobby group, Americans for Generational Equity. Intergenerational equity broadly encompasses the idea that young and old should have comparable access to opportunities, including public policy benefits. The debate, which spawned some 356 print media articles according to Marshall, Cook and Marshall (1991) in the United States, has received limited attention at best in Canada.

TABLE 1

Age Structure: Canada and United States
1987

| White | United States | | | Canada |
	African American	Other	Total	Total
% age 0-14				
20.5	27.0	26.6	21.5	21.2
% age 65+				
13.0	8.2	6.6	12.2	10.9
Total "dependency" ratio (0-14 + 65+ /15-64)				
50.4	54.3	48.8	50.9	47.2

Source: Statistics Canada. 1990. Report on the Demographic Situation in Canada, 1990. Current Demographic Analysis by Jean Dumas. Ottawa: Minister of Supply and Services, 1990, p. 71.

Of interest in this chapter is that the intergenerational equity discussion, for the most part, skips over social equity and family issues in linking demographic age groups to public policy issues. This skipped step is very important to understanding who the children and older people in question actually are and the basis of their claims on public policy (Quadagno, 1989). Briefly put, the young who make claims on public funds are not all the young but the poor who in the United States are differentially African American and Hispanic. As is clear in Table 1, these groups differ appreciably from the white population in being more youthful and having significantly smaller proportions of older people. The old, in sharp contrast, are differentially white and better off (not in poverty to the same degree), have longer life expectancies and firmer claims to public pensions. Family is particularly important because neither old nor young exist in vacuums but have connective links to one another, largely through family, to the middle-aged group, those of labor force age. What this middle generation is doing in relation to the young, the old, and society generally, through taxes and contributions of time and other resources matters greatly to public policy and yet is largely overlooked. Thus, the intergenerational equity issue, framed typically in terms of demographics, may be essentially a social equity issue, mediated in the immediate realm by family as well as collectively by society.

In Canada, the social policy/demographics discussion has taken a different form. Instead of attention being focused on issues of intergenerational equity, there is considerable attention to how significantly public policy in such diverse arenas as pensions, health care and immigration is driven by an aging population (e.g. McDaniel, 1987; Foot, 1988). Assumptions, seldom explored or even questioned, tend to be made by both the public in general and policy-makers about increased costs of pensions and health care as a direct consequence of population aging. Immigration policy, long an issue of public interest in Canada, becomes seen by some as the answer to Canada's low birth rate—the underlying and most important cause of population aging. Although the perceived "problem" of population aging does not reveal any ameliorative effect from immigration nor do health care costs appear to have as much to do with aging as with dying, both dimensions are ignored in the face of the "demography as destiny" argument. Ignored as well are the multitude of ways in which families mediate in demographic aging and public policy challenges.

Demographic predictions in the past have been notoriously off the mark, foreseeing neither the baby boom after World War II, nor the contemporary baby bust. This record is somehow forgotten in today's world where demographic predictions are taken very seriously indeed. Predictions related to human phenomena tend to have an aspect that does not characterize predictions in other realms in that they may be self-fulfilling. The classic example of this, still taught in many introductory sociology courses, is that if depositors at a bank believe the bank to be insolvent and act as if it is insolvent, the bank becomes insolvent as a direct result of the depositors' beliefs and actions. The depositors withdraw all their money at once, leading to the collapse of the bank. Predictions which relate demographic futures to public policy tend to have a self-fulfilling aspect not because individuals act to make them true but rather because explaining rising costs of pensions and health care in terms of demographic aging is so simple and alluring. A "quick fix" explanation has a feeling of substance that closer scrutiny may suggest is really ephemeral.

Demography is distinctly abstract, expending great amounts of energy not looking at human beings and behavior directly, but only as aggregate trends, seemingly beyond human will. An example is that demographers tend to talk about fertility as if it were somehow divorced from sexual politics and gender issues. Perhaps it is the lifelessness of demography that, ironically, makes demographic predictions seem so compelling to social policy. Lost in futurists' looks at the social and economic world is that present demographic trends are the result of human behaviors. Yet projections seem to loom larger and become more real than anything we can do by dint of human will. There is a tyranny in the prediction, a transcendence of the human when demographic projections are invoked. Thus, demographic aging becomes a "problem" to be solved by social policy rather than an expected outcome in societies sufficiently well off to be able to control their fertility at a level they can support and similarly to control disease and mortality so many people can live long lives.

One last point about social policy built on demographics. A popular perception is that crises in public policy will loom large when the baby-boomers retire early in the next century. This is clearly an understanding premised on demographic determinism: demand for public services is thought to be driven by sizes of age groups. The reality, as pointed out by Myles (1991), is that the caregiving crisis is already upon us, not resulting from increased demand for care but from decreased supply of caregivers as more and more women, the principal caregivers in our society, work in the paid labor force and are less available for informal caregiving. Other factors matter too, such as decreased access to the appropriate level of formal care and the greater prevalence of chronic health problems. Focusing on demographic trends has caused policy-makers to miss this current crisis while instead attending to some future crisis, which may or may not occur. Social policy built in response to demographic trends may not be the best policy. In summary, demographics, while important, are only one part of the complex of issues which challenge social policy in aging societies. Other issues include social equity, family resources and distribution within families as well as gendered division of labor in the workplace and in the family.

FAMILY AND SOCIAL POLICY

Family, in both the United States and Canada, has recently become a hot public policy concern. Day care and reproductive rights have been not only actively debated but the subjects of distinctly interventionist policies, or attempts at policies, in both countries. Quebec has implemented policies intended to raise the birth rate, in part with the intention of countering demographic aging by increasing the numbers of young people (Caldwell & Fournier, 1987; Laurin, 1984; Sheppard, 1988). Family issues, with a decidedly demographic component have never been so central to the public policy agenda as now. Nor have families been referenced for their ideological value as much as they are currently. Family policies are shaped as much by wishful thinking and nostalgia as they are by societal changes. Although the circumstances in which families live have changed dramatically—the demise of the family wage being among the most notable of these changes—the ideologies with which the family is imbued have changing less rapidly. Family has become mythologized, so that it is still expected to be the warm private place of yesteryear, even as we know we behave differently in contemporary families. Tensions abound between family as lived reality and family as ideal, with many politicians seeming keen to capitalize more on emotional illusions than everyday family realities.

Family policies have captured the interest of politicians, both north and south of the 49th parallel. Although most public policies have some implications for families, family policy *per se* (policies that are specifically intended to work toward the benefit of families) have received, until recently, limited attention in public policy circles. The prevalent notion has been that family is private, no one's business but one's own. The ideology of familism, of family as everything to us, a private place where we can be sheltered from the stresses of the public world, is one of the prevalent myths on which the North American conception of the welfare state depends (Baines, Evans, Neysmith, 1991; Walker, 1991). Yet, it has been made evident, with empirical research, that the family is the single most dangerous of social institutions, with risks of being beaten and murdered higher within the family than in the most crime ridden of cities. Myths prevail in the face of overwhelming evidence to the contrary, so strong is the ideology of familism.

Family policies have built on the myth of the caring, large extended family, a myth which works to instill in people a sense of responsibility to fulfill family caregiving obligations (Kaden & McDaniel, 1990; Baines, Evans, & Neysmith, 1991). It is thought that families abandon their elderly today, whereas in times gone by, we all lived in happy three-generation families, gathering around elderly relatives' bedsides as they uttered their last words. The reality is that few families in the past had older relatives who lived sufficiently long for their grandchildren to get to know them (Gee, 1990). Only the very well-to-do had life expectancies long enough to experience three-generation families; the vast majority lived in two-generation families, with parents in the 19th century barely surviving the children's growing into adulthood (Gee, 1990).

The notion of family as a private realm, also a myth, has policy implications. Family has always functioned in the interest of the larger society, giving birth to new members, socializing them to be productive members of society, teaching the young society's values, such as caring for the old and infirm, and performing other socially valuable functions. Essential to the social roles that family plays is service to the economy and the state (Baines, Evans, & Neysmith, 1991; McDaniel, 1990). Although not always explicit, family exerts a generally conservative influence on society by encouraging workers, students, and housewives to sacrifice their senses of injustice in the workplace, the schools, and the home, "for the good of the family." The family's needs are thought to take priority over the needs of individuals. Paradoxically, threats to family, in either form or function, tend to be viewed by the state and the public policy apparatus as a cause for concern and policy action. When policy-makers devote their attention to family issues, it is typically because they see families as no longer adequately meeting the functions they want families to perform. Social welfare policies, for example, tend to reinforce a conception of family as an economic unit with dependents and a wage earner (Baines, Evans, & Neysmith, 1991). Some see demographic aging as another threat to family and family caring as state policy, since there are more members of families, both young and old, demanding care and attention.

In summary, recent public policy attention to family has been based as much, if not more, on myths and illusions about families than on hard empirical facts. Family policy may need a jolt of contemporary family reality to best meet the needs of aging societies.

ISSUES AND INTERCONNECTIONS

Public policy in the social realm has always been built on uneasy compromises. The thorny fields out of which social policy grows, regardless of its country of origin, include the dilemmas of private versus public provision and administration of services. Challenges are ongoing, without ever being fully resolved. For example, although health care in Canada is public, nursing home care typically is not. In the United States, although health care is generally private, there are a growing number of public and semipublic schemes and growing government involvement with health insurance schemes. The question of whether responsibility for the aged, the infirm, and the dependent lies with family or the state remains unresolved.

Characterizing much public policy debate with respect to aging and family is the dilemma of entitlement versus need. The entitlement argument holds that recipients of benefits (pensions, health care, housing subsidies, etc.) are entitled to benefits as a function of some universal criterion—in this case, passing a particular age. The need argument favors some assessment of means for receipt of benefits. In Canada, need is replacing universality (a concept long held dear to most Canadians) with the elimination in 1989 of universal access to Old Age Security (a pension available previously to anyone over the age of 65), by taxing back OAS for all high income earners (Gee & McDaniel, 1991). This is at present being challenged in the courts. That the so-called "claw-back" ceilings are not indexed to cost of living means that by 2019 (according to current estimates), those with incomes as low as $20,000 (Canadian) annually will have their OAS taxed back. Entitlement involves other issues as well such as who is thought to be deserving of a pension. The question is an increasingly real one, as unions in the 1990's in both the United States and Canada strike not for increased wages but for job security and benefits issues. Pension benefits are becoming scarce and much sought after in the work place. Pensions for homemakers are an entitlement issue with family implications. Some argue that society cannot afford to pay for the retirement of those who work at home and that pension provision for homemakers and displaced homemakers (who are divorced with no marketable skills) is essentially a family matter. Others argue that homemaking is an invaluable service to society and should be pensionable. The means of entitlement is a public policy issue with family relevance. Typically, pensions are either provided through links to the paid work force or by universal eligibility, but some spouses and dependent children of pensioners receive pensions on the basis of family status. The public policy challenges here are real as spouses who separate can now split pension credits in Canada (Gee & McDaniel, 1991). The argument has been made in the courts in the past few years that a combination of entitlement by family status and by work force contributions may be most appropriate for some women, whose earned ' pensions are inadequate as a result of child raising responsibilities. The debate continues.

Entitlement debates occur on the other side of the issue, too. Who is expected to pay for pensions? Is it we ourselves, our families, our spouses, the government, companies for which we work? Public policy in Canada is shifting more and more to individual responsibility by offering tax incentives for retirement savings while making few reforms to the public pension system. In the United States, private responsibility, not only for pensions but also for health care, has been a guiding principle for some time. "Harmonization" of service delivery means that services, or the connections among services, are reduced. This places more onus on families, usually a euphemism for women in families, to take on more work in caring for sick, old, or disabled relatives (Baines, Evans, & Neysmith, 1991; Myles, 1991; Walker, 1991). This is part of the caregiving crunch mentioned earlier. Sometimes the term of choice is "community" rather than family, but the result seems to be the same: that more women take on more responsibility, out of concern, guilt, or the simple reality that there is no one else to do it for no or very low pay (Baines, Evans, & Neysmith, 1991; Kaden & McDaniel, 1990; Neysmith, 1989).

Interconnections between demographic aging and family exist at other levels, too. Demographic aging is perceived as a force which alters family relationships and the family's role in society. In an aging society, the old are said to replace the young as dependents. This is made vivid in the concept of dependency ratio, an abstract demographic term having no bearing whatever on actual dependency (Foot, 1988; McDaniel, 1986, 1987, 1990). The concept is an overly simple proxy for economic dependency of both old and young on those of labor force age. Dependency ratio, as a demographic concept, may be a useful indicator of changing age structure, but as an indicator of economic or familial dependency, it is misleading and suggestive of relationships that may or may not exist and largely do not exist in society. Dependency ratios mask real human relationships by abstracting them to age deterministic categories: if one is over age 65, one is dependent, while a person of 18 is considered, in demographic terms, to be independent. Dependency ratios have gathered further baggage over the years—they have been transformed, largely by their allure to public policy-makers, into a sort of mirror image of what they actually are. Dependency in the familial sense does not fully imply burden, it is suggestive of mutuality and of benefits that may not be tangible. Dependency in familial terms, only becomes a "problem" when transposed into public policy and public purse terms.

In summary, several dilemmas characterize public policy on family and aging including that of public versus private provision, entitlement versus need, family versus state responsibility, and the large dilemma of mutuality versus burden within families.

DEMOGRAPHIC AGING AND FAMILY:
TRENDS AND PROSPECTS

Attention must be given in this chapter to trends and patterns of demographic aging and family in order to provide substance to the contentions made. No attempt is made to be comprehensive nor is an attempt made to make direct or systematic comparisons of United States and Canadian trends. Work appears elsewhere for both the United States (Kobrin, 1981 among others) and Canada (Gee, 1990; McDaniel, 1986, among others), and comparing Canada and the United States (Statistics Canada, 1990, Part II: United States/Canada comparisons).

In a global sense, the United States and Canada have similar patterns of demographic aging as shown in Table 1. Neither is at the advanced stage of demographic aging of some European countries, such as Sweden (16.5% 65+ in early 1980's) or what was West Germany (15.3%), or the United Kingdom (15.2%). Canada, slightly less demographically old than the United States, is one of the youngest of the industrialized countries. The United States population is more diverse, with the white population having appreciably more older persons and fewer younger than African American or "other" non-white populations. Table 1 reveals that African American and "others" have very small proportions in the older age groups in the United States but significantly more in younger groups.

TABLE 2

Life Expectancy by Sex and Class
Canada late 1970's

	Life Expectancy		Disability-Free Life	
	M	F	M	F
Overall	70.8	78.3	59.2	62.8
Income Level				
Lowest	67.1	76.6	50.0	59.9
Middle	70.9	78.5	61.1	64.3
Highest	73.4	79.4	64.3	67.5

Source: Adapted from Wilkins, Russell, & Owen Adams. 1983. "Health Expectancy in Canada, late 1970's: Demographic, Regional and Social Dimensions," *American Journal of Public Health* 73(9):1078.

The gender gap in aging is one of the most fundamental ways in which family and demographic aging intersect. Women outlive men in both the United States and in Canada, with the result that older families look very different than younger families and have different needs. Table 2 shows the differences in overall life expectancy by gender in Canada in the late 1970's. In 1982, women at age 60 could expect to outlive men of the same age by 5 years; women at age 70 could expect, on average, to live another 15.1 years, and men 11.6 years (McDaniel, 1986). The gender gap is comparable in the United States. This has a number of fundamental implications for public policy with respect to family and aging. Women are much more likely to be widows than men and significantly more likely to be living alone (for those over 65, women in Canada are more than three times more likely to be living alone; for those over 80, it is more than five times more likely) (General Social Survey 1990, Cycle 5, unpublished as yet). As shown in Table 2, women are likely to live more of their later years in disability than men with less well-off women facing disability earlier. And women are more likely to experience poverty in their later years than men, as shown in Table 3. All this leads women to be more probable candidates for care receipt by families as well as for health care and institutionalization in the last years of life.

TABLE 3

Poverty Levels for Older People
Canada (1986) and United States (1987)
by Sex and Family Status

	United States				Canada	
	Total		African American		Total	
%	M	F	M	F	M	F
In Families	6.0	7.0	17.4	23.8	13.2	25.0*
Unattached	18.7	43.5	24.8	63.6	33.1	50.1

* For Canada, the poverty figures for families are for Female-headed and Male-headed families.

Note: Definitions and poverty lines differ in the United States and Canada, as does the social services "safety net."

Sources: Canadian data: National Council of Welfare, Progress Against Poverty, 1987. United States data: United States Bureau of the Census, Current Population Reports, Population Profile of the United States, 1989. Special Studies Series P-23, No. 159, 1989.

Socio-economic differences have a profound effect throughout life and in the experiences of old age, too. In the United States, race is an imperfect euphemism for class. As seen in Table 1, African Americans and "others" have substantially lower proportions in the older age categories. In part the differences are the result of higher birth rates and larger proportions in the younger age groups among these "minority populations." But it is also a result of the lower life expectancies of African Americans and "others" relative to whites (Schulz, 1991). A similar pattern of differences is apparent in Canada as seen in Table 2. Those in the lowest socio-economic classes have the lowest life expectancies and the greatest risks of living in disability. This is particularly apparent for the lowest income level men, who experience disabilities at age 50 on average. As income levels rise, so do life expectancies, with women at each income level outliving men. It is clear then that for both the United States and for Canada, gender and class matter to the public policy challenges of aging, although neither clearly emerges as significant in pure demographic analyses.

The remarkable growth among persons living alone (Harrison, 1981) in both Canada and in the United States reflects preference and housing availability as well as changing demographic and family patterns. Older women comprise a significant part of the growth in those living alone in Canada, and in the United States research has revealed that living arrangements of older unmarried women in both countries are a function of the availability of kin (Stone, 1988; Wolf, Burch & Matthews, 1990; Wolf & Soldo, 1988). If relatives do not exist or are not available, older people will most frequently live alone. The kin who are most likely to have older relatives live with them, or to live with older relatives, are the same as those who most often help older relatives. They are differentially female, geographically proximate, and healthy, with the unmarried getting some priority as better choices compared to the married. These patterns are empirically validated in a model developed by Walker (1991).

Demographic aging is embedded in the fabric of societies in which it is occurring. The simple cause is superb control over fertility, providing fewer young entrants to society and consequently elevating the average age of the total population as well as the proportion of the total comprised by those in the older age categories. Increasing life expectancy, in the most industrialized countries only makes some small contribution to the overall change. The reality then is that demographic aging is the consequence of many members of a society deciding to limit their fecundity patterns. It is not surprising then that demographic aging is a sign of affluence, of societies in sufficient control over death and disease that they can control birth rates with the confidence that most of those born will grow to adulthood. This is strikingly apparent in the United States data shown in

Table 1, where the demographic picture for whites is one of control and increased longevity, with decreasing proportions of youth. The picture for African Americans and "others," however, is one of less control and contentment. The "others" category parallels demographic patterns in many Third World countries, while that of African Americans is slightly, but not significantly, better.

TABLE 4

Demographic Indicators of Parents' Lives
Canada

| | Birth Cohort | | | |
	1860	1910	1930	1960
Average # children & surviving to age 20	3.2	2.4	3.3	1.6
Median age at:				
first birth	26.6	25.2	23.2	25.0
last birth	37.2	29.0	29.5	26.8
"empty nest"	57.2	49.0	49.5	46.8
% adult years spent with children	78.2	58.0	57.8	41.9
# years spent in empty nest	6.8	17.0	21.0	30.2

Source: Adapted from Gee, Ellen. 1990. "Demographic Change and Intergenerational Relations in Canadian Families: Findings and Social Policy Implications," *Canadian Public Policy* 16(2): 193.

Demographic reflections of changing family patterns over time are revealed in Tables 4 and 5, adapted from Gee (1990). Table 4 shows how much family life cycles have changed in Canada over the last century or so. While it is well known that average family size has declined precipitously, it may be less well known that the probabilities of survival to age 20 have increased impressively. What is truly remarkable are the changes in average age at significant life events. While average age at first birth has hardly changed at all, average age at last birth has declined dramatically, from close to 38 to almost 27. A woman born in 1860 spent almost eleven years bearing children, while a woman born in 1960 spends, on average, less than two years. The experience of the last child leaving home occurs almost ten years earlier than it did a century ago. And, if increases in life expectancy are considered, the amount of one's lifetime spent in raising children over the past century has been nearly halved, while the number of years spent in a family in which the children are grown has increased five-fold. Putting family changes in long-term context reveals how very much family patterns have changed in the lifetimes of a few generations.

The policy implications of these changes are enormous, with both the structure of family and the timing of life events altered. Family defines lesser parts of our lives and thus assumes a different place in the public mind. Policies that define us in the 1990's as only (or centrally) familial will simply be out of touch with contemporary changes in the family life course.

Another manifestation of demographic change on the family front is that more adult children, even well into middle age, have living parents (Gee, 1990). Table 5 shows the dramatic increase in those at age 60 with surviving parents, from 2 percent for the 1860 cohort to a projected 23 percent for those born in 1960. Those with surviving parents at age 40 have almost doubled over the course of this century, while those with surviving parents at age 50 have increased almost four times. This means that middle-aged Canadians are facing, in large numbers, the challenges as well as the joys of having a generation older than they, something that their parents were much less likely to experience. The majority of these older parents are healthy and living autonomously, so it is not necessarily true that their presence creates greater pressures on adult children, but as the parents age, the challenges can multiply.

TABLE 5

Proportion of Children
With at Least One Surviving Parent
Canada

Birth cohort

		1860	1910	1930	1960*
Proportion					
	at age 40	42	61	73	82
	at age 50	16	33	49	60
	at age 60	2	8	16	23

*Projected
Source: Adapted from Gee, Ellen. 1990. "Demographic Change and Intergenerational Relations in Canadian Families: Findings and Social Policy Implications," *Canadian Public Policy* 16(2):192.

Taken together, Tables 4 and 5 indicate marked changes in family structures in North America (while the data are Canadian, similar shifts have occurred in the United States as well). Families have become more vertical, with more generations in each, and less horizontal, with fewer children per family. This change is among the most salient for families and aging in public policy terms (Binstock & George, 1990; Schulz, 1991). It means, essentially, that as family size declines and numbers of generations increase, there are fewer and fewer members of the middle generation to care for the old and for the young. This is one of the primary dimensions to the present caregiving crunch. The other fundamental factor, as mentioned earlier, is a decline in the supply of caregivers, most often women, as more women take paid employment to support their families.

In sum, although both Canada and the United States are demographically aging, neither is among the oldest societies in the world, and both countries have wide gaps between subpopulations that are older and younger. The gender gap in life expectancy means that older families are more often female, whose needs differ from those of males, and who are more likely to live alone in their later years. The shape of our lives in families has changed dramatically over the last century, with smaller portions of our lives being spent having and raising children but longer portions spent as adult children of aging parents.

POLICY INTERPRETATIONS OF AGING AND FAMILY

How changes in family and in demographic structure are translated into policy remains something of a mystery since the filters which form a crucial part of the process are not clearly visible and their functions are less than transparent. Nonetheless, it seems apparent that there is a vital role played by perspective and ideology. Demographic and family trends and patterns, in and of themselves, have no intrinsic meaning. The meaning comes from the perspective through which they are viewed and the ideology that serves as the impetus to public policy. Demographic aging, for example, can be interpreted as a sign of a society's or a subgroup's affluence and its control over the causes of death. Or, it can be interpreted as a sign of demographic decline—a society which is dying out—and more importantly, economic quandries (a zero or low growth economy). Interpretation depends on the perception of what is happening societally and how demographic and family changes are seen to fit into the bigger picture. One interpretation or the other is not inherent to demographic or family trends.

Ideological coloring of the supposed links between demographic aging and family change is made more likely because of the levels at which these changes occur. Demographic change is indirect, the collective and often unintended result of millions of individual decisions: demographic aging as the consequence of reduced fertility, for example. Family change is seen closer up and with less public distance. Family is thought to be a private preserve. Few people understand, even those familiar with data and theories about the family, that their families are seldom typical. So, for demographic analyses used in public policy, there is the distancing that the collective perspective allows -- policymakers may say that policies emanate directly from demographic changes in age structure to explain why costs of certain services cannot be met. And, for family, there is the tendency for public policy to stay away unless families are seen to be "problem families," and then policy interventions are likely to be direct and aimed toward "normalization," or restoring the family to what is ideologically defined as normal.

Public policy challenges posed by demographic aging and family changes involve issues of gender and of class. Gender is important because of women's positioning in family and society as caregivers and because women live longer than men (Baines, Evans, Neysmith, 1991; McDaniel, 1990). Women as carers and as cared for carry with them accumulated inequalities. A woman who has trouble balancing work and caring for older relatives is at risk both at work and at home (Baines, Evans, & Neysmith, 1991). She will have little time to care for herself or plan for her own retirement. Yet the challenges she faces are largely invisible to policymakers who limit their focus to the future of pensions and health care.

Public policy challenges of demographic aging and family are also class issues. The better off experience aging and the crunch of generational demands, because they tend to live longer, and, as importantly, they have fewer children. The less well-off struggle for survival and with greater demands from the young. The challenge to public policy is that, in the United States primarily, but to a lesser degree also in Canada, these two profoundly different realities exist in a single society. The obvious question is, how to accommodate the uniqueness of both groups.

To make the class aspect of public policy more concrete, an example is in order. Taxes are at issue in the United States because the interests of the older, better off, white population and the younger, poorer, non-white populations are not automatically seen as conqruent. It is largely the former group that is lobbying, effectively, for policies for the old and the aging. The less politically organized non-whites are having more difficulty getting the interests of their children onto the public agenda. In debate after debate, the issue of not paying taxes for "someone else's children" is raised as if the interests of children are separate from society's interests. This debate has been cast into the framework of generation and family and has deeply affected tax policies at local and state levels.

What are some of the research challenges of the future? There are many, only a few of which can be discussed here. Exploration and explication of the means by which sociodemographic trends get translated into public policy issues and ultimately into public policies would be high on the list of what should be done. There is often more rhetoric than substance in this area. The fundamental research question is what exactly is meant by the concepts of burden, dependency, and caregiving? These terms are bandied about in discussions and debates about demographic change and public policy, yet more is assumed than actually known about what they mean to people in various contexts and what they mean to policymakers.

Explorations of some of the contradictions between family and life in the public sphere could be beneficially explored in future research. For example, how is it that caring within the family is seen as costless to individuals and to society, whereas caring by society is defined as costly? Many other contradictions could be usefully examined under the bright light of empirical research.

The need persists for research on aging, particularly research on the interconnections among macro-level phenomena, such as demographic aging and family change, to be guided by theory. Too often research in this area is driven by the whims and fashions of the day, or by rank empiricism, neither of which lead generally toward the accumulation of a solid body of knowledge.

The policy challenges are less clear. Certainly what seems essential are policies for caring, outlined by Walker (1982; 1991). This reorientation of public policy priorities would put an end to the common practice of pitting so-called interest groups against each other. It would also reveal the ways in which present-day policies rely on an unrealistic, actually never existent, model of the family as a private place where all caring occurs. Current policy seems to assume that families have a state sanctioned monopoly on caring that would somehow be compromised were policy itself caring or were caring to be done anywhere else but in the family. The,onus of responsibility for caregiving is thus cloaked in the ideological baggage of the sancity of family values.

Policy of the future would see families and family change as well as demographic aging, more realistically, in socio-historical context rather than as free-floating challenges to policymakers. This would enable development of policies that are enabling to families, to older people, and to society. Policies that punish people, even inadvertently, for living in families that are not seen as typical or for living "too long" are not policies that should be encouraged.

In sum, policy making on family and aging, like social policy making in general, is an inexact process. It is deeply colored by ideology, with the dimensions of class and gender too often overlooked. Research and policy of the future face many challenges. Perhaps one of the most serious is the need for researchers and policymakers to work, genuinely, together to develop frameworks and perspectives that enhance understanding of the complex issues involved in demographic aging and family change.

THE 1990'S AND BEYOND

What does the future hold for public policy on demographic aging and family? Two contrasting scenarios come to mind. The first is a continuation of what we have now. The costs of demographic aging, to the extent there are costs, are largely borne by families. Families, and most notably women in families, tend to serve as elastic cuffs between large-scale demographic changes and individuals. If numbers of generations increase, the responsibility for dealing with this change falls to families. If fewer adult children exist in the future, as a result of declining birth rate and family size, then more responsibility for older relatives will fall to fewer family members. And if neglect or abuse of elder relatives occurs, then family members are held accountable as individuals, regardless of how they may be trying to cope with no or only limited supports.

The elasticity of families in coping with these and other demographic changes in light of largely unsupportive and unsympathetic social policies is not infinite. Like the costs of childbearing which are largely absorbed by women whose income and educational opportunities are limited, often very seriously, as a result, the costs of elder care cannot be infinitely absorbed without costs to society. Middle-aged women who are caregivers under stress today will become the old women of tomorrow. Their needs will be greater for health care, for social care, for pensions and economic supports. Playing off the needs of the middle-aged with those of the old and the young places all at a disadvantage.

The second scenario is a brighter one but requires a sharp shift in the current public policy orientations of both the United States and Canada. The likelihood of such a shift will be discussed momentarily. State policy that encourages the family to be the central player in elder care must, first of all, change. As Walker emphasizes (1991), existing state policy which perpetuates a narrow view of family as carrying all the responsibilities that society cannot do otherwise, must end. New challenges of equity are posed for public policy: to sort out the life cycle inequities that result from women's roles as carertakers, of both young and old, and render women less able to be competitive for the best opportunities that society can offer. In this scenario, women and men would be equal in the opportunities the workplace can offer as well in the demands and pleasures of family life. Dependency would no longer be equated with burden, as it would emerge that reciprocal family interactions balance entitlement with obligations, both in family and in society.

How likely is such a shift in public policy? Some might argue that it is nothing short of a Polyanna dream, sketched in pastels and hope. In times where deficits and bottom lines are mentioned in every second sentence policymakers and media pundits utter, this scenario may seem remote indeed. But, there is a bottom line side to the scenario: it could easily save money in a serious way. This could happen in two ways: first, it could save in the short-term, by enabling more people, particularly women, to contribute productively, at a time when labor force skills and brainpower are in short supply indeed. And in the longer term, it could enable more older people to live into old age healthy and with less stress in their lives. This would result in considerable savings to families, to society, and to us as we age.

In short, there is considerable reason for optimism, provided we readjust our public policy approaches soon. We must acknowledge that a crisis for families in caregiving is not something to be concerned about at some future point but that it is upon us now. And we must develop policies that adequately reflect this reality.

REFERENCES

Baines, C., Evans, P., & Neysmith, S. (Eds.) (1991). *Women's caring: Feminist perspectives on social welfare.* Toronto: McClelland and Stewart.

Binstock, R. & George, L. (Eds.) (1990). *Handbook of aging and the social sciences (3rd edition).* San Diego: Academic Press.

Caldwell, G. & Fournier, D. (1987). The Quebec question: A matter of population. *Canadian Journal of Sociology*, 12,16-41.

Connidis, I. (1989). *Family ties and aging.* Toronto: Butterworths.

Dalley, G. (1988). *Ideologies of caring: Rethinking community and collectivism.* London: Macmillan.

Dulude, L. (1987). Getting old: Men in couples and women alone. In G.H. Nemiroff (Ed.), *Women and men: Interdisciplinary readings in gender,* (pp. 323-339). Toronto: Fitzhenry and Whiteside.

Foot, D. (1988). *Policy implications of demographic change in Canada.* Ottawa: Employment and Immigration Canada.

Gee, E. (1990). Demographic change and intergenerational relations in Canadian families: Findings and social policy implications. *Canadian Public Policy,* 26, 191-199.

_____, & McDaniel S. (1991). Pension politics and challenges: Retirement policy implications. *Canadian Public Policy,* 27, 456-472.

Harrison, B. (1981). *Living alone in Canada: Demographic and economic perspectives.* Ottawa: Statistics Canada.

Hooyman, N. (1990). Women as caregivers of the elderly: Implications for social welfare policy and practice. In D. Biegel & A. Blum (Eds.), *Aging and caregiving theory, research and policy.* (pp. 221-241). Newbury Park, CA: Sage.

Jutras, S. (1990). Caring for the elderly: The partnership issue. *Social Science and Medicine,* 7, 763-771.

Kaden, J., & McDaniel, S. (1990). Caregiving and care-receiving: A double bind for women in Canada's aging society. *Journal of Women and Aging,* 2, 3-26.

Kobrin, F. (1981). Family extensions of the elderly: Economic, demographic and family cycle factors. *Journal of Gerontology,* 36, 370-377.

Kyriazis, N. & Stelcner, M. (1986). A logit analysis of living arrangements in Canada: A comparison of the young and old. *Journal of Comparative Family Studies,* 17, 389-402.

Laurin, C. (1984). *For Quebec families: A working paper on family policy.* Quebec Minister of Social Affairs, Gouvernement du Quebec.

Marshall, V., Cook, F., & Marshall, J. (1991). Conflict over generational equity: Rhetoric and reality in comparative context. Paper presented at Spencer Foundation Conference, San Francisco.

McDaniel, S. (1986). *Canada's aging population.* Toronto: Butterworths.

_____.(1987). Demographic aging as paradigm in Canada's welfare state. *Canadian Public Policy,* 13, 330-336.

_____. (1990). Towards family policy in Canada with women in mind. Feminist Perspectives, #17, 1-23. Canadian Research Institute for the Advancement of Women.

_____, & Gee, E. (Forthcoming). *Aging and social policy in Canada.* Toronto: Butterworths.

Myles, J. 1991. Editorial: Women, the welfare state and caregiving. *Canadian Journal on Aging*, 10, 82-85.

_____, & Quadagno, J. (1991). Explaining the difference: The politics of old age security in Canada and the United States. Paper presented at Spencer Foundation Conference, San Francisco.

_____, & Quadagno, J. (1991). *States, labor markets and the future of old age*. Philadelphia: Temple University Press.

Neysmith, S. (1989). Closing the gap between health policy and the home-care needs of tomorrow's elderly. *Canadian Journal of Community Mental Health*, 8, 141-150.

Preston, S. (1984). Children and the elderly: Divergent paths for America's dependents. *Demography*, 21, 435-457.

Quadagno, J. (1989). Generational equity and the politics of the welfare state. *Politics and Society*, 17, 353-376.

Rosenthal, C. (1987). Aging and intergenerational relations in Canada. In V.W. Marshall (Ed.), *Aging in Canada: Social perspectives (2nd edition)*. (pp. 311-342). Markham, Ontario: Fitzhenry and Whiteside.

_____. (1990). Family issues in institutional care of the elderly. Presented at the meetings of the Canadian Gerontology Association, Victoria, British Columbia, November.

Schulz, J. (1991). *Economics of population aging*. New York: Auburn House.

Sheppard, R. (1988). Quebekers offered $3,000 bonus to have larger families. *Globe and Mail*, 13 May, A10.

Statistics Canada. (1990). Report on the demographic situation in Canada, 1990. *Current demographic analysis* (by Jean Dumas). Ottawa: Minister of Supply and Services.

_____. (1991). *Caring communities: Proceedings of the symposium on social supports*. Ottawa: Minister of Supply and Services.

Stone, L. (1988). *Family and friendship ties among Canada's seniors: An introductory report of findings from the General Social Survey*. Cata. no. 89-508. Ottawa: Statistics Canada.

Ungerson, C. (1987). *Policy is personal: Sex, gender and informal care*. London: Tavistock.

Walker, A. (1991). The relationship between the family and the state in the care of older people. *Canadian Journal on Aging*, 10, 94-113.

_____. (Ed.). (1982). *Community care: The family, the state and social policy*. Oxford: Blackwell Martin Robertson.

Wolf, D., Burch, T., & Matthews, B. (1990). Kin availability and the living arrangements of older unmarried women. *Canadian Studies in Population*, 17, 49-70.

_____, & Soldo, B. (1988). Household formation choices of older unmarried women. *Demography*, 25, 387-403.

CHAPTER 6

Developing a Home Care System to Meet the Needs of Aging Canadians and Their Families

Shelia M. Neysmith

One of the internationally recognized strengths of the Canadian health care system is the way in which it has put in place a mechanism that guarantees to all residents a set of specified services, ensures that providers will co-operate in delivering them, and clears away financial impediments that might block access to those services.

It is important to be clear, however, on what is and is not guaranteed under the Canada Health Act. The argument developed in this chapter is that the categories of services covered, primarily hospital costs and physician fees, are not those that are increasingly seen as essential to promoting good *health*. In fact, if current legislation and funding regulations do not shift their emphasis, they will actively work against the future well-being of older persons and their families. It is this area that public policy is challenged to address.

In this chapter I (1) look at those features of the Canada Health Act and its companion legislation that make them so successful; (2) argue that because of its importance to the quality of life of both elderly individuals and their families, home care services need similar structures to promote their development; (3) outline some of the hurdles to be overcome in developing social care policies that promote equity across the different family situations that characterize the aging Canadian population. Each of these issues will be discussed in terms of how they affect elderly persons in their public lives as citizens possessing rights and obligations and in their private lives as members of families with whom they share particular social histories.

THE UNDERPINNINGS OF A UNIVERSAL HEALTH CARE SYSTEM

The piece of legislation that people think of when they laud the Canadian health care system is the Canada Health Act of 1984 which brought together the Hospital Insurance and Diagnostic Services Act of 1957 and the Medical Care Act of 1966. All of these federal acts are actually sets of arrangements for developing public hospital and medical services within each province. The Canada Health Act rests on five principles: public administration, comprehensiveness, universality, portability, and accessibility. These ensure that all Canadians, young and old, have a right to covered services. What is less obvious to the casual observer is the companion piece of legislation, the Established Programs Financing Act, 1977, which also allows federal money to flow into provincial programs, but also has a provision for equalization payments that are critical to achieving national standards in a country marked by regional disparities. The provinces have jurisdiction to define the specifics of their health care programs. But unless the above criteria are met for designated services, they do not receive federal reimbursement for their expenditures.

The financing of long-term care reflects the historical struggle of federal and provincial authority that characterizes the Canadian political economy. It is a particularly heated and very sensitive issue at the moment as Canadians struggle to incorporate the demands of Quebec and our aboriginal peoples, along with the ongoing jockeying for position by all provinces, into a revised vision for the nation. These economic and political realities necessarily affect the climate within which Canadians are trying to determine the future service needs of an aging population.

At the time of writing there is mounting concern about the shrinking proportion of federal funds going into provincially provided services. They are no longer tied directly to economic growth. The following figures give a flavor for the rapidity of this decline: in 1986

Federal transfers were held to economic growth minus 2 per cent; in 1989 it was the same formula but minus 3 per cent; in 1990 a freeze until 1992-1993 was imposed, then transfers would be based on GNP growth minus 3 per cent; in 1991 the freeze was extended until fiscal 1995-1996 (National Council of Welfare, 1991:17).

A question arising from these data is at what point will the shrinking contribution of the federal government result in an erosion of its ability to influence national standards? Figure 1 depicts the situation in 1988. It also captures some of the tension between the two levels of government around who has control over financing. The federal Tax Transfer slice, for instance, is claimed by both Federal and Provincial governments.

Figure 1
SOURCES OF FUNDS FOR HEALTH CARE, 1988 - 1989

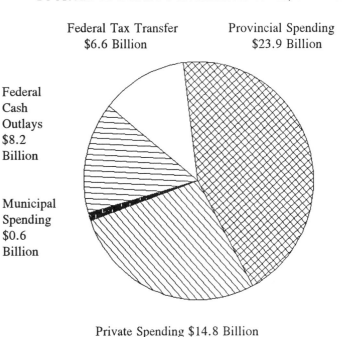

Federal Tax Transfer
$6.6 Billion

Provincial Spending
$23.9 Billion

Federal
Cash
Outlays
$8.2
Billion

Municipal
Spending
$0.6
Billion

Private Spending $14.8 Billion

Source: National Council of Welfare. Funding Health and Higher Education: Danger Looming. Ottawa: Minister of Supply and Services Canada. 1991 p. 2.

Besides challenging the amount of federal allocations, the provinces are also clamoring to have all health funds transferred directly to them, along with the indirect authority now residing at the federal level. However, claims of provincial autonomy and variation have to be carefully weighed against the implications of this scenario for inter-provincial equity. For instance, for elderly persons with low incomes, provincial home care programs can apply for funds under the Canada Assistance Plan (CAP). This is attractive because CAP is still a 50-50 cost shared program. However, some provinces also use CAP criteria for determining a user fee level; while in others the identical service has no change.

One can argue that there are positive aspects to provincial autonomy, and indeed we have examples of extremely creative policy leadership in some provinces. Manitoba is perhaps the best known example for long-term care and Quebec for the development of local community service centers (CLSC's). However, it is equally true that at present Canada can be described as a country with ten provincial and two territorial systems of long-term care. There is no mechanism, as there is with the Canada Health Act, to actively encourage the development of nation-wide guarantees of home care services while traditional incentives for institutionally based medical care remain in place.

Over the years the above Acts have become critical vehicles for encouraging Canada to maintainwide standards on covered services. Obviously services that are partially reimbursed by federal dollars are cheaper for the provinces to deliver. One might wonder at the lack of political pressure to change what services are covered, given evidence demonstrating the limited impact of medical care on the health of the community. Data continue to show that morbidity rates vary by income; that it is not so much individual lifestyle as environmental issues that affect health; that strengthening communities and supporting families are essential if health is to be promoted; that social circumstances outside the sphere of medical care remain important determiners of health (Epp, 1986; McDaniel, 1986 Wilkens; Adams & Brancker, 1989; WHO, 1988).

In Canada the term "healthy public policy" has emerged in recent years to capture these ideas. In both federal and provincial policy documents there is considerable discussion of a changing vision of good health. The idea of healthy public policy emphasizes the importance of broader policy issues in the promotion of health. Ensuring health for all, especially those groups that do not fare so well under current arrangements, is seen as a multisectoral and collaborative process that must include affected constituencies. This perspective runs counter to professional norms of specialization that so often result in fragmentation (Pederson et al., 1988). Unfortunately, the actuality of program implementation does not always reflect the rhetoric of empowerment, community development, and social action on the determinants of health that the phrase healthy public policy implies. Similarly, it has yet to modify the types of health care services guaranteed under the Canada Health Act. It is a change in these ingredients that will affect the well-being of people as they age.

THE POWER THAT RESIDES IN DELIVERY MECHANISMS: A WEAKNESS OF WELFARE PLURALISM

Organizational structures are not neutral pathways for delivering resources, but a narrow focus on service goals can obscure this. Recent long-term care policy discussions have emphasized the centrality of home care programs. An important justification for developing such services is that they are desired by old people and their families. Leaving aside for the moment just what such preference statements mean, these documents go on to discuss how supporting kin carers will be facilitated. Many Provinces are experimenting with various types of assessment teams and service coordinators. The goal of these strategies is to reduce duplication and customize service packages in order to better meet the needs of older persons and their families. Community care schemes include volunteers, neighbors, friends, and family members as part of the service delivery "team." There are usually mechanisms for covering the costs incurred by informal helpers while a coordinator has funds to purchase services from voluntary and market providers. Case managers are encouraged to mix and match; the important point is the procurement of services, not the auspice of who provides them. These organizational innovations in service delivery are not peculiar to Canada. They are, for example, also being reported extensively in the United States (Kane & Kane, 1987; Kemper, 1990), the U.K. (Baldock, 1990; Davies & Challis, 1986) and Australia (Howe, Ozanne, & Selby, 1990)

Several aspects of this focus on the coordination of services warrant examination. One is the assumption in these discussions that a welfare pluralist model of service provision is unproblematic. A recent Ontario policy paper on long-term care, *Strategies for Change* (1990), for example, emphasizes the importance of coordinating assessments and services to support informal carers yet is silent on the issue of provider auspice.

Welfare pluralists envision a variety of providers; the state, voluntary agencies, private markets, and informal networks. Welfare states have always incorporated the voluntary, informal, and commercial sectors but during the 1980's the legitimacy of public sector dominance in the delivery of services was challenged. Many pluralists maintain that the state should act as regulator and financier, but its role in delivery should be reduced and that of the other sectors correspondingly increased (Johnson, 1987). It is the pluralist model is that underlies the organization of home care in most provinces.

The twin goal of procuring services while containing cost distracts attention from an analysis of the pathways of service provision. Are there hidden costs in alternate pathways? Where should responsibility rest? Can the current organization guarantee country wide coverage and some kind of national standards? Welfare pluralists do not enter into these types of discussion. Yet they are key questions in discussion of social justice which focuses on the what and the how and judges policy outcomes in terms of their distributional effects.

Consistent with the pluralist model is the vision of the state as enabler and partner. Public funds are made available for setting up and supporting the co-ordination of services, providing the provinces with grants that can be used to develop services under a mixture of models, paying per diems to various service groups. Language referring to "building partnerships," however, does not encourage one to be critical of who the partners are—the emphasis is on bridging, not examining the condition of the building materials or the structure of the land upon which each end of the building rests.

Welfare pluralists criticize public services as not only inadequate and of poor quality but as also being bureaucratic, centralist, and authoritarian. These are not unfounded accusations, but the implication that if delivered through the other sectors these problems would not exist is equally open to question.

For instance, whether or not the provision of home care services by the private sector is superior in terms of quality, efficiency, or access remains a matter of heated debate but limited research in the United States and Canada (Gray, 1986, quoted in Bergthold et al., 1990).

In welfare pluralism decentralization is invariably linked with participation as a mechanism for the wider distribution of power. This assumes that people want to participate, both as consumers and direct service providers, and that such participation leads to empowerment. It might, in so far as people exercise some control over an area of their lives. But the power differentials within western market economies are built into our economic and social structures. One could even argue that the time and effort dispersed in local level service delivery actually diverts people from pursuing political action (Johnson, 1987).

Indeed available research examining participation based on an interest group model suggests that consumers have not had a big impact in changing health care systems (Bjorkman, 1985; Fontana, 1986). One explanation might be that the pluralist model of social policy is based on interest group theory. Interest group theory is not centrally concerned with explicating those structural aspects of our society that shape the context within which group activity, including the actions of elderly persons and their families, takes place. It allows for minor skirmishes among the players but basic power relationships remain in place.

An area where this struggle is increasingly visible is around the relative costs of different home care personnel. Quality control issues in home care have surfaced in the last few years especially around the heavy reliance of home care organizations on low paid paraprofessionals (Harrington & Grant, 1990; Szasz, 1990). For example, such persons are not covered by Medicaid in the United States. Although the funding specifics are different in Canada, these low paid, primarily female service personnel are also the backbone of our home care programs. Yet provincial policy papers situate case managers as the key players (Ontario, 1990). The discussion is about balancing the contradictory demands made on case managers as advocates, assessors of need, and controllers of resources. We hear little about the contradiction facing homemakers, for instance, as they try to balance the personal care requirement of their elderly clients, expectations of kin, territorial disputes with health and social service professionals and the demands stemming from their own, usually low income, families. Despite the call by Kane (1989) for research on paraprofessionals, we have limited knowledge about this important sector of the service labor force.

While no provincial home care program is as restrictive as the United States Medicare in terms of days of service, or as Medicaid in its eligibility criteria, nevertheless, the following statement about the California system captures the issues facing Canadian home care service workers:

> Our home care system includes a broad range of personnel, including nurses, case managers, therapists, social workers, and paraprofessional such as homemakers, home health aides, and chore workers. Of these personnel, paraprofessionals account for an estimated 70-80 percent of the home-delivered long-term care (Kemper, Applebaum, & Harrigan, 1987). At the same time, paraprofessional services tend to be most problematic in terms of quality (Riley, 1989). Ironically, the success of home care depends largely on homemakers and home health aides who are often poorly paid, poorly supervised, and inadequately trained. In addition, annual turnover rates among personal care workers are estimated at 60-70 percent industry wide (Feldman, 1988), making it very difficult for agencies to ensure quality and continuity of care. Major causes of attrition among home care workers include low pay and lack of benefits, lack of recognition and opportunity for advancement, feelings of isolation, burnout related to job stress, and personal problems (Canalis, 1987), (Applebaum & Phillips, 1990:446).

To raise questions about situational givens such as auspice and wage scales is to risk having oneself branded as an idealist, an academic, an avoider of the nuts and bolts of the hard decisions that have to be made within current economic realities—not in some hoped for future; people need imperfect services now, not ideal ones next year. At the risk of being so labelled, I would argue that the content and organization of services, the *what* and the *how*, are precisely the questions that must be addressed in the remaining years of this century before our aging population peaks. Cost containment was the issue of the 1980's; elderly persons and their families are surely entitled to a more creative policy thrust in the 1990's.

In Canada, as in the United States, home care services are targeted to the frail and sick elderly immediately after hospitalization. However, Canadian data (Shapiro, 1990) like those coming out of the United States documents that patients are being discharged earlier, that home care is increasingly being used as a hospital replacement service (Bergthold et al., 1990; Fischer & Eustis, 1989). If hospitals are no longer providing as much care, then the question is who is picking it up? The answer seems to be: home care programs and the informal care system.

The pluralist model does not recognize that the formal and informal service worlds operate according to very different organizational and power rules. Over the last decade officials enforcements of the importance of family, friends and neighbors, and the essentially subsidiary role of formal statutory sector services in providing care have been underscored by forceful political rhetoric (Glendinning, 1990; Neysmith, 1991). This definitional issue is explored in the following section.

GUARANTEEING A SOCIAL MODEL OF CARE

In Canada our service model is one of welfare pluralism—under siege by fiscal and constitutional crises. Provincial long term care policies reflect these political realities. Nevertheless, as there will be increasing numbers of people needing home care services in the years to come, it is essential to examine how the family, the state and the employment histories of women intersect. These three domains are intrinsically intertwined. As long as they are treated in isolation we ignore the nature of these bonds. It is the linkages, central to assessing the impact of programs, that are emphasized in the following discussion.

What kinds of services are seen as enabling elderly people to live longer in the community? The crucial ingredient seems to be the availability of a kin caretaker. Beyond that, in terms of formal services, they are the familiar mix of home health care, respite and homemaking, meal and transportation services, and supportive housing. In other words, those services that help people to manage independent living, services that either support or relieve families of the responsibility that they carry on an ongoing basis. These services currently are not available to all Canadians under uniform terms and conditions; rather they are available to some depending on locality and accidents of family structure. I argued above for universal guarantees and national standards for physician and hospital services. We do not have similar mechanisms to guarantee services such as homemakers despite the fact that they are a key ingredient in the community based services announced as a priority in virtually all provinces.

Although we are strong in our current long-term care documents on the importance of informal caretakers, and recognize the need to support them, we are short on the specifics of just how this is to be done (Lister, 1990). Statements recognizing the contribution of kin in making it possible for old people to remain in their own homes are no longer good enough. The issue is what kinds of support are needed? For what kinds of families? For whom within the family? From what areas will resources be withheld so that they can be put into home care? Finally, who will determine what is needed?

One way of understanding the dual focus in policy discussions on co-ordination and support of families, while emphasizing the necessity of controlling costs, is to cast the home care drama in terms of the discourse on need interpretation versus that of economic rationalism. Interpreting people's needs is a very political act usually undertaken by providers, not users, of service. People's needs are not pregiven and unproblematic; those who interpret needs also shape them. Thus, in professional translations, political issues tend to get interpreted into legal, administrative and/or therapeutic matters (Fraser, 1989). The consequence of this is that these systems execute political policy in a way that appears non-political and tends to be depoliticizing (Young, 1990).

The legislation and funding of our health and social service system are critical because they structure the definition of need. This defining, or redefining, is part of the process of categorizing people so that they qualify as legitimate service users. In order to get services to flow, needs have to be assessed and articulated in a way that allows them to fit into service categories. Indeed, the ability to do this is the mark of a skilled professional service provider. At the same time, however, the process encourages clients to bring their lived experiences into closer alignment with that of their administratively defined situation. An example is the extremely popular service of respite care. This service is thought of very positively by many. (Lawton, Brody, & Saperstein, 1989; Neysmith, 1987). However, the very existence of such a service defines the situation of the family caregiver as one from which she/he needs periodic rest and recovery in order to carry on. Its existence in no way questions the current set up of who does the caring and in fact reinforces a familial model of care.

The notion of a general preference for informal care is just too simplistic. It varies by type of help needed, person doing it, history of the relationship and *what is available* as a *realistic option*. Here research, such as that by Daatland in Norway, suggests alternative policy directions. He compared people's preferences for help in 1969 with what they chose in 1981:

> Norwegian elderly people today are clearly more aware of public help and services compared to the late 1960's, and a growing number of them prefer public rather than family help. A study in Oslo found that a majority would turn to public services when in need of long-term help, even when children were living close by. Children or other informal helpers were preferred over the public services only when there was a need for short-term assistance. The growing preference for public help is taken primarily as a response to increased availability of public services, and not as a reflection of weaker inter-generational solidarity (Daatland, 1990:1).

This returns us to the question of what types of services we want to guarantee that old people and their families have access to? For both demographic and political economy reasons the research that might best inform Canadian decisions is more likely to be found in the European literature than in that coming out of the United States. In these countries, although its role may by hotly debated, the state is always assumed to be a key actor. This permits the policy-making starting point to move from a residual perspective which assumes that families are a social safety net to one that asks "What kinds and how much formal care is necessary so that no family member is forced to substitute informal care for formal care." (Hokensted & Johansson, 1990)

In recent comparative assessment of the situations in Denmark and Great Britain, Siim (1990) notes that since the introduction in Denmark of state responsibility for social care of children and the elderly there has been a dramatic rise in both social expenditures and social employment. By the mid-1980's 70 per cent of women were employed in "care work," i.e., day care institutions, homes for the elderly, health and education institutions—a situation that may explain the well developed Danish feminist critique of caring labor.

Furthermore, between 1962 and 1977 the number of old people living with their children dropped significantly: for men over 80 it fell from 41 per cent to 22 per cent; the percentage of same-aged women fell from 27 per cent to 11 per cent. Studies also found a downward trend in contact between elderly persons and their children. During the same time period there was no increase in the cost of social care services provided for old people living in their homes, e.g., home-helps, home nursing, care work, and housing support (Olesen, 1981 quoted in Siim, 1990).

As in the Daatland (1990) study, Siim concludes that the above situation does not reflect changing family solidarity norms. Rather, it resulted from a policy change that gave high priority to providing services to elderly persons in their homes. Such data suggest that studies of preference can only be meaningful when they are interpreted within the context of what respondents understand as the possible. Secondly, such research points to budgetary implications. A home care system designed to meet the needs of both old persons and their families would seem to require a major reallocation of resources into the expansion of low tech non-professional services like home helps.

BALANCING INDIVIDUAL RIGHTS AND FAMILY RESPONSIBILITIES

In the are of long-term care, Canada seems to be pursuing a policy of family responsibility buttressed by formal services to fill in gaps and reinforce areas where k****in care is thin. Although funding for home care services has increased over the years, its proportion of the health care budget has not. There has been little attempt at reducing funds from the traditional paths of hospital and physician costs. Without a massive infusion of funds that can only result from reallocation of dollars, it seems unlikely that we will develop the level of home care services that change people's preference for relying on kin care.

In defining the need for home care, the family, the economy, and the state interact in a political arena where traditional assumptions about the distribution of rights and responsibilities are being challenged (Minkler & Estes, 1991; Neysmith, 1991; Ungerson, 1990). Care of the elderly has recently broken out of its traditional definitional bonds of family obligation where all agreed it was a private trouble, but it has not yet been relocated to the arena of public responsibility. Rather, at present it can best be described as a contested conceptual area with rival discourses: there are the health care professionals, e.g., social workers, physicians, nurses, administrators, who are concerned with areas of responsibility and delivery mechanisms; there are oppositional movements, e.g., feminists, activist groups of elderly, ethnic groups who focus on the inequities in service systems; there are reprivatization discourses which try to repatriate care of dependent persons back into the family and/or into the market economy.

Whatever the outcome of the debate, those most affected will be women. Women will continue occupying a variety of positions over their individual life courses: as caregivers to a variety of family members, as paid care providers where most will not be able to command high salaries, and finally, if they are fortunate, as recipients of some of the services they provided to others for so many years.

All social and health services are officially gender neutral. However, they impact differentially on men and women. This has been particularly well documented in the area of care for dependent persons (Abel & Nelson, 1990; Barusch & Spaid, 1989; Brody, Dempsey, & Pruchno, 1990; Stoller, 1990; Prushno & Resch, 1989; Spitze & Logan, 1989; Ungerson, 1990; Young and Kahana, 1989.) Because care for dependent family members is still primarily the responsibility of women, even in countries with advanced social service programs (Wearness, 1990; Siim, 1990), rules and regulations enhancing family obligations actively hinder women's ability to make gains as labor force participants or as citizens engaged in political behavior in the larger community outside of the family.

For instance, as Canadian citizens women are entitled to an indexed Old Age Security (OAS) pension; as members of the labor force they are enrolled in the portable indexed Canada Pension Plan (CPP) that covers all employees. However, in 1989 half of OAS recipients qualified for the income tested Guaranteed Income Supplement (GIS). These combined sources of income still left over forty percent of persons, both women and men, over sixty-five hovering at the poverty (Grenon & Bernard, 1989). Only those with a history of good jobs and subsequent access to employment related pensions avoid this fate. However, the average CPP benefit of $295.00 per month compared to men's $500.00 per month. The irony of the situation is highlighted when one is informed that at that time the maximum GIS benefit was $387.00 per month (National Health and Welfare Canada, 1991). Since both systems are indexed, it is the employment histories of women that lead to poverty. Leaving aside the strengths or weaknesses of these pension mechanisms, it is the family obligations of women that impede their ability to profit from pension benefits that reflect one's track record in the paid labor market.

As this example illustrates, programs based on quite different premises frequently converge in the lives of individuals. Young (1990) argues that social programs can be categorized into two groups: one set is oriented toward individuals and tied to participation in paid work; the other is tied to their membership in families. In the former people are defined as rights bearing, possessive individuals; in the latter they are seen as dependent clients. Women reside in both these definitional categories, but their responsibilities in the latter affect their ability to make use of the rights and privileges associated with the former. Although they cross the boundaries in their daily lives, the consequences of their co-existence is not recognized in areas such as pension policy and home care services. Increasing awareness during the 1980's of the social creation of dependency has resulted in social policies which encourage elderly people to remain in the community as long as possible, but the policy thrust has also emphasized individual rather than social responsibility for maintaining independence. What has actually occurred is a shift in the locus and nature of dependency. The rhetoric of individual responsibility translates into people being more dependent on private sources of support. The language of citizen entitlement has been replaced with that of family obligation and a much softer form of social responsibility which can be discharged through neighborliness and voluntarism (Abrams and Bulmer, 1985; Allen, 1988; Lee, 1985)

FUTURE DIRECTIONS

So what are the policy questions of the 1990's—after we get over encouraging families to do what they are already doing; after we acknowledge that family members are at a premium, indeed they are a scarce resource; after we realize that home care has to be conceptualized beyond that which is not institutional care; and after we come to terms with the fact developing home care services means the reallocation, not the saving, of dollars?

I would suggest that the issues to be faced are very similar to those which confronted Canadians when we acknowledged that access to medical care was a citizen's right, not a privilege. To do otherwise meant that certain groups suffered disproportionately. At that time we talked about minimal guarantees that all Canadians were entitled to.

The demographic trends discussed by McDaniel in Chapter 5 of this volume were push factors in forcing an examination of current health care services. However, debate tends to be limited to issues important to the health care delivery system, namely, how do we coordinate various types of services and mesh formal and informal care?

From a provider's point of view, trying to establish agreed-upon areas of professional authority is important for maintaining sanity as well as safe guarding claims to particular expertise. However, the relative power of these players in the formal system is considerably more than that of those who make up the informal system. Old people, their families, carer support groups, friends and neighbors experience what it means to be frail and in need of help. But the way they respond is shaped by the content and organization of services. Empowering these players is critical to the future development of a community based model for supporting elderly persons. Although this theme has emerged recently in the healthy public policy documents referred to earlier, it has yet to be realized in the design of the majority of our service systems.

As argued earlier, participation does not automatically result in a redistribution of power. Rather I am suggesting that it is a necessary, if not sufficient, condition for promoting social change. A public health consultant, captures this theme:

Unless we become comfortable thinking simultaneously in both personal and structural ways, we risk losing sight of the simultaneous reality of both. If we focus only on the individual, and only on crisis management or service delivery, we risk "privatizing" (rendering personal) the social and economic underpinnings of poverty and powerlessness. But if we only focus on the structural issues, we mystify the plight of the powerless and people in crisis. (Labonte, 1990:67)

The position taken in this chapter is for a strong public sector presence in future home care services. This entails a role for the state that goes well beyond that of financier; it argues for a public sector that takes leadership in defining policy direction and developing delivery systems. This model is not consistent with a pluralist vision of a state which primarily collects and disperses resources and/or one where responsibility for co-ordination depends on the cooperation of local service providers. These players cannot be expected to support, let alone initiate, policies that may be important nationally even if not in the best interest of their particular agencies. Service area boundaries, the reduction of some services and the promotion of others, changing per diem rates, the gathering of uniform statistics are just some of the examples where a broader authority is needed. Such authority can be vested at the provincial level. Manitoba and Quebec have been singularly successful in achieving this. However, a federal presence is needed for ensuring equity in long-term care services across the country. Federal legislation was necessary for guaranteeing hospital and medical services. There is no reason to believe that these economic and political realities will differ for home care services. Accomplishing this would entail considerable negotiation between federal and provincial governments. However, as the earlier discussion noted, such negotiations are inherent to the Canadian Federal system. It was possible to achieve national guarantees of medical under the Canada Health Act. There is nothing inherently different in doing likewise for home care services.

The second issue to be confronted will be the development of home care programs that support elderly persons and their various familial arrangements without any assumptions as to what these might be. A focus on elderly persons, rather than their carers or families, would help prevent the social creation of dependency because it positions elderly persons as citizens with their own set of claims. Programs that help kin carers may benefit elderly persons but not necessarily so.

Thirdly, in designing future service systems the lifelong demands made upon, and commitments of, women need to be placed front and center. These are the persons who provide most of the hands on daily care. Future policy debate would center upon examining the types of programs we have in place to balance these claims and promote well-being amongst both givers and receivers of care.

Recognizing the structural basis of existent inequities also means that we cannot see the problem of how to get informal caring work done as something to be settled within the family. Such position flies in the face of our knowledge of the consequences of power differentials existent within families (Eichler, 1988). Yes, the majority of women say they chose to care and they express very positive feelings about caring for their elderly family members. Also, there are many elderly male spouse caregivers. However, neither of these observations addresses the question of why so many more women than men are doing it. Choices, like preferences, are circumscribed by what is considered possible. In the political context of caregiving men and women have different options available to them (Baines, Evans, & Neysmith, 1991).

Fourthly, welfare pluralists have legitimately criticized the organization and content of services delivered through large public agencies. However, these are characteristics of bureaucracies that can develop under voluntary and proprietary as well as public auspice. The argument made here for a strong public sector is that without this there will be no structural mechanism for elderly persons and their families to make claims or argue for entitlements based on rights of citizenship. Home care services in the future as in the past will be primarily paid for out of public monies. The challenge is how to ensure that those citizens who are structurally disadvantaged are treated equitably. This hurdle is passed in many pluralists' discussions.

The tremendous popular support that the Canada Health Act enjoys exists because its universal benefits are visible to all; they are not seen as primarily benefitting the poor. Scholars have argued that one of the lessons of the crisis of the welfare state is a recognition that it is difficult to frontally attack universal programs (Mishra, 1984; Myles, 1989). Such programs are used by too many middle class voters to permit this to be a political possibility. However, as the earlier discussion on EPF Act demonstrated, Canadians are currently experiencing a decrease in the financial support accorded to many of our public programs. This fiscal squeeze, combined with the promotion of a mixed auspice approach to service delivery, will inevitably lead to a weakening of the principles underlying programs. We can predict that home care will be supported, or criticized, depending on its design. If services are limited, and a funding mechanism put in place that is not sensitive to auspice, then those old Canadians and their families with resources will be able to exercise a degree of choice not available to others and pressure to target tax-supported services to only the "most needy" will result in residual public services used primarily by the poor. Such programs are much more susceptible to cutbacks as the history of public welfare programs so amply documents.

The policy issue might be phrased in terms of "which way do we want to tip the dependency scale?" There are different types and contexts of dependency. In this chapter I have argued for a shift from "private" dependency on kin care to "public" dependency on services and a strong state presence in the design as well as the funding of services. This position is premised on an understanding of vulnerability which sees it as arising from both natural and social circumstances. Frail elderly persons will always require help with activities of daily living. However, how we define need, design services, and organize their delivery will result in programs enhancing or diminishing social vulnerability. This is the policy challenge facing Canadians as we determine what services aging persons and their families will have a citizen's claim to in the twenty-first century.

REFERENCES

Abel, E. & Nelson, M., (Eds.), (1990). *Circles of care: Work and Identity in women's lives.* New York: State University of New York.

Abrams, P. edited by M. Blumer. (1985). Policies to promote informal Care: Some reflections on voluntary action, neighborhood involvement and neighborhood care. *Ageing and Society*, 5, 1-19.

Allen, G. (1988). Kinship, responsibility and care for elderly people. *Ageing and Society*, 8, 249-268.

Applebaum, R., & Phillips, P. (1990). Assuring the quality of in-home care: The "Other" challenge for long-term care. *The Gerontologist*, 30, 444-450.

Baines, C., Evans, P., & Neysmith, S. (Eds.), (1990) *Women's caring: Feminist perspectives on Social Welfare.* Toronto: McClelland & Stewart.

Baldock, J. (1991). England and Wales. In R. Kraan & A. Evers (Eds.), *Care for the elderly: Significant innovations in three European countries.* (pp. 45-69). Boulder, Colorado: Westview Press.

Barusch, A. & Spaid, W. (1989). Gender differences in caregiving: Why do wives report greater burden? *The Gerontologist,* 29, 667-676.

Bergthold, L., Estes, C., & Villaneuva, A. (1990). Public light and private dark: The privatization of home health services for the elderly in the United States. *Home Health Services Quarterly,* 11, 7-33.

Bjorkman, J. (1985). Equity and social policy: Conceptual ambiguity in welfare criteria. *Comparative Politics* 17, 16-32.

Brody, E., Dempsey, N. & Pruchno, R. (1990). Mental health of sons and daughters of the institutionalized aged. *The Gerontologist,* 30, 212-219.

Canada. Canada Health Act, (1984). Now, *Revised Statutes of Canada,* 1985. Ch. C-6.

Daatland, S. (1990). What are families for? On family solidarity and preference for help. *Ageing and Society,* 10, 1-16.

Davies, B., & Challis, D. (1986). *Matching resources to needs in Community care.* Aldershot: Gower.

Eichler, M. (1988) *Families in Canada today: Recent changes and their policy consequences.* Second Edition. Toronto, Ontario: Gage Educational Publishing Company.

Epp, J. (1986). *Achieving health for all: A frame work for health promotion.* Ottawa: Health and Welfare Canada.

Fraser, N. (1989). *Unruly practices: Power, discourse and gender in contemporary social theory.* Minneapolis, Minnesota: University of Minnesota Press.

Fischer, L., & Eutis, N. (1988). DRGs and family care for the elderly. *The Gerontologist,* 28, 383-390.

Fontana, L. (1986). Political ideology and local health planning in the United States. *Human Relations,* 39, 541-556.

Glendinning, C. (1990) Dependency and interdependency: The incomes of informal carers and the impact of social security. *Journal of Social Policy,* 19, 469-497.

Grenon, A.,& Bernard, M. (1989) *The financial situation of Canadian pensioners (Pension Survey, 1987). Research Note.* Income Security Programs. Ottawa: Health and Welfare Canada.

Harrington, C., & Grant, L., (1990) The delivery, regulation, and politics of home care: A California case example. *The Gerontologist*, 30, 451-461.

Health Promotion Directorate. (1989). *Health inequities II.* Ottawa: Health and Welfare Canada.

Hokensted, M., & Johansson, A. (1990) Caregiving for the elderly in Sweden: Program challenges and policy initiatives. In D. Biegel & A. Blum (Eds.) *Ageing and Caregiving: Theory, Research and Policy* (pp. 254-269). Newbury Park: Sage Publications.

Howe, A., Ozanne, E., & Selby, C. S. (Eds.). (1990) *Community care policy and practice: New directions in Australia.* Clayton, Victoria: Monash University.

Johnson, N. (1987). *The welfare state in transition: The theory and practice of welfare pluralism.* Brighton, Sussex: Wheatsheaf Books Ltd.

Kane, N. (1989). The home care crisis of the nineties. *The Gerontologist*, 29, 24-31.

Kane, R. (1989). Toward competent, caring paid caregivers. *The Gerontologist*, 29, 291-292.

_____, & Kane, R. (1987). *Long-term care: Principles, programs and policies.* New York: Springer.

Kemper, P. (1990). Case management agency systems of administering long-term care: Evidence from the channelling demonstration. *The Gerontologist* 30, 817-824.

Labonte, R. (1990). Empowerment: Notes on professional and community dimensions. *Canadian Review of Social Policy/Revue canadienne de politique sociale,* 26, 64-75.

Lawton, M. P., Brody, E. & Saperstein, A. (1989). A controlled study of respite service for caregivers of Alzheimer's patients. *The Gerontologist*, 29, 8-16.

Lee, G. (1985). Kinship and social support: The case of the United States. *Ageing and Society,* 5, 19-38.

Lister, R. (1990). Women, economic dependency and citizenship. *Journal of Social Policy,* 19, 445-467.

McDaniel, S. (1986). *Canada's aging population.* Toronto and Vancouver: Butterworths.

McGilly, F. (1990). *An introduction to Canada's public social services: Understanding income and health programs*. Toronto: McClelland & Stewart.

Minkler, M., & Estes, C. (Eds.) (1991). *Critical perspectives on aging: The political and moral economy of growing old*. Amityville, NY: Baywood Publishing Company Inc.

Mishra, R. (1984). *The welfare state in crisis*. Brighton, Sussex: Wheatsheaf Books Ltd.

Myles, J. (1989). *Old age in the welfare state: The political economy of public pensions*. Second edition. Lawrence, Kansas: University of Kansas Press.

National Council on Welfare. (1991). *Funding health and higher education: Danger looming*. Ottawa: Minister of Supply and Services Canada.

_____. (1990). *Pension Reform*. Ottawa: Minister of Supply and Services.

National Health and Welfare. (No date). *Canada pension plan contributors/cotisants du régime de pensions du Canada* 1987. Ottawa: Date Development and Analysis Division. Programs Policy, Appeals and Legislation Directorate. Income Security Programs Branch. Health and Welfare Canada.

Neysmith, S. (1991). From community care to social model care. In C. Baines, P. Evans & S. Neysmith (Eds.). *Women's caring: Feminist perspectives on social welfare* (pp. 272-299). Toronto: McClelland & Stewart.

_____. (1987). S.P.R.I.N.T.'s *Respite program: An evaluation*. Unpublished Research Report. Toronto.

Ontario. Ministry of Community and Social Services. Ministry of Health. Office of Senior Citizens' Affairs. Office for Disabled Persons. (1990). *Strategies for change: comprehensive reform of Ontario's long-term care services*. Toronto: Queen's Printer.

Pederson, A., Edwards. R., Kellner, M., Marshall V., & Allison, K. (1988). *Coordinating healthy public policy: An analytic literature review and bibliography*. Prepared for Health Services and Promotion Branch. Health and Welfare Canada. Ottawa: Minister of Supply and Services.

Pruchno, R., & Resch, N. (1989). Husbands and wives as caregivers: Antecedents of depression and burden. *The Gerontologist*, 29, 159-165.

Siim, B. (1990). Women and the welfare state: Between private and public dependence. A comparative approach to care work in Denmark and Britain. In C. Ungerson (Ed.). *Gender and caring: Work and welfare in Britain and Scandinavia* (pp. 80-109). London: Harvester Wheatsheaf.

Shapiro, E. (1991). Home Care: Where is it and where should it be going? In L. Wells (Ed.) *An aging population: The challenge for community action* (pp. 18-42). Toronto: Governing Council, University of Toronto.

Spitze, G., & Logan, J. (1989). Gender differences in family support: Is there a payoff? *The Gerontologist, 29,* 108-113.

Stoller, E. (1990). Males as helper: The role of sons, relatives, and friends. *The Gerontologist, 30, 200-235.*

Szasz, A. (1990). The Labour impacts of policy change in health care: How federal policy transformed home health organizations and their labor practices. *Journal of Health politics, Policy and Law,* 15, 191-210.

Ungerson, C. (Ed.). (1990). *Gender and caring: Work and welfare in Britain and Scandinavia.* London: Harvester Wheatsheaf.

Wallace, S. (1990). The no-care zone: Availability, accessibility, and acceptability in community-based long-term care. *The Gerontologist,* 30 254-261.

Wearness, K. (1990). Informal and formal care in old age: What is wrong with the new ideology in Scandinavia today? In C. Ungerson (Ed.), *Gender and caring: Work and welfare in Britain and Scandinavia (pp. 110-132).* London: Harvester Wheatsheaf.

Wilkins, R., Adams, O., & Branker, A. (1990). Changes in mortality by income in urban Canada from 1971 to 1986. Statistics Canada. *Health Reports.* 1: 137-174.

World Health Organization. (1988). *Healthy public policy—strategies for action: The Adelaide recommendations.* Geneva: WHO.

Young, R. & Kahana, E. (1989). Specifying caregiver outcomes: Gender and relationship aspects of caregiving strain. *The Gerontologist,* 29, 660-666.

Young, I. (1990). *Justice and the politics of difference.* Princeton, New Jersey: Princeton University Press.

NOTES

1. Although the historical specifics are beyond the scope of this newspaper in terms of developing future strategies, it may be useful to recall that federal funds originally matched provincial expenditures when Medicare was first established in 1966. This was no small incentive in convincing the provinces to join. During the seventies it became clear that although federal dollars were at stake, the federal government had no control over the rising health budget. The current formula, of daunting complexity, is based on three principles: (1) the payment of "block grants" to provinces calculated in terms of their "fiscal capacity"; (2) the giving up of tax points if the provincial government develops programs in the designated areas; (3) both of these be publically accounted for and the federal contribution acknowledged; see McGilly (1990) for an exceptionally readable version of this legislation).

2. Specifically, these are defined as goods and services which are medically necessary and distributed by licensed medical practitioners and organizations for the purpose of maintaining health, preventing disease and diagnosing and treating injury, illness, or disability (The Canada Health Act, 1984, Section 2).

3. Empowerment can be seen as existing at three levels: interpersonally it is the experience of a potent sense of self, enhancing self-esteem and self-efficiency; interpersonally, it is the construction of knowledge and social analysis based upon personal and shared experiences; and, within communities, it is the cultivation of resources and strategies for personal and socio-political gains (Health Promotion directorate II, 1989:10).

4. When assessing the feasibility of this option it is instructive to look at how Australia has instituted a national Home and Community Care policy. There are important differences between the two countries, for example, Australian states have a smaller tax base than Canadian provinces. Nevertheless, the similarities suggest that, to modify an earlier observation on the Canadian health care system, "if there's a will; there's a way."

CHAPTER 7
Policy Failure in Geriatric Acute Care: The Impact on Family Caregivers[*]

Carolyn J. Rosenthal, Victor W. Marshall, and Joanne Sulman

The effects of policy inadequacies at a macro- or structural level have an undeniable impact on individual family members at a micro-level. In this chapter, we look specifically at how the failure to develop explicit and adequate policies in medical care for the elderly is evidenced in Canada (Chappell, 1988; Marshall, 1989; Shapiro & Roos, 1981) and elsewhere (Kane, 1987; Lagoe & Decker, 1991; Shaughnessy, 1991) by a persistent inability to appropriately discharge acute care hospital geriatric patients to suitable long-term care facilities once the acute medical episode has passed. Increasing numbers of acute hospital patients are old, and a significant proportion of them suffer protracted stays once hospitalized. They and their families become unintended victims of health care policies and policy gaps. Our goals are to: (1) describe the structural situation in which many elderly are inappropriately hospitalized; (2) explore the causes of this situation in policy terms; (3) describe the effects of being caught up in these circumstances on patients and their families, drawing on a study based in one hospital in a Canadian province; and (4) recommend policy directions at the hospital level and at a broader societal level to help ameliorate this problem.

THE PROBLEM OF LONG-STAY PATIENTS IN ACUTE CARE HOSPITALS

Arguably, many older patients in Canadian acute care hospitals do not belong there and are inappropriately housed while awaiting placement in chronic care hospitals or nursing homes (Aronson, Marshall & Sulman, 1987). Paget (1983) estimated this proportion for Canada as a whole to be between 10 and 20 percent of acute hospital beds. A decade ago, Gross and Schwenger (1981) calculated that 12.7 percent of Ontario's hospital beds were so occupied. A more recent report says, "Inadequate access to in-home and community support services results in the over-use and inappropriate use of higher-cost services; for example, more than 10 percent of Ontario's 17,000 acute care hospitals beds are used by people who, in fact, require long-term care and support services" (Strategies for Change, 1990). In Toronto, where the data presented below were collected, a 1984 survey suggested that 13.9 percent of acute care beds were occupied by patients awaiting discharge (Metropolitan Toronto District Health Council, 1984).

The situation these figures depict is referred to by a number of terms: administratively necessary days, inappropriately placed patients, or the pejorative "bed-blocking" patients (Aronson, Marshall & Sulman, 1987; Fisher & Zorzitto, 1983). These terms imply that the long-stay phenomenon is important primarily at the level of the health care system in that it affects the availability of acute care beds. As well, there is an implied blame on the patients themselves. The presence of long-stay geriatric patients in acute hospitals, however, is hardly the fault of patients. Nor is it the fault of uncaring families. The real cause of the long-stay problem is public policy—or, as we argue below, policy failure. In this perspective, patients and families are more accurately viewed as victims with no control over the root causes of long-stay but bearing its consequences.

Locating the cause of the long-stay problem in the aging population or "bed-blocking" patients diverts attention away from policy. Our argument in this chapter is that the roots indeed lie at the policy level as do the solutions. Attention to patients and families should not be in the context of how they "cause" the problem but rather how they are affected by it. We thus begin our chapter with an examination at the policy level, then examine the effects of policy on the families of patients, and turn finally to interim and long-term recommendations.

POLICY FAILURES AND DILEMMAS CAUSING THE LONG-STAY PROBLEM

The causes of protracted stays are multiple (Beatrice, 1979). The long-stay patient situation is frequently attributed to a shortage of long-stay beds, i.e., to a dearth of nursing home and chronic hospital beds (Shaughnessy, 1991). This misconstrues the problem in the Canadian context and, particularly, in the metropolitan Toronto context. Toronto has an ample per capita, age-adjusted stock of long-term care beds. The problem, rather, is with the placement and movement of patients through the various levels of the long-term care system. The system is clogged because: community-based services are inadequate to support a large enough percentage of the frail elderly at home; the two levels of intermediate care, homes for the aged and nursing homes, are insufficiently coordinated with each other and with heavier care chronic hospitals; it is in their interests to accept patients whose needs for care are light, often not serious enough to justify institutional care but which could be met through community-based services; rehabilitation programs in the hospitals do not foster an aggressive approach to discharge; and, discharge planning is not adequately developed at any level of care.

Inadequate development of community-based services

In Canada, long-term care policy is a provincial rather than a federal matter. In contrast to the rest of the country, the four western-most provinces have well-developed long-term care policies and programs (Kane & Kane, 1985; Marshall, 1989). In Ontario, policy development concerning community-based services for the aged has floundered. The recent history of policy considerations in Ontario is captured by three reports issued over a five year period. *A New AGEnda* was issued by the Minister for Senior Citizen's Affairs in 1986 under a Liberal government administration, but no significant change occurred. In 1990 a new position paper, *Strategies for Change: Comprehensive Reform of Ontario's Long-Term Care Services*, was issued by the offices of four cabinet ministers (for health, community and social services, senior citizens' affairs, and disabled persons). This document was issued shortly before the fall of the Liberal Government, and the New Democratic regime which followed prepared yet another "public consultation paper," *Redirection of Long-Term Care and Support Services in Ontario* (1991).

The 1986 report was not restricted to long-term care or community care issues, but it did note that appropriate community-based services, including those which would be alternatives to extended care in nursing homes or homes for the aged, were not widely available. It intoned that all of the strategies discussed—"health promotion, education and research, community services, and enhancement of hospital services—are specifically intended to reduce and, ideally, to eliminate preventable and inappropriate institutionalization" (A New AGEnda, 1986:7). The report then made a commitment: "We will undertake a major revision and rationalization of the extended care program and also address complementary issues in adjacent services such as residential care and rest homes." Improved assessment and placement procedures were included in the changes to be made in the system.

Four years later, the catalogue of problems with the long-term care system was repeated in the *Strategies for Change* report, which, as noted above, suggested that deficiencies in community-based care led to more than 10 percent of acute care hospital beds being occupied by inappropriately placed persons (Strategies for Change, 1990:9). This document described the current system of community-based services as lacking in coordination and availability. It noted that administration is "complex and cumbersome, with over 750 different administering bodies. Comprehensive planning is difficult. Access and eligibility criteria are confusing, and services cannot meet the complex and changing needs of persons requiring personal support and care" (Strategies for Change, 1990). It recommended a series of changes which for the most part followed a consultant report (Price Waterhouse, 1988): coordination of access to services, integration and consolidation of in-home services, and expansion of community-based support services, including support for informal caregivers.

The change of government resulted in inaction for two years, before the consultation paper on *Redirection of Long-Term Care and Support Services in Ontario* reproduced most of the recommendations of the previous government's report, and called for more discussion. The net result has been a persistent failure to seriously address the lack of coordination in the system, and the underdevelopment of its community care aspects.

Inadequate coordination of homes for the aged and nursing homes

In Ontario, the three levels of institutional long term care other than the acute hospital are, in descending order of intensity, the chronic hospital, the nursing home, and the home for the aged (Levels of care and their designation differ slightly from province to province in Canada. See Kane & Kane, 1985). In Ontario, chronic hospitals are publicly run under the authority of the provincial Ministry of Health. Nursing homes are almost wholly privately run under the authority of the Ministry of Health and, because they are reimbursed by the Ministry, financially dependent upon it. Homes for the Aged are run largely by municipalities or religious and charitable associations on a non-profit basis, and they fall under the authority of the Ministry of Community and Social Services. In fact, about half of clients in homes for the aged are extended care patients with the need levels of nursing home patients, and the home receives reimbursement from the Ministry of Health for these patients (Funding and Incentives Study, n.d.). *The Strategies for Change* and *Redirections* documents propose to eliminate the distinction between homes for the aged and nursing homes, and the latter document also recommends development of support services for people in designated housing units, providing "...24-hour services needed for seniors and people with disabilities to remain in their own communities" (Redirections, 1991). In addition, current policy is questioning the continued existence of the chronic hospitals (Council of Chronic Hospitals, 1991).

Structural interests in accepting low need-for-care patients

In Canada there are also provincial variations in reimbursement mechanisms for hospital and long-term care. Hospitals are generally reimbursed on global budgets which take into account the number of active treatment beds, and the maximum number of such beds is typically regulated by government. This is the case in Ontario. Reimbursement within the acute hospital does not vary by level of care. In the acute hospital, the long-stay patient awaiting discharge obviously consumes fewer services and resources than an acutely ill patient. Thus, the presence of such patients in appreciable numbers allows some trimming of hospital costs. However, these patients, who in the acute hospital consume fewer resources, are heavy-care patients in the nursing home or chronic hospital contexts. Nursing homes receive the same amount of funding per patient regardless of the amount of care required. In such circumstances, the incontinent, severely cognitively impaired, or otherwise heavy-care patient is not likely to be especially desirable. The 1990 and 1991 policy reports both recommend reimbursement mechanisms which take into account the greater needs of heavy-care patients in nursing homes. One obvious consequence of such a revision could be greater hospitableness toward patients with heavier care needs.

Inadequate development of rehabilitation programs

Despite the advantages accruing from the presence of chronically ill geriatric patients, acute care hospitals are not designed for the care of such patients. This is despite the fact that a very large percentage of acute care patients are old. In Ontario, the average length of stay for those aged 65 or more was 14.8 days in 1985-6, compared to 9.0 days for the total population; and 43.6 percent of the total number of days of acute hospital care was accounted for by persons age 65 or older (Ontario Gerontology Association, 1986).

As one example of the type of program needed, in the hospital which was the site of the present study one of the authors established a group program for long-stay cognitively, physically, and socially impaired elderly patients, with the goal of maintaining functional status following recovery from the acute episodes which had prompted hospitalization. Although apparently successful, the program was temporarily terminated due to its failure to garner institutional support in the form of additional funding. Staff time dedicated to the program was an add-on and had to be sacrificed due to increased pressures as the number of long-stay patients in the hospital grew (Sulman & Wilkinson, 1989). Further interdisciplinary advocacy eventually brought about the development of an intermediate care geriatric unit to address the unique needs of these patients. It is clear, however, that such programs are rather fragile. Their implementation and continuation depends upon successful negotiation of the gauntlet of bureaucratic policies. If the negotiation fails, responsibility for ameliorative strategies becomes shifted, by default, to informal care providers.

Problems with discharge planning

Discharge planning serves an essential gate-keeping function in the long term care system. Currently, in Ontario and across Canada, it is the focus of considerable concern about the coordination between the acute care hospital and other components of the long-term care system. Beatrice (1979) notes that discharge planning is part of, and affected by, other aspects of the long term care system: "All aspects of the system push each other. As ADs (administratively necessary days) increase, or are generated by more rigorous utilization review, the pressure on the long-term care system is multiplied. If growth in long-term care resources is slow, the existing resources will be allocated to the more 'desirable' patients (private pay or mildly impaired) or by the most aggressive and skilful discharge planners. The more disabled patients will wait and the less sophisticated hospitals will incur more ADs" (Beatrice, 1979:3).

The dynamics of this system are undoubtedly affected by macro-level features of the health care system. Beatrice (1979) notes that, in Massachusetts, large, urban hospitals have fewer problems with ADs than smaller hospitals, and he attributes the difference to their greater resources for "trading" with nursing homes. That is, a hospital refers patients who will be private pay to a nursing home only if that nursing home in return accepts some of the public pay patients waiting for placement. In the

Canadian context, with extensive public support for nursing home and home for the aged care, such leverage may be less than in the United States. However, priority acceptance of acutely ill nursing home patients into the acute hospital could be a basis for negotiation of more rapid placement. In Manitoba, Shapiro, Roos, & Kavanagh (1980) found the major cause of long stays in the acute hospital to be the hospital-nursing home link. Patients had the right to stay in hospital until they gained admittance to the nursing home of their choice, while nursing homes could refuse to admit selected patients. Long-term care institutions tended to avoid admitting patients with behavioral problems. In the United States, the system of diagnostic-related groupings (DRG's) effectively eliminates the freedom of choice of the patient to remain in hospital. A model which limits the ability of the long-term care facility to select out the lighter-care patients is found in British Columbia. In that province, most long-term care facilities are enrolled in the provincial Long Term Care Program, in which a condition of membership is the obligation to accept patients referred by the local area Program office. These offices attempt to equitably distribute "difficult to place" patients among institutions (Coordination of Long Term Care Services Task Force, 1983). The extent to which a jurisdiction provides financial resources to acute hospitals or long term care institutions is therefore a structural factor affecting the leverage which can be exercised on components of the system to facilitate the appropriate placement and flow of patients to various levels of care.

THE IMPACT OF LONG-STAY ON FAMILIES

While reform across the long-term care spectrum, from the acute hospital to community-based services, continues to be discussed and debated by bureaucrats, health care and social service providers, older people continue to become ill and be hospitalized. It is not an exaggeration to say they and their families are in a sense victimized by the near-paralysis of protracted policy discussion. We now consider the impact of this policy dilemma on the families of long-stay acute care geriatric patients by examining data from an empirical study conducted by the authors.

First, a note of caution. It is difficult to separate the effects of ill health (of a patient or family member) from the effects of length of stay itself. Because this is not a comparative study of different medical care settings, we do not know definitively if the patients or their families would fare better or worse if the patients were discharged from hospital and placed in a long-term care facility or even returned to their home or the home of a family member. Nonetheless, some reasonable inferences can be made about the consequences of long-stay in acute care settings by examining the limited follow-up data we have and by careful interpretation of interview responses.

The purposes of presenting the descriptive data are: (1) to build a profile of the situations of these families; (2) to see whether and how various dimensions change over time, and (3) to examine the effects of transfer out of the acute hospital and into a long term care setting.

The study on which we draw involved interviews with patients in a Toronto teaching hospital and their primary caregivers (who were usually family members). All patients age 65 or older for whom a discharge planning form was completed to initiate placement in a long-term care facility, from whom consent was obtained, and whose attending physician gave consent, were enrolled in the study shortly after the discharge planning form was completed. The data gathering period extended from spring 1987 to autumn 1989. A patient response rate of 78 percent was obtained. For each patient, the "person most involved with the patient these days" was identified by social work staff; in 95 percent of cases, this "primary caregiver" was a family member. Eighty-four primary caregivers were enrolled, with a response rate of 95 percent. Data were gathered at three-month intervals until two data-points following discharge or, for a small number of cases, the end of the study.

To explore the impact of long-stay on families, we compare descriptive data on family members at the time of entry into the study (Time 1) and six months later (Time 2). The analysis is limited to those 49 family members whose relative either was still in the acute hospital at Time 2 or had been placed in a long-term care facility. At Time 2, the relatives of 21 of these family members (43%) were still in the acute hospital, while 28 (57%) had been transferred to a long-term care facility.

TABLE 1
Sample Characteristics, Comparing Those Who Remain in Acute Setting and Those Who Are
Transferred to a Long-term Care Facility at Time 2.

	All	Acute Care	Long-term Care
Length of stay—mean number of months from time of admission to hospital to Time 2:	12.7	18.4	8.5
N	49	21	28
Type of long-term care facility for which application made: chronic hospital			
N	18	12	6
(%)	(37)	(57)	(21)
nursing home			
N	29	9	20
(%)	(59)	(43)	(71)
home for the aged			
N	2	0	2
(%)	(4)	(0)	(7)
Family caregiver's relationship to patient:			
spouse N	10	6	4
(%)	(20)	(27)	(14)
child N	27	11	16
(%)	(55)	(52)	(57)
other N	12	4	8
(%)	(24)	(19)	(29)

The impact of long-stay versus transfer to long-term care

Several characteristics of family members are displayed in Table 1 and reveal differences between those whose relatives remained in the acute hospital and those whose relatives were transferred to a long-term care facility.

The first difference relates to the length of stay from the patient's admission to the acute care hospital and the Time 2 data gathering point. While the period between initial data gathering (Time 1) and Time 2 was six months, patients had been in the hospital for varying lengths of time prior to entry into the study. (Entry occurred either once application was made for long-term care or some time after that, not at the time of admission to hospital.) As Table 1 shows, patients who were transferred to a long-term care facility by Time 2 had a shorter total length of stay (by 10 months) than those who remained in the acute hospital. This suggests that they were easier to place than those who were still in the acute care setting.

The second difference relates to the type of facility for which application was made. The majority of patients transferred to long-term care had applications made to nursing homes or homes for the aged, while the majority of patients who remained in the acute hospital were characterized by applications to chronic hospitals, which provide a heavier level of care closer to that of acute hospitals. Thus, the type of facility requested helps explain the greater length of stay for the group in acute care at Time 2 noted above.

The third difference shown in Table 1 relates to the family member's relationship to the patient. Among the family members of patients remaining in the acute hospital, a higher proportion were spouses and a lower proportion were "other" (i.e., neither spouses nor children). Spouses tend to maintain heavier care patients at home longer than do other categories of caregivers. Hence, the hospitalized patients with spousal caregivers in the study were heavier care patients and thus more difficult to place. Patients without spouses had been admitted to hospital at lighter levels of care; they were thus easier to place.

These differences should be kept in mind when interpreting the data presented below. They lead us to expect that among relatives of the patients still in acute care, responses on various indicators of the impact of the patient's hospitalization will be more negative than responses of relatives of patients who were transferred to long term care. A final point of caution is that the sample is very small. The analysis and discussion are therefore pursued in an exploratory spirit.

Table 2 displays frequencies on a number of indicators at Time 1 and Time 2 for the sample as a whole, for the sub-group of family members whose relative remained in the acute setting, and for the sub-group whose relative was transferred to long-term care. By comparing the groups over time, it is possible to make some inferences about the impact of protracted stay in the acute care setting.

We first discuss the indicators which point to a negative impact of long stay. These are frequency of visiting, the presence of depressive symptomatology, a negative impact on the respondent's relationship with his/her spouse, and a negative impact on getting housework done.

Visiting is an important way in which family members monitor patient care and indeed provide direct care to their relatives. The location of the acute hospital in the downtown core of the city may be a barrier to visiting, both because of distance from residential areas and because of the cost of parking. Therefore, we expected that visiting might increase following transfer to long-term care. This pattern did appear in the data, in that there was a slight increase in visiting among the long-term care group, along with a slight decrease in the acute hospital group.

The percentage of respondents whose score on CES-D indicated the presence of *depression* remained constant among the acute hospital group, while it decreased among the long-term care group. A second indicator bears mention, although the numbers are extremely small. Among respondents who were married and whose spouse was not the patient, the proportion saying the hospitalization had a negative impact on the *spousal*

TABLE 2
Comparison of Family Caregivers Whose Relative Remained in Acute Hospital with Those
Whose Relative Was Transferred to a Long-term Care Facility

	ALL		ACUTE HOSPITAL		LONG-TERM CARE		TOTAL Ns
	T1 N %	T2 N %	T1 N %	T2 N %	T1 N %	T2 N %	ALL AC LTC
Last visited today/yesterday	21 (43)	21 (43)	9 (43)	7 (33)	12 (43)	14 (50)	49 21 28
Depressed (16 or higher on CES-D)	16 (53)	20 (41)	8 (57)	8 (57)	10 (50)	6 (30)	34 14 20
Burden - mean score	22.8	12.4	20.1	10.8	24.4	13.4	32 12 20

Some aspect of care is tiring/stressful	34 29 (69) (59)	17 13 (81) (62)	17 16 (61) (57)	49 21 28
Tension between respondent and patient	12 8 (58) (16)	5 2 (24) (10)	7 6 (25) (21)	49 21 28
Tension between respondent and other family members	23 9 (47) (18)	7 3 (33) (14)	16 6 (57) (21)	49 21 28
Not enough rest	22 17 (45) (35)	11 9 (52) (43)	11 8 (39) (28)	49 21 28
Feel too many demands	15 18 (31) (37)	6 8 (29) (38)	9 10 (32) (36)	49 21 28
Feel torn between patient's needs and own needs	25 22 (51) (45)	11 9 (52) (43)	14 13 (50) (46)	49 21 28
Feel uncomfortable when visiting	25 19 (51) (39)	13 8 (62) (38)	12 11 (43) (39)	49 21 28
Negative effect on time for recreation	24 18 (67) (50)	11 8 (73) (38)	13 11 (62) (52)	36 15 21
Negative effect on financial situation	7 2 (20) (5)	3 1 (20) (7)	4 1 (20) (5)	35 15 20
Negative effect on getting housework done	16 10 (46) (29)	6 5 (40) (33)	10 5 (50) (25)	35 15 20

Negative effect on health/stamina	19 13 (54) (37)	10 7 (71) (50)	9 6 (43) (29)	35 14 21
Negative effect on relationship with spouse (if spouse not the patient)	5 2 (28) (11)	2 2 (33) (33)	3 0 (25) (0)	18 6 12
Negative effect on relationship with children	7 6 (23) (20)	2 3 (17) (25)	5 3 (28) (17)	30 12 18
Staff not listening	19 16 (40) (33)	10 9 (48) (43)	9 7 (33) (26)	48 21 27
Very/somewhat satisfied with medical treatment	34 32 (83) (78)	14 15 (74) (79)	20 17 (91) (77)	41 19 22
Very/somewhat satisfied with nursing care	30 32 (71) (76)	12 14 (63) (74)	18 18 (78) (78)	42 19 23

relationship remained the same in the acute hospital group, while it decreased among the long-term care group. A negative impact on the respondent's *getting housework done* was more evident among the acute hospital group.

Two indicators point to more negative results among the long-term care group, compared to the acute hospital group. Family members whose relative was transferred to long-term care showed little decrease in the proportion who reported *feeling uncomfortable when visiting* the patient, while such feelings did decrease among the acute hospital group. These feelings of discomfort may be related to adaptation to the move to a long-term care facility. *Satisfaction with medical treatment* rose very slightly among the acute hospital group, while it declined somewhat among the long-term care group. This finding no doubt reflects the difference in availability of physicians in the university-affiliated acute hospital as opposed to nursing homes and other long-term care facilities.

On the majority of indicators examined, there were no differences between the two groups of family members. Specifically, there were no differences in *caregiver burden, tension with other family members, not getting enough rest*, feeling that there were *too many demands*, feeling *torn between the patient's needs and one's own needs, reporting a negative* impact on one's *financial situation* or *health and physical stamina* as a result of the patient's hospitalization. As well, two variables related to hospital care, *satisfaction with nursing care* and *feeling the staff do not listen*, showed no differences between the two groups.

Caregivers whose relative remained in the acute hospital showed much greater decreases in the proportion saying an *aspect of care was tiring or stressful*, compared with caregivers whose relative was transferred. This may be because patients who remained in the hospital needed greater care than those who were transferred, leading to more professional intervention. In contrast, in long term care facilities, families may be expected to provide a greater amount and range of assistance than is the case in acute care settings.

Feeling the hospitalization had a negative effect on time for recreation decreased in both groups over time but fell more sharply for caregivers whose relative remained in the acute hospital than for those whose relative was transferred. This may be because visiting was less frequent, freeing more time for recreation. For those whose relative was in long-term care, some increase in time for recreation may have resulted because the facility was usually closer to home than the acute hospital, requiring less travel time.

Although very few caregivers reported a negative effect of the hospitalization on their relationships with their children, the proportion rose slightly in the acute hospital group and fell slightly in the long-term care group. The same pattern of improved relationships after transfer to a long term care facility can be seen on the indicator of conflict with one's spouse. These trends may reflect the uncertainty regarding the patient's future that remains for the acute hospital group. In contrast, for the long-term care group, decisions have been made and families no longer feel "up in the air."

Summarizing the findings described in the study, we found that on some indicators, caregivers in the acute care group showed more negative patterns than those in the long-term care group, on other measures the reverse was true, and on still other measures there were no differences.

Long-stay does appear to have a negative impact on caregivers in two important respects: mental health and close family relationships. The greater persistence of depressive symptomatology among the acute hospital group may be related to other factors we have not explored, but it seems reasonable to speculate that it is due to some degree to the ongoing uncertainty about the patient's future. The finding that caregivers' close family relationships also suffer to a greater extent when the patient remains in the acute care setting is of concern in that it suggests an erosion in vital sources of socioemotional support.

The patient's transfer to long-term care, however, seems to have its own negative concomitants, although in an evaluative sense it might be argued that these are less serious than those associated with long-stay. That is, phenomena such as feeling uncomfortable when visiting and feeling less satisfied with medical treatment do not strike at the heart of personal well-being the way that depression and altered family relationships do.

Perhaps ironically, the data suggest that on many indicators family members are neither advantaged nor disadvantaged by the long-stay situation. (Patients, of course, may be another matter. For a discussion focusing on patients, see Marshall, 1987.) Feelings of burden, fatigue, too many demands, and conflict between the patients' and their own needs are similar, on the whole, whether relatives remain in acute hospitals or are transferred to long-term care facilities. These findings may be attributable to family responsibility and devotion that motivate families to worry, visit, monitor, and provide care regardless of the patient's location. It may also be that each type of care setting has its own strengths and weaknesses, with neither setting providing caregivers with enough confidence in patient care that they feel able to reduce their own role performance to fully manageable levels. For families whose relative remains in the acute setting, one advantage lies in the fact that in such a setting technical care will be readily available if needed. This may well provide families with a sense of security about their relative's medical care, although satisfaction with other aspects of care is similar across settings.

POLICY RECOMMENDATIONS

The first section of this chapter outlined policy failures and policy dilemmas leading to the long-stay situation in which elderly patients remain for long periods of time in acute hospitals. Because chronically ill geriatric patients in acute settings are unlikely to receive care that is aggressively targeted to their special needs (Sulman et al., 1987), one would expect the families of these patients to experience greater negative impact of the patient's hospitalization than would be the case if their relatives were in appropriate, long-term care facilities. In the second section of the chapter, it was seen that the impact of the long-stay situation on family caregivers was more negative in some important respects, although the overall pattern was for similarities across settings. As well, on some indicators the long-term care setting was associated with a more negative impact, although it might be argued that these areas were less serious than those associated with the acute hospital in that they were less related to caregiver well-being.

One of the reasons that neither type of setting was found to be clearly better or worse for caregivers may be that, in the real as opposed to the ideal world, each type is a mixed blessing. Acute hospitals do not provide appropriate levels and kinds of care for long-stay geriatric patients, but they may well provide a sense of security to patients and families because of their technical resources and because people have negative views of long-term care institutions. One would expect long-term care facilities to provide more suitable care, but in reality these institutions vary widely in quality and may fail to meet their care mandate (Tarman, 1990). Thus, it may well be that neither type of facility adequately meets the needs of elderly patients or their families.

The primary issue, whatever the setting, is to provide better care to patients, leading to less distress and worry for families. Given the persistence of the long-stay situation in acute care, it is imperative to explicitly address the needs of long-stay patients and their families in the acute hospital. That is, rather than simply viewing the long-stay situation as a "problem," we need to recognize the needs of the patients and their families whose lives are profoundly affected by policies over which they have little control and about which they have less knowledge.

Developing more appropriate care for long-stay patients and their families includes providing special programs and services and promoting rehabilitation in the acute care setting. On the surface, this might seem to contradict current policy directions in Ontario (Evans, 1987; Spasoff, 1987; Government of Ontario, 1991) and elsewhere in Canada that express support for a shift of health resources toward the community sector. However, the simple substitution of inadequate alternatives in the community is an increasingly common but expensive error. In this regard, Canada and the United States share a common plight. The acute hospital can do some things more effectively than any other setting; a recognition and exploitation of the acute hospital's potential role in helping to return elderly patients to the community could have very positive benefits. Intensive, short-term rehabilitation of the elderly is one of the areas that acute hospitals could address very well, if resources were allocated for that purpose, since highly trained rehabilitation staff working in well-equipped units are often already in place. Elderly patients would benefit, and family members, who feel helpless when their spouse or parent is denied rehabilitation, would be reassured that their relative's needs are not viewed as a low priority. However, short-sighted policies often divert scarce rehabilitation resources away from geriatric patients in order to deal with hospital deficits or other priorities. Thus, some patients who might otherwise return to the community, or who, with intensive rehabilitation, might require a lighter level of care, can become long-stay patients awaiting more costly chronic care.

In general, however, acute hospitals lack incentives to allocate resources to fully address the distinctive needs of long-stay elderly patients and their families (Marshall, 1987). Although program initiatives might well result in cost savings, through returning patients to the community or maintaining them at lighter levels of care, these savings would be primarily realized not by the hospital itself but rather by other sectors. Ironically, an added disincentive is the fact that long-stay patients can be of benefit to hospital budgets since the current global budgeting formula for acute care institutions has the effect of rewarding the covert transformation of acute care beds to chronic care beds (Aronson et al., 1987).

The need for aggressive intervention with chronically ill geriatric patients is, of course, not limited to the acute care setting. Long-term care settings, while in theory more appropriate than the acute hospital for the patients in our study, themselves often fail to provide the programs and treatments that would benefit patients. Similarly, as the policy documents we reviewed above so strongly argue, chronically ill elderly residing in the community may not have access to the kinds of services and programs they need.

A recent editorial on the persistence of backlogs of long-stay patients in the United States (Shaughnessy, 1991) suggests that the causes of the problem are either a severe shortage of hospital beds or a severe shortage of nursing home beds. These causes can be ruled out in our case study: the causes of the long-stay problem lie primarily with a policy failure to put into place an integrated, coordinated, broad-spectrum program of long-term care. The problem is not with the lack of understanding of the design features of such a program. We have seen that its basic aspects are well precedented in other Canadian provinces and well described in policy documents and "discussion papers." The problem, then, is largely with a failure of policy implementation.

Ultimately, the solution to these problems is three-fold: (1) to direct initiatives toward maximizing the functional independence of elderly persons who require maintenance or regular supervision; (2) to recognize the critical need in many families for additional supports; and (3) to develop an enhanced model of continuity of care that ensures that gains made in the acute care setting are sustained in the community or in long-term care. Although efforts to improve coordination are being made, the continued fragmentation of policies relating to treatment of the elderly in acute care, long-term care, and the community helps to perpetuate a high rate of institutionalization, and also contributes to the continuation of stress experienced by caregivers, regardless of the location of the patient.

A key element in new policy initiatives for the chronically ill elderly and their caregivers is attention to the linkages among community agencies, acute care hospitals, and long-term care institutions. As long as each arena is funded separately, with few incentives to coordinate care, the current fragmentation will continue. Unfortunately, continuity of care appears to be in no one's interest except that of patients and their families. The frail elderly person with recent onset of confusion who is brought to a hospital emergency department by an exhausted family member is ill served by the usual combination of reassurance, a prescription, and a phone number for Meals-on-Wheels. Without rapid, coordinated intervention in the community, this person will likely become a candidate for long stay in an acute care institution. Given the extreme underfunding of services to provide care in the community and the lack of an integrated, coordinated long-term care system which emphasizes community-based care, the problem of long-stay patients in the hospital, with its attendant stresses on family members, can be expected to persist and to increase as the number of very old people increases in our population.

We have argued throughout this chapter that older people and their families are the victims rather than the causes of the long-stay problem. However, it is very likely that a widespread view of the aging population as the cause of the problem will continue. Policymakers will no doubt go on pointing to the need to "free" acute care beds, implying that long-stay patients are "blocking" those beds. As well, policymakers will continue to gravely refer to the burdens the aging population places on our health care system and the near-intolerable demands the system will face in the future. There may be a subtle or not-so-subtle implication that we have already reached the breaking point with respect to long-term care beds, resulting in the spillover of chronically ill elderly into acute care beds. Such reasoning is an example of "apocalyptic demography" (Robinson, 1991), in which the long-stay phenomenon becomes seen as yet one more indication of the growing crisis in health care, caused by the aging of the population. Our argument in this chapter has been quite the reverse. The long-stay problem is not "caused" by population aging but by inadequacies in policies and policy implementation. The difficulties that are seen today in Ontario in shifting the health care system to be better able to deal with chronic illness relate, in part, to reallocating resources away from the very powerful acute care sector. Blaming societal aging in general, or individuals and families in particular, for the long-stay problem merely diverts attention from the real causes of the problem and obscures the kinds of solutions that might provide the appropriate and high quality care that older people and their families deserve. Social scientists have long employed the concept of "blaming the victim" to identify misguided explanations and interpretations of one or another undesirable experience. In Canada current policy discussions about long-stay patients in short-stay hospitals often fall prey to the same sort of logic. This chapter's goal has been to point out that this is simply not the case. Protracted stays are not the "fault" of patients and families but rather are the result of the policy and implementation process. This process, once identified, should be amenable to control and redirection, with the result that all affected parties, including patients and their families, will experience more satisfactory outcomes.

*The authors gratefully acknowledge the research support of Health and Welfare Canada and the Ministry of Community and Social Services of Ontario. Rosenthal acknowledges the support of the Ontario Ministry of Health through a Career Scientist Award.

REFERENCES

A New AGEnda: Health and social services strategies for Ontario's seniors. (1986). Toronto: Government of Ontario.

Aronson, J., Marshall, V., & Sulman, J. (1987). Patients awaiting discharge from hospital. In V.W. Marshall (Ed.), *Aging in Canada: Social perspectives, 2nd edition* (pp. 538-549). Markham, Ontario: Fitzhenry and Whiteside.

Beatrice, D. (December, 1979). Briefing paper: Administratively necessary days. Internal report prepared for the Massachusetts Department of Public Welfare.

Chappell, N. (1989). Long-term care in Canada. In E. Rathbone-McCuan & B. Havens (Eds.), *North American elders. United States and Canadian comparisons*, (pp. 73-78). Westport, CT: Greenwood Press.

Coordination of long term care services task force (CLTCS). (1983). A review of a selected sample of coordinate long term care service models in Canada and other countries. Manuscript, pp. 30 + 3.

Council of Chronic Hospitals of Ontario. (October, 1991). *Chronic care hospitals and the redirection of long-term care services*. Toronto: Council of Chronic Hospitals of Ontario.

Evans, J. (1987). Toward a shared direction for health in Ontario. Report of the Ontario Health Review Panel. Toronto: Government of Ontario.

Fisher, R. H. & Zorzitto, M. L. (1983). Placement problem: Diagnosis, disease, or term of denigration? *Canadian Medical Association Journal,* 129, 331-334.

Funding and incentives study (n.d.). Prepared by Stevenson Kellogg Ernst and Whinney for the Health Care System Committee, Premier's Council on Health Strategy. Toronto: Premier's Council on Health Strategy.

Gross, J., & Schwenger, C. (1981). _Health care costs for the elderly in Ontario: 1976-2026_. Toronto: Occasional Paper 11, Ontario Economic Council.

Health for all Ontario. (1987). Report of the Panel on Health Goals for Ontario. Toronto, Ministry of Health, Government of Ontario.

Kane, R. (1987). Issues in the delivery of long term care services in the United States. In M.J. Gibson (Ed.), _Income security and long term care for women in midlife and beyond: U.S. and Canadian perspectives. Proceedings of the U.S./Canadian expert group meeting on policies for midlife and older women_, (pp. 14-21). Washington, D.C.: American Association of Retired Persons.

_____, & Kane, R. (1985). _A will and a way: What the United States can learn from Canada about caring for the elderly_. New York: Columbia University Press.

Lagoe, R., & Decker, K. (1991). Long-term care patients in acute care beds: A community-based analysis. _The Gerontologist_, 31: 438-446.

Marshall, V. (1987). Older patients in the acute-care hospital setting. In R. Ward & S. Tobin (Eds.), _Health in aging: Sociological issues and policy directions_, (pp.194-208). New York: Springer.

_____, Rappolt, S., & Wilkins, S. (1989). _Models for community-based long term care_. Prepared for Health Policy Division, Policy, Planning and Information Branch, Health and Welfare Canada.

Metropolitan Toronto District Health Council. (1984). _Long term care bed needs in Metropolitan Toronto_. Toronto.

Ontario Gerontology Association. (1989). _Fact book on aging in Ontario_. Toronto.

Paget, A. G. (1973). Acute care hospitals: Their role in long-term care. _Dimensions in Health Service_, 60, 28-29.

Price Waterhouse. (November 1989). _Operational review of the Ontario home care program: Final report_. Toronto: Ontario Ministry of Health.

Redirection of long-term care and support services in Ontario. (1991). Toronto: Ministry of Community and Social Services, Ministry of Health, and Ministry of Citizenship, Government of Ontario.

Robertson, A. (1991). The politics of Alzheimer's disease: A case study in apocalyptic demography. In M. Minkler & C. Estes (Eds.), _Critical perspectives on aging: The political and moral economy of growing old_, (pp. 135-150). Amityville, New York: Baywood.

Shapiro, E., Roos, N., & Kavanagh, S. (1980). Long term patients in acute care beds: Is there a cure? *The Gerontologist* 20, 342-349.

_____, & Roos, N. (1981). The geriatric long-stay hospital patient: A Canadian case study. *Journal of Health Politics, Policy and Law*, 6: 49-61.

Shaughnessy, P. (1991). Editorial. Somebody's sleeping in my bed: The hospital, the nursing home, and near-acute care. *The Gerontologist*, 31, 436-437.

Strategies for change. Comprehensive reform of Ontario's long-term care services. (1991). Toronto: Ministry of Community and Social Services, Ministry of Health, Office for Senior Citizens' Affairs, and Office for Disabled Persons, Government of Ontario.

Sulman, J., & Wilkinson, S. (1989). An activity group for long-stay elderly patients in an acute care hospital: Program evaluation. *Canadian Journal on Aging*, 8, 34-50.

Tarman, V. (1990). *Privatization and health care: The case of Ontario nursing homes.* Toronto: Garamond Press.

CHAPTER 8
Advance Directive Policy in Canada: The Impact on Older People and Their Families*
Eric M. Meslin and Kara Sutherland

Families have always been faced with making difficult decisions for each other regarding matters of health. These decisions, whether admitting an older relative to a long-term care institution or a more urgent decision to consent to necessary medical treatment, are made more difficult when families are unaware of the wishes of the person. Families wishing to care for older relatives face a difficult ethical conflict when such wishes are not known: in the absence of specific instructions, how should families act in the best interests of their relative?

Some of the most important mechanisms for achieving these goals to date have been advance directives. These instruments—both instruction directives such as "living wills" or proxy directives such as durable powers of attorney—are now the focus of medical, legal, and philosophical discussion in Canada and the United States. The emergence of advance directives can be linked to several factors, including a societal concern that patients are not permitted to determine the type of care they would prefer to have begun or withdrawn (President's Commission, 1983), that terminal illness is not well managed by physicians (Fisher & Meslin, 1990; Heintz, 1988; Eisendrath & Jonsen, 1983), that an aging population will want to include end of life decisions in their discussions with their families, and to other more general speculations about the usefulness or futility of medical care (Schneiderman, Jecker, & Jonsen, 1983).

Some of these issues can be studied empirically both prospectively and retrospectively. There is already evidence of the value of empirical research for purposes of developing the content and style of advance directives (Emanuel et al., 1990) and of assessing the attitudes of patients, families and clinicians towards completing these documents (Singer & Hughes, 1991). The introduction of the *Patient Self-Determination Act* in the United States (1991) provides ample opportunities to evaluate the outcomes of public policy when measured against the values and intentions which precipitated it. Under this legislation, all publicly funded hospitals must now inform patients of advance directives and their right to refuse treatment and comply with the existing state law regarding advance directives. (Patient Self-Determination Act, 1990; High & Turner, Chapter 3).

Similar opportunities exist in Canada to assess the impact on older persons, their families, and the provinces. Unlike the United States, however, no federal legislation has been enacted. Still, many important questions still have not been adequately answered. Some of these concerns are procedural: what should advance directives look like? Who should be permitted to complete them? Ought all patients upon hospital admission be provided with a form? Other questions are more substantive: what medical treatments can be refused or requested in an advance directive? Can patients while competent reliably predict what kind of treatment they would want if they became incompetent in the future? What happens when people change their mind?

While this information is certainly valuable, it is clear that any policy shift that would permit or encourage the use of advance directives (in contrast with one that would discourage or prohibit their use) raises ethical issues for older persons and their families that must be assessed on ethical grounds as well. Largely missing from this discussion of advance directives, therefore, has been an ethical assessment of the effect that this development in public policy will have on older persons and their families. If advance directives are to be codified in Canadian public policy in the same way that virtually all of the United States has done (Areen, 1991), it is appropriate to consider the moral content of that public policy and to understand more clearly the problem that advance directives are intended to solve. The purpose of this chapter, therefore, is to examine the ethical implications of this public policy development in Canada and in particular to discuss these implications in terms of the effect on older persons and their families. We intend to do three things: first, we will explain what advance directives are and what factors have contributed to their development. Second, we will examine the status of advance directives in Canada and the likely prospect of their widespread adoption. Here we will pay special attention to the similarities and differences with the United States approach to the problem that advance directives intend to resolve. Finally we will consider the ethical implications that this development in public policy will have on older persons and their families. In particular, we will suggest that traditional philosophic categories of analysis, particularly the appeal to ethical principles, will need to be adjusted to account for the increasing role of families in decision making.

BIOETHICS AND ITS INFLUENCE ON ADVANCE DIRECTIVES POLICY

Three related developments have converged to form the present context in which advance directives policy discussions take place. First, medical advance has contributed numerous technologies to a growing list of wondrous services: cardiac pacemakers to regulate heart function; sophisticated ventilation and respiration machinery to restore and maintain a homeostatic breathing environment; drugs and biologics that enhance immune function and combat pesky bugs; several methods for delivering medically supplied hydration and nutrition; medical imaging, such as CAT scans; and various resuscitation procedures (Bronzino, Smith, & Wade, 1990). Taken together, these advances have contributed to a climate in health care in which people believe that if there are technological solutions to medical problems, the technologies ought to be used.

Second, social movements such as the civil rights movement, the women's movement, and the consumer movement have stressed the rights and empowerment of previously powerless groups. In health care this has been manifested in the patient's rights movement, for example, as patients and their families began to demand a greater role in clinical decision making (Annas, 1982). The most striking feature has been the increasing importance in both law and bioethics given to the doctrine of informed consent (Rosovsky & Rosovsky, 1990; Faden & Beauchamp, 1986).

Third, academic philosophy began to turn its attention to the moral problems in medicine and health care. Early texts, such as Ramsey's *The Patient As Person* (Ramsey, 1970), provided an initial impetus for applying moral theory to such problems as withholding and withdrawing treatment, organ transplantation and informed consent. In the late 1970's, Beauchamp and Childress' *Principles of Biomedical Ethics* (1979) provided a philosophic account of how to apply fundamental ethical principles to moral problems in medicine, health policy and research. The principles of autonomy, beneficence, non-maleficence and justice are now fixtures in the bioethics literature. In particular, the principle of autonomy has assumed increasing importance in both theory and practice (Dworkin, 1988). It also serves as the philosophic starting point for advance directives.

Technology, empowerment, and ethical reflection have combined to pose a challenge for individuals, their families, and society: how should the empowered older person plan his or her life? Can society afford the costs of implementing advance directives? What are the implications for families of legislating these documents? These are the questions that advance directives policy must address.

ADVANCE DIRECTIVES

What are advance directives and how do they work? Following King's recent definition, an advance directive is "a written statement that is intended to govern health care decision making for its author, should he or she lose decisional capacity in the future" (King, 1991). Patients who are mentally competent to make treatment decisions on their own behalf do not require advance directives, nor do they require others to decide on their own behalf. There are many patients who, for specific reasons lack decision making capacity. A large number of patients with dementia are lacking this ability; so do patients who are permanently mentally incapacitated resulting from stroke, trauma, or failed resuscitation attempts. These are the persons for whom advance directives are believed to provide the greatest service: previously competent patients for whom decisions regarding treatment (or non-treatment) will need to be made.

Informal advance directives have a long history in medicine. For centuries people have been telling friends, family members, and physicians *verbally* how they want to be treated. This history also includes letters, written mostly by physicians, which were usually limited to withholding or withdrawing treatment (Humphrey and Wickett, 1986). They bore some resemblance to the early versions of the "Living Will," in that both were anticipatory declarations, and also some resemblance to some recent advance directive documents which specify details of treatment (e.g., cessation of ventilator after 3 min. of anoxia). Still, both verbal disclosures and letters have an element of informality to them. Moreover, they were difficult to implement if the individuals to whom the verbal disclosure was made was unavailable at the time the decision needed to be made. Similarly, letters could be mislaid or forgotten. Neither carried legal force. More formal documents were thought to be needed.

INSTRUCTION DIRECTIVES

Two types of formal advance directives exist: instruction directives and proxy directives. Instruction directives, like the "Living Will" issued by organizations such as the Society for the Right to Die and Dying with Dignity, allow individuals to specify those medical procedures they would want provided or foregone once they are incompetent to make such directions themselves. These decisions include the initiation or withdrawal of medical therapies such as surgery, antibiotics, medically supplied hydration and nutrition, and cardiopulmonary resuscitation. The advantages of a Living Will are numerous. Fisher and Meslin (1990) identified three: they permit advance expression of a patient's preferences recognizing the importance of the patient's own evaluation of quality of life; they promote communication about medical care at the end of life with family, friends, and health care professionals; and they demonstrate respect for the patient as an autonomous person. Singer identified others including the reduction of emotional distress of family members who may be faced with these decisions, and the reduction of psychological distress of health care providers who are concerned about making the wrong decision (Singer et al., 1992). Any policy regarding advance directives is based on the assumption that it is always morally preferable to act as the patient would have wanted and that it is better to have discussed these important matters before the time that a decision would need to be made.

The development of living wills have also raised a number of concerns; for example, early living wills tended to include ambiguous language such as "terminal illness," "heroic measures," and "extraordinary treatment," terms that had not been well defined (President's Commission, 1983). On the other hand, some of the recent versions have been quite complex including different combinations of treatments and medical conditions (Emanuel & Emanuel, 1989). This is a problem similar to that found in hospital consent forms where balancing the need to be comprehensive against the value of putting the information on one readable form becomes a legal and ethical tradeoff.

Other concerns are that their use could paradoxically restrict patients' rights by subtly compelling those persons without a living will to submit to care they otherwise would not have wanted; that they may negatively affect the physician-patient relationship by reducing it to a mere contractual arrangement lacking any human interaction (Fisher & Meslin, 1990), and the difficulty in making assessments of future preferences for care (Singer et al., 1992; Robertson, 1991). Many of these problems have been discussed by philosophers. For example, Dresser (1989) has suggested that living wills are the contemporary version of the classical problem of personal identity: is the incompetent patient for whom a medical decision must be made *the same* person as the one who completed a living will while competent? Philosophers have also wondered whether living wills really do allow individuals to express their preferences or wishes. This is an epistemological question that turns on the notion of how certain we are (or need to be) that a wish written on a document really is the settled judgment of that person since this involves a certain amount of interpretation (Juengst & Weil, 1989). Similarly, deciding whether an individual really wants to die, wants to have her pain treated, to be institutionalized, or to have an equivalent quality of life to the one she enjoyed before her medical condition are complicated, value-laden questions. Living wills are not sophisticated enough to include both preferences and values. (Cambert, MacIver-Gibson & Nathanson, 1990; Meslin & Abrhamsohn, 1991).

PROXY DIRECTIVES

Several of these objections have been overcome with the development of proxy directives, sometimes called a Durable Power of Attorney.[1] Whereas instruction directives designate *decisions* a competent person would make about medical treatment, proxy directives are intended to allow persons to designate an *individual* to make decisions on their behalf when they are no longer competent to do so themselves. Modelled after the power of attorney for financial matters, the Durable Power of Attorney extends this same authority to health care decisions. The benefits of Durable Powers of Attorney parallel those of the Living Will but, unlike the living will, provide a mechanism for allowing substitute decision makers to exercise limited discretion in complying with the wishes and preferences of a previously competent patient. The problems too are similar to those of the Living Will although the chief difficulty devolves from having medical decisions once removed from the person for whom they must be made.

Taken together, however, the Living Will and Durable Power of Attorney provide a comprehensive mechanism for empowering older persons at a time when they are most vulnerable. By designating through a living will what an older person would want done in the event of mental incapacity, and designating through a Durable Power of Attorney a person (quite likely a family member) to carry out their wishes and act in their best interests, there is some assurance that advance planning will be accomplished to the satisfaction of the person.

CANADIAN PUBLIC POLICY ON ADVANCE DIRECTIVES

The public policy approach in Canada has similar features to that of the United States but is unique in several respects. Canadians watched with interest the deliberation of the United States Supreme Court in the case of Nancy Cruzan (Cruzan, 1990). The Court was asked to decide whether the State of Missouri could require that there be clear and convincing evidence of an incompetent patient's wishes to discontinue medical treatment. Although it agreed that Missouri could require this standard, the Court also acknowledged that there is a right to refuse treatment. Like the United States, Canada has a rich history in case law that reflects the evolution in the standards of disclosure required of physicians in order to obtain an informed consent, and what may count as an informed refusal. The 1980 Supreme Court of Canada case of *Reibl v. Hughes* (1980) established the "reasonable person standard" in much the same way that *Canterbury v. Spence* (1972) did in the United States

It now appears that early concern about the drawbacks of legalizing living wills (Fisher & Meslin, 1990) has been tempered by an increase in support in Canada for these documents. Interestingly, however, Canadian courts have yet to encounter any cases like those involving Karen Ann Quinlan (1976) or Nancy Cruzan, where resolution of a difficult medical treatment decision required judicial intervention. There may be a number of explanations for this. First, some have pointed to the decidedly less litigious environment in Canada as compared to the United States. Indeed, in a recent analysis of malpractice claims in Canada, Robertson (1991) found that in the ten years since *Reibl* was decided, there has been little impact on the frequency or severity of malpractice claims. A second reason may be that the decisions to initiate or withdraw medical care from patients have remained within the context of the relationship between families, patients, and health care professionals. However, it is difficult to assess the extent to which mutual or shared decision making about medical care is occurring and whether conflicts arise that cannot be addressed within such relationships.

A third reason may be the lack of public involvement in policy discussions in Canada on this issue. Unlike the United States, where the President's Commission reports led to legislative initiatives in virtually every state (Areen, 1991), Canadian public policy has moved slowly. With the notable exception of the Law Reform Commission of Canada's reports on criteria for the determination of death (LRCC, 1981) and euthanasia (LRCC, 1982), and an a set of professional guidelines (CMA, 1984), little national attention has been focused on the broader topic of decision making at the end of life for older persons. Yet even in the case of the LRCC, it has been argued that its impact has been minimal. (Indeed, it is worth noting that neither of the LRCC reports have resulted in law reform in

Canada, and, as described below, only two provinces have enacted legislation on advance directives).

The comparison between the United States and Canadian approaches to public policy in this area deserves mention if only to indicate a possible explanation for the vacuum with respect to the Canadian situation. Some authors have noted stark difference in the products of the President's Commission and LRCC. Browne (1988) and Winkler (1988) both observed that the President's Commission spoke clearly on the appropriateness of legislating living wills and of adopting the "substituted judgment" standard for incompetent patients, while the LRCC (1982) vacillated on these issues. Winkler (1988) points to the ambiguity with respect to whether there is a presumption that incompetent patients could want any treatment thought to be beneficial to them. He also suggests that where the President's Commission supports the direct involvement of family members in making a substituted judgment, the LRCC acknowledges the importance of consultation but grants primary authority to physicians.

On the same issue of foregoing treatment Browne (1988) illustrates the LRCC's ambiguity in drawing attention to its initial liberal view with respect to the concern for overall patient welfare and then subsequently turns to a conservative position when trying to apply a quality of life standard to such decisions. He further points to this ambiguity in the LRCC's position on legislating living wills. The LRCC, Browne argues, waffles—initially recommending that living will should have legal force and then later in the same report, rejecting the concept. In the absence of a public forum for discussion, the opportunity to clarify these issues was lost.

These reasons for a low Canadian profile on advance directives policy are admittedly speculative. In fact, at the time of this writing (December 1991) several cases of patients (or their families) expressing a desire to have medical treatment discontinues have been reported in the media, and a few brought to court. One of those which may establish Canadian case law involves Nancy B., a young woman in Montreal, who is completely incapacitated by Guillain-Barre Syndrome and has requested that she be disconnected from her ventilator. A decision is expected early in 1992. This case and others will likely mobilize public interest in advance directives. Already there is some legislative interest.

CURRENT LEGAL STATUS OF ADVANCE
DIRECTIVES IN CANADA

Two provinces have passed legislation regarding advance directives, Nova Scotia (1989) and Quebec (1989), both of which permit the use of proxy directives where patients are incompetent. No Canadian province has passed legislation regarding instruction directives or "living wills." This is likely to change, as evidenced by both existing case law and recent introduction of several legislative initiatives in other provinces. The case law dates, at least, to 1983, when the British Columbia Court of Appeal held that it was not mandatory to force feed a patient (British Columbia, 1983). More recently, the Ontario Court of Appeal unanimously held in 1990 that a physician was liable for administering a blood transfusion to a Jehovah's Witness. In this case, *Malette v. Shulman* (1990), a woman was brought unconscious to hospital following a car accident but carried a card indicating her explicit refusal of blood transfusions. Some have argued that the card may be regarded as an advance directive (Singer & Lowy, 1991).

Other legal events that indicate the extent of the Canadian shift toward legalizing advance directives include the preparation of a discussion paper by the Manitoba Law Reform Commission which endorses the use of advance directives and a legislative mechanism for their adoption (Manitoba Law Reform Commission, 1990) and a comprehensive legislative package introduced by the Ontario government in May 1991. This package included two pieces of legislation, the *Consent to Treatment Act* (1991) and the *Substitute Decisions Act* (1991), which collectively would establish mechanisms for legally recognizing living wills and durable powers of attorney for personal care.

The legal background to advance directives policy in Canada also must be framed in terms of the *Charter of Rights and Freedoms* which became law as part of the *Constitution Act* in 1982. Madame Justice Rivet (1990) has observed that three of the Sections of the *Charter* are particularly relevant to health care: *Section 7* defines certain specific rights and protection:

Everyone has the right to life, liberty, and security of the
person and the right not be deprived thereof except in
accordance with the principles of fundamental justice.

Section 15(1) describes the protection against discrimination that all
Canadians are entitled to before the law:

Every individual is equal before and under the law and
has the right to the equal protection and equal benefit of
the law without discrimination and, in particular, without
discrimination based on race, national or ethnic origin,
color, religion, sex, age, or mental or physical disability.

These two Sections illustrate how the *Charter* resembles elements
of the American Bill of Rights. However, what distinguishes them is *Section
1* of the *Charter* which outlines the permissible limits on fundamental rights:

The *Canadian Charter of Rights and Freedoms* guarantees
the rights and freedoms set out in it subject only to such
reasonable limits prescribed by law as can be
demonstrably justified in a free and democratic society.

Individual rights are fundamental under these Sections but not
absolute, so we can only speculate how the *Charter* might affect advance
directives policy in Canada. If one of the purposes of advance directives
policy in Canada is to ensure that certain rights to receive or reject health
care services are protected, then it is likely that any legal challenges to
those policies could eventually be adjudicated by reference to those
Sections. For example, it is possible that a family could sue a hospital (or
province) because the advance directives policy deprived an older relative
of the right to life, liberty, or security of person (Section 7) or because he
or she was discriminated against on the basis of age or physical or mental
disability (Section 15). We suspect, however, that it would be more likely
that a family would sue a hospital or province for *failing* to establish
advance directives policy since the *Charter* could be interpreted as dictating
that there should be such policies to protect the liberty and security of the
person or to ensure that individuals were not discriminated against. We also
suspect that the *Charter* could be invoked if an existing advance directives
policy did not permit individuals to express their desire not to receive a

particular medical treatment, such as hydration or nutrition (which is the case, for example in the *Oklahoma* and *Connecticut* statutes). On the other hand, *Section 1* might be used if an advance directives policy permitted individuals to request medical treatments that were very costly. It might be unfair on grounds of distributive justice to honor such requests when it would deprive others of more needed or more beneficial treatment. This more widespread acceptance of the specific social obligations to the individual as recognized in the *Charter* would make the policy shift towards advance directives potentially at odds with the ethic of health care in a universal system.

THE FIT BETWEEN CANADIAN HEALTH POLICY AND ADVANCE DIRECTIVES

It seems assured that Canada will follow the United States lead of legislating advance directives, province by province, thus establishing mechanisms for patients and families to effect treatment decisions that are consistent with individual preferences. This is not surprising, given that Canadians do share many values of Americans, including concern for the protection of individual rights and the promotion of well-being, and yet as we noted with respect to the *Charter* there are some fundamental differences. Clark argues (Chapter 1) that the goals or ends of the two countries are different. Americans, he argues extols the Declaration of Independence's "life, liberty, and the pursuit of happiness," while Canadians appeal to the virtues of "peace, order, and good government" emerging from the *Constitution Act* (1867) which created Canada. (*Section 1* serves to uphold these values.)

Still, despite some common themes that emerge from Canadian and United States perspectives on individual rights Canadian health policy evolved in a very different way from that in the United States. Given the particular difficulty that Canadians have faced throughout their history in defining their own identity, any analysis of those shared values regarding life-sustaining treatments and advance directives will more difficult to conduct. A proxy for those values can be found in some of the social institutions Canadians value, particularly in health care. Clark's analysis is a helpful start to frame the sociologic terrain of public policy in Canada. Doern and Phidd (1988) have deepened this analysis by describing the normative content of Canadian public policy as involving several *ideologies* (liberalism, conservatism, and socialism), *dominant ideas* (efficiency, individual liberty, stability of income, redistribution and equality, equity, natural identity, and regional diversity); and *ideas and paradigms* (the "curative" as contrasted with the "preventative" approach to health care.)

Even this brief analysis indicates that Canada and the United States may share some common ideologies (conservatism and liberalism) but not others (socialism) and some dominant ideas (individual liberty, efficiency) but not others (equality, equity, regional diversity). Perhaps the most obvious difference between the two countries is with respect to health care. Indeed, as Taylor has observed, the reasons are complex:

> If we were to ask why, when Canadian and United States societies appear to be so much alike, Canada has a nationwide, universal program of medical insurance but the United States does not, the answers would be both numerous and complex—and inevitably incomplete. Many of the explanations, however, would focus on the differences in political systems: in the allocation of powers between the national and the state or provincial governments, in the respective legislative bodies and their relationship to the executive, in the system of political parties and their objectives, in the influence of relevant interest groups, and, not least, in the differences in citizens' views on what the role of government in society should be. (Taylor, 1990:1)

Health care may be the best example of an institution that is valued so much differently in each country. Doern and Phidd (1988) suggest that it is one of the paradigms that distinguish the two countries. Health care is constitutive of the social and economic history of the country and is regarded as a collective good rather than an item to be purchased. The Canadian health care system is a publicly administered system, funded out of general tax revenues. This fact is not only of historical or political interest but of specific medical interest: not every medical procedure that a competent patient in the United States decides to request or refuse through an advance directive is available to his or her Canadian counterparts. While this fact has been chiefly responsible for some of the criticisms of the Canadian health care system (Crows & Ferrier, 1991), it does not reflect the whole picture. Canadians and specifically older Canadians and their families are not placed in the type of financial jeopardy resulting from costly medical care that their American counterparts are.

What is becoming more clear, however, is that older Canadians will be the first to assess their health care needs from a range of perspectives: individual preferences, collective goods, and cost. The obvious outlet for this discussion is the issue of whether advance directives policy will be assessed on grounds of cost-effectiveness rather than patient's rights. We suspect that as the funding issue takes the center stage in Canadian health policy (as it appears to be), Canadians may be expected to make the kinds of trade-offs that American families have been forced to make for years.

So far, this discussion has focused principally on the substance of advance directives and the structure of public policy development for implementing them. Next we examine the problems advance directives may create for families and the way that philosophical reflection may explain these problems more clearly.

THE DILEMMA OF FAMILIES: WHICH PHILOSOPHY EXPLAINS THEIR INVOLVEMENT?

In the wake of the *Cruzan* decision concerns have already been expressed in the United States regarding the legal role of families in decision making (Pawlson, 1991). For example, Baron argues that there is no need to go to family members when deciding whether to continue treating a patient in a persistent vegetative state, because there is a growing appreciation of the presumption that such patients would want to have medical support terminated (Baron, 1991). In contrast (but not necessarily in contradistinction), King asserts that families should have "the presumptive right to make major medical decisions for incompetent adult patients" (King, 1991). Baron and King are not at odds, since the former is making an observation about a factual matter, and the latter is making a claim about a normative one. It is the normative issue that requires some further assessment.

The approach to medical care based on the principle of respect for autonomy has become an increasingly prevalent one. It is now an ethical imperative to receive informed consent from patients before any medical treatment is administered, and, in fact, the law in both in Canada and the United States requires it (Browne, 1988). Moreover, there is increasing recognition that patients have certain moral and legal rights to be directly involved in decisions about their medical care, particularly the right to consent to medical treatment and to refuse it. (Rosovsky & Rosovsky, 1990; MacDougall, 1988) This discussion has been extended to recognize some of these same moral and legal rights where patients are decisionally incompetent (Weisstub, 1990), because in situations where those decisions may affect the quality of the life of patients, it is ethically preferable to attempt to honor the decisions the patient would have made were they able to do so. In an environment where individual values are thought to trump all others, the ethical imperative for advance directives policy would be clear: establish policies that maximize the opportunities for individual preferences to be satisfied. Unfortunately (or fortunately), decision making involves others, besides the individual.

Those who are involved in providing care for others may and frequently will have different values, beliefs, and experiences than the individuals who are receiving care. These differences may be among older people and their families (Danis et al., 1988) or between patients and their formal caregivers (Kohn & Menon, 1988; Thomasma & Pellegrino, 1987). It is somewhat surprising, therefore, that little attention has been paid to the role of the family in decision making at the end of life, and, specifically the impact that public policy governing this domain will have on families.

Differences in fundamental values can lead to disagreement about appropriate treatments confusion and treatment delays. Often these disagreements are due to a failure on the part of individuals to plan for a time when they will be unable to make medical decisions and communicate these decisions unambiguously. Much discussion is already taking place about planning for decisional incapacity which is regarded as a neglected area in ethics and aging (High, 1987). But it is also the case that differences in the values held by individuals (even those related by blood, marriage, or other arrangement) create difficulties for decision making. The family is often thought of as a logical surrogate decision maker for the incompetent patient, since they are more likely to know what values the patient held than a physician or nurse who did not know the patient well. Physicians are even less able to reliably predict the decisions of their patients. In fact, various empirical studies have shown that there is a low rate of agreement between decisions made by patients about their care and those made by physicians, families or other proxies on their behalf (Ouslander, Tymchuk, & Rahbar, 1989; Uhlmann, Perlman, & Kain, 1988).

Families are expected to make a substitute judgment which in effect will ensure the preferences of the previously competent patient are respected. Advance directives allow the family to carry out those wishes, whether that be through an instruction directive or a Durable Power of Attorney. In the absence of any advance directive a family can act in what they take to be the best interests of their relative, relying on a personal assessment of quality of life and informed by the perception of patient expectations. What was learned from the *Cruzan* decision, however, was that families with the best intentions may be limited in their ability to make medical decisions for an incompetent older relative. Moreover, court decisions do not deepen our understanding of these dilemmas. Here, philosophic rather than legal explanation may be helpful. The case of a competent elderly woman who refuses a suggested medical treatment that may hasten her death may be described in terms of the conflict between the respect owed to this decision and the obligation to prevent a harm from occurring. This dichotomy—between respecting autonomous decisions and acting in the patient's medical best interests—may be summarized using the convenient shorthand of ethical principles where the "conflict" is between the principle of respect for autonomy and beneficence.

This may be convenient but it is unsatisfactory for the philosophic reasons we address below and, more importantly, for older persons and their families. It is unsatisfactory to individuals and their families because it fails to account for the richness of context and human biography that characterizes the relation between caregiver and patient. This would be easy to resolve if it were the case that all families always acted in unison and always held the same values as their relatives. Unfortunately, families may not always in the best position to act in a family member's best interest (Pellegrino & Thomasma, 1987). They may not know the patient well, especially if they have not lived with or near them. Molloy recently referred to this as the "daughter-from-California-syndrome" (Molloy, 1991) to indicate the difficulties that occur when a distant relative arrives at an institution to act on behalf of an incompetent patient. In other instances, families may not endorse or condone the patient's values because they are at odds with each other. Families may also be prone to feelings of guilt and responsibility for the patients' illness, which may translate into decisions to pursue more intensive care than that which the patients may have chosen. In other words, families are often vulnerable to decision making based on factors external to the patient that inhibits their role as surrogate decision maker.

The philosophic problem is somewhat more complex and abstract but, we think, relevant to analyzing both individual cases and policy: it concerns the effects of applying philosophical principles to cases. We suggested above that it is philosophically unsatisfactory to mechanistically reduce cases (or worse, patients) to principles. It is unsatisfactory for philosophers because it is still an open question as to whether principles alone are sufficient to ground a moral theory that is useful in clinical decision making (Jonsen & Toulmin, 1988). While we do not believe that this type of "principlism" (Clouser & Gert, 1990) is what Beauchamp and Childress intended in their work, the clinical reality may occasionally demand a fine-tuning of these action-guides. For example, some have maintained that by concentrating too much on the concept of patient autonomy, the interests of the family have been ignored. Hardwig has extended the concept of autonomy to include families as well as patients and argues that, "in many cases family members have a greater interest than the patient in which treatment option is exercised. In such cases, the interests of the family members often ought to override those of the patient" (Hardwig, 1990). This interpretation of autonomy is at odds with the prevailing legal and ethical principles of self-determination, one that has taken twenty years of jurisprudence and bioethical argument to achieve. On the other hand, jurisprudence rarely blazes the trail towards new interpretations of ethical responsibility and obligation, so it is not helpful to look there for advice. Hardwig's central point, as we see it, is that families tend to share in each other's interests—he calls them "connected interests"—and because of this interrelationship it is appropriate to make decisions considering the consequences to others:

> Because the lives of those who are close are not separable, to be close is no longer to have a life entirely your own to live as you choose. To be part of a family is to be morally required to make decisions on the basis of thinking about what is best for all concerned, not simply what is best for you (Hardwig, 1990:6).

We can see then, that by using principles, deciding whose interests ought to prevail might be seen as a conflict over whose autonomy ought to be respected most. (This is what we mean by principlism being unsatisfactory.) Surely there is more at work in an ethical assessment of the case of a family deciding about treatment for another family member.

Appealing to ethical principles helps to frame the type of potential conflicts but will not provide the context or narrative history necessary to understand the needs of the older person and their families. Still, there has been progress. Consistent with the multi-principled approach above, Beauchamp and McCullough (1984) have described two traditional models of moral responsibility in physician-patient relationships: an "autonomy" model and a "beneficence" model, each of which are derived from their respective principles. The autonomy model is intended to focus on empowering individuals with respect to the choices they make. The beneficence model focuses on acting for the welfare of the individual. These models are not themselves free of difficulty as the authors themselves recognize:

> The conflict generated by the [autonomy and beneficence] models is an inescapable dimension of medical practice: a conflict between the patient's best interests understood from the perspective of medicine and the patient's best interests from the perspective of the patient....Medicine as known in the West has inherited a complex history, and physicians presently must determine their responsibility to their patients in terms of both of these models. This is a basic demand in medical ethics because adopting one model *exclusively* will result in the sacrifice of significant values....(Beauchamp & McCullough, 1984:50-51)

One implication of Beauchamp's and McCullough's assessment may be that neither model alone will generate the kinds of obligations and responsibilities that characterize the relationship between health professionals, older persons, and their families. Even if Beauchamp and McCullough's conclusion is reasonable (and we believe it is), it will be necessary to look beyond a principle-driven approach to a more contextually-informed one. This it seems, is more in keeping with the recognition of the notion of interdependency and familial responsibility that emerges when one looks at the effect of illness on patients and caregivers

(Cohen, Meslin, & Shulman, 1991; Hardwig, 1990). If one of the problems that advance directives policy intends to solve is the fear of not being able to directly plan one's life, we think such policy should be motivated by concerns for the competent person now, the incompetent person they may become, and their family throughout this period.

Part of this fine-tuning of principlism as the philosophic foundation for our moral responsibilities to patients and family members presumes that *care* needs to be included as a central feature of the relationship. One version of this ethic is a communitarian one where decision making involves a public conception of the good (Cunningham, 1991). A community that decided in advance what policy they would want to be governed by would enjoy all the advantages of anticipatory planning. This type of ethic has been suggested by Emanuel (1987) with respect to medical treatment:

> A clear policy known in advance would also preempt the
> need for families to engage in lengthy and distressing
> court battles over the termination of medical care of their
> loved ones. (Emanuel, 1987:19).

A second version of this ethic is more relevant to the discussion of the effect of such policies on families. Recent feminist philosophers such as Gilligan have argued that a different voice, what she calls a voice of care, can be identified in women as distinct from men (Gilligan, 1982). This ethic recasts not only the way moral theory is understood but also the way individuals understand their relationship to others. For example, women tend to focus on moral problems within their own context, emphasizing responsibility with and interconnectedness to others. In contrast, men focus on moral problems from the perspective of rights and duties. Gilligan called the former a voice of care and the latter a voice of justice. We hope that this type of ethic will soon become part of the structure of relationships in health care in general, because it most closely approximates the type of moral concern within families. Translating such an ethical commitment into public policy will be difficult, but not impossible, particularly since models of the care ethic already exist in nursing (Fry, 1989).

CONCLUSION

As Canada moves to adopt a legislative solution to a problem that can be defined as medical, technological, social, and ethical, it is necessary to take stock of the implications for older persons and their families and society. Advance directives are the product of an ethic of individualism that responds to a particular feature of that problem, namely, the legitimate concern around the control over one's life. However, as the population "ages and greys," it will be even more necessary to consider other features of the problem for which advance directives are a possible solution. These include the fit between health policy and individual preferences in a universal health care system and the relationship between individual and collective interests at both the family and societal levels. We have not argued that advance directives are dangerous or problematic (although there are some legitimate problems to be worked out), nor have we hailed their arrival. Rather, we have examined the way that the inevitable move toward adoption of advance directives policy in Canada both parallels and diverges from that traced out in the United States and concluded that we have much to learn as we go. Short of sitting back and waiting for the public policy to unfold we have suggested that several factors influence Canadian policy development including the shared philosophic and legal values within the system and the unique features of the family in medical decision making. Some of these bear repeating.

1. Advance directives, both instruction and proxy, offer several benefits to older persons and their families, specifically the opportunity to jointly plan for a time when important medical and health decisions will need to be made. These benefits cannot be realized without first addressing important limitations. The recognition that collective decision making in health care is process oriented as much as outcome oriented may be primary. Here, we recognize that one of the serious drawbacks of advance directives is their focus on treatment *decisions*, whether by an individual him/herself (as in the Living Will) or by others (as in the Durable Power of Attorney), rather than on the

process of communication, and about the values underlying those decisions.

2. While there is much to be learned from the United States experience with respect to advance directives policy, it should be possible to structure a Canadian strategy that recognizes the important differences in political process as much as the important similarities in shared values. This strategy will need to account for philosophic, cultural, and legal values that shape the process of public policy. It may also need to account for the economic realities facing the Canadian health care system.

3. If families are to be valid surrogate decision makers for their older relatives, then a contextual ethic of care can be operative here. In this sense we take "care" to include a broader concept of community care and a narrower one of relationship between and among identified individuals; as such it represents a more accurate description of the type of relationship families could hope to achieve with respect to their members.

These elements need amplification and elaboration. We suggest these as elements only to provide an opportunity to reflect on some of the philosophical assumptions and difficulties underlying advance directives policy development.

*We wish to gratefully acknowledge the assistance of Rhonda Fox and Janey Kim-Cave for their meticulous typing of this manuscript.

REFERENCES

Annas, G. J. (1982). The emerging stowaway: Patients' rights in the 1980s. *Law, Medicine, and Health Care*, 10: 32-45,46.

Areen, J. (1991). Advance directives under state law and judicial decisions. *Law, Medicine, and Health Care*, 19, 91-100.

Baron, C. H. (1991). Why withdrawal of life-support for PVS patients is not a family decision. *Law, Medicine and Health Care*, 19: 73-75.

Beauchamp, T. L., & Childress, J. F. (1989). *Principles of biomedical ethics*, 3rd ed. New York: Oxford University Press.

_____, & McCullough, L. B. (1984). *Medical ethics: The moral responsibilities of physicians*. Englewood Cliffs, NJ: Prentice-Hall.

[British Columbia] *Re Attorney General of British Columbia and Astaforoff* (1983), 6. C.C.C. (3d) 498 (B.C.C.A.).

Bronzino, J. D., Smith, V. H., & Wade, M. L. (1990). *Medical technology and society: An interdisciplinary perspective*. Cambridge, MA: MIT Press.

Browne, A. (1988). Foregoing life-sustaining treatment: The Canadian law reform commission and the President's commission. In J. E. Thornton & E. R. Winkler (Eds.), *Ethics and aging: The right to live, the right to die* (pp. 172). Vancouver: The University of British Columbia Press.

Cambert, P, MacIver-Gibson J., & Nathanson, P. (1990). The values-history project: An innovation in surrogate medical decision making. *Law, Medicine and Health Care*, 18, 202-212.

Canadian Charter of Rights and Freedoms. Part I of the *Constitution Act, 1982*, Schedule B of the *Canada Act 1982* (U.K.), 1982, c.11.

Canadian Medical Association (1984). Joint Statement on Terminal Illness. *Canadian Medical Association Journal*

Canterbury v. Spence (1972) 464 Fr. 2nd (D.C.Cir), 772.

Clark, P. G. (1992). Public policy in Canada and the United States: Individualism, familial obligation, and collective responsibility in the care of the elderly. (this volume)

Clouser, K. D., & Gert, B. (1990). A critique of principlism. *Journal of Medicine and Philosophy*, 15, 219-236.

Cohen, C. A., Meslin, E. M., & Shulman, K. I. (1991). Dementia at home: Ethical issues and clinical realities. In J. Berg, H. Karlinsky, & F. Lowy (Eds.), *Alzheimer's disease research: Ethical and legal issues* (pp. 317-330). Toronto: Carswell.

Connecticut Removal of Life Support Systems Act, Conn. Gen. Stat. Ann. 19a-570 to 19a-575.

Consent to Treatment Act, 1st Sess., 35th Leg. Ont., 1991.

Cruzan v. Director, Missouri Department of Health, 110 S. Ct. 2841 (1990).

Danis, M. et al. (1988). Patients' and families' preferences for medical intensive care. *Journal of the American Medical Association*, 260: 797-802.

Dresser, R. S. (1989). *Advance directives, self-determination, and personal identity*. In C. Hackler, R. Moseley, & D. E. Vawter (Eds.), *Advance directives in medicine* (pp. 155-170). New York: Praeger.

Dworkin, G. (1988) *The theory and practice of autonomy*. New York: Cambridge University Press.

Eisendrath, S. J., & Jonsen, A. R. (1983). The living will: Help or hindrance? *Journal of the American Medical Association*, 249: 2054-2058.

Emanuel, E. J. (1987). A communal vision of care for incompetent patients. *Hastings Center Report*, October/November: 15-20.

Emanuel E. & Emanuel, L. (1989). 'The medical directive': A new comprehensive advance care document. *Journal of the American Medical Association*, 261: 3288-3293.

Emanuel, L. L., Barry, M. J., Strekle, J. D., & Emanuel, E. J. (1990). A detailed advance care directive. *Clinical Research*, 38: 738A.

Faden, R. R., & Beauchamp, T. L. (1986). *A history and theory of informed consent*. New York: Oxford.

Fisher, R. H., & Meslin, E. M. (1990). Should living wills be legalized? *Canadian Medical Association Journal*, 142: 23-26.

Fry, S. T. (1989). The role of caring in a theory of nursing ethics. *Hypatia*, 4: 88-103.

Gilligan, C. (1982). *In a different voice*. Harvard University Press.

Hardwig, J. (1990). What about the family? *Hastings Center Report*, 5-10, 5.

Heinz, L. J. (1988). Legislative hazard: Keeping patients living against their wills. *Journal of Medical Ethics*, 14: 82-86.

High, D. M. (1987). Planning for decisional incapacity: A neglected area in ethics and aging. *Journal of the American Geriatrics Society*, 35: 814-820.

High, D. M., & Turner, H. B. (1992). Advance directives, surrogate health decision making, and older families. (this volume)

Humphrey, D., & Wickett, A. (1986). *The right to die: understanding euthanasia*. New York: Harper and Row.

Jonsen, A. R., & Toulmin, S. (1988). *The abuse of casuistry*. Berkeley, CA: University of California Press.

Juengst, E. T., & Weil, C. J. (1989). Interpreting proxy directives: Clinical decision-making and the durable power of attorney for health care. Inc. Hackler, R. Moseley & D. E. Vawter (Eds.), *Advance Directives in Medicine* (pp. 21-37). New York: Praeger.

King, N. M. P. (1991). *Making sense of advance directives*. Dordrecht: Kluwer Academic Publishers.

King, P. A. (1991). The authority of families to make medical decisions for incompetent patients after the *Cruzan* decision. *Law, Medicine and Health Care*, 19: 76-79.

Kohn, M., & Menon, G. (1988). Life Prolongation: View of elderly outpatients and health care professionals. *Journal of the American Geriatrics Society*, 36: 840-844.

Krasny, J., & Ferrier, I. R. (1991). A closer look at health care in Canada. *Health Affairs*, 10: 152-158.

Law Reform Commission of Canada. (1981). *Criteria for the determination of death: Report no. 15*. Ottawa: Minister of Supply and Services.

Law Reform Commission of Canada. (1982). *Euthanasia, aiding suicide and cessation of treatment: Working paper no. 28*. Ottawa: Minister of Supply and Services.

MacDougall, D. J. (1988). The right to participate: Ending discrimination against us elderly. In J. E. Thornton & E. R. Winkler (Eds.), *Ethics and Aging* (pp. 127-141). Vancouver: University of British Columbia Press.

Malette v. Shulman (1990), 67 D.L.R. (4th)321(Ont.C.A.).

Manitoba Law Reform Commission. (1990). *Discussion paper on advance directives and durable power of attorney for health care*. Winnipeg: Manitoba Law Reform Commission.

Meslin, E. M., & Abrahamsohn, G. (1991) The intellectual will: A model for eliciting values about medical treatment decisions. Presented at the Canadian Association of Gerontology, Toronto, Ontario, October 24.

Molloy, D. W., Clarnette, R. M., Braun, E. A., Eisemann, M. R., & Sneiderman, B. (1991). Decision making in the incompetent elderly: "The daughter from California syndrome." *Journal of the American Geriatrics Society*, 29, 396-399.

[Nova Scotia] *Medical Consent Act*, R.S.N.S. 1989, c.279.

[Oklahoma] *Natural Death Act*, Okla. Stat. tit. 63, 3101-3111.

Ouslander, J. G., Tymchuk, A. J., & Rahbar, B. (1989). Health care decisions among elderly long-term care residents and their potential proxies. *Archives of Internal Medicine*, 149: 1367.

Pawlson, L. G. (1991). Impact of the *Cruzan* case on medical practice. *Law, Medicine and Health Care*, 19: 69-72.

Pellegrino, E. D., & Thomasma, D. C. (1988). *For the patient's good: The restoration of beneficence in health care.* New York: Oxford University Press.

President's Commission for the Study of Ethical Problems in Medicine and Biomedical and Behavioural Research. (1983). *Deciding to forego life-sustaining treatment: ethical, medical and legal issues in treatment decisions* (pp. 139-141). Washington, DC: US Government Printing Office.

[Quebec] *Public Curator Act*, S.Q. 1989, c.54.

Quinlan [1976], 70 N.J. 10, 355 A.2d 647, cert. denied, 429 United States 922

Ramsey, P. (1970). *The patient as person.* New Haven: Yale University Press.

Reibl v. Hughes 1980 2 S.C.R. 880, 114 D.L.R. (3d) 1, 14 C.C.L.T. 1, 4 LL. Med. Q. 209, 33 N.R. 361, 14 C.C.L.T. 1.

Rivet, M. (1990). Allocation and rationing of health care resources: Patients' challenges to decision making. Presented at Canadian Institute for the Administration of Justice, Toronto, October 1990.

Robertson, G. (1991). Informed consent ten years later: The impact of *Reibl v. Hughes. The Canadian Bar Review*, 70: 423-447.

Robertson, J. A. (1991). Second thoughts on living wills. *Hastings Center Report*, 21: 6-9.

Rosovsky, L. E., & Rosovsky, F. A. (1990). *The Canadian law of consent to treatment.* Toronto: Butterworths.

Schneiderman, L. J., Jecker, N. S., & Jonsen, A. R. (1990). Medical futility: Its meaning and ethical implications. *Annals of Internal Medicine*, 112: 949-954.

Singer, P. A. & Hughes, D. L. (1991). Family physicians' attitudes towards advance directives. *Clinical Research*, 39: 416A.

Singer, P. A. & Lowy, F. H. (1991). Refusal of life-sustaining treatment, the *Malette* case, and clinical decision making under uncertainty. *Annals of the Royal College of Physicians and Surgeons*, 24, 401-403.

Singer, P. A. et al. (1992). The Center for Bioethics discussion paper on advance directives. *Canadian Medical Association Journal*, (in press).

Substitute Decisions Act, 1st Sess., 35th Leg. Ont., 1991.

Taylor, M. G. (1990). *Insuring national health care*. Chapel Hill, NC: University of North Carolina Press.

Thomasma, D. C., & Pellegrino, E. D. (1987). The role of the family and physicians in decisions for incompetent patients. *Theoretical Medicine*, 8, 83-292.

Uhlmann, R. F., Pearlman, R. A., & Cain, K. C. (1988). Physicians' and spouses' predictions of elderly patients' resuscitation preferences. *Journal of Gerontology*, 43: M115-121.

Weisstub, D. N., Chairman. (1990). *Enquiry on mental competency: Final report*. Toronto: Queen's Printer for Ontario.

Winkler, E. R. (1988). Foregoing treatment: Killing versus letting die and the issue of non-feeding. In J.E. Thornton & E.R. Winkler (Eds.), *Ethics and aging: The right to live, the right to die* (pp. 155-171). Vancouver: The University of British Columbia Press.

NOTES

1. In different jurisdictions, this is referred to as a Durable Power of Attorney for Health Care or Durable Power of Attorney for Personal Care.

2. This is especially interesting given that most advance directives refer to "family" within the body of the document. For example, the Concern for Dying document (1990) begins: "To my family, my physician, my lawyer and all others whom it may concern...." It goes on to indicate those upon whom the expressed wishes are to be binding: "By means of this document, which I intend to be legally binding, I direct my physician and other care providers, my family, and any surrogate designated by me or appointed by a court, to carry out my wishes."

3. This should not be confused with the proper place of emotion in decision making. We would expect families to become emotional about decisions to continue or forego medical treatment for a patient precisely because it is a family member.

PART III

Comparisons and Conclusions

CHAPTER 9
Conclusion
Carolyn J. Rosenthal and Jon Hendricks

Our overall purpose in compiling this volume was to sketch the political and economic underpinnings of domestic policies concerning older people and examine how these underpinnings circumscribe family connections. More specifically, we had four objectives. First, we wanted to link the individual experience of aging to the domestic policies and programs that constrain or enhance older people's lives. Second, we wanted to move beyond a focus on individual aging to the level of the family. Individuals do not age in isolation but rather as part of families. Looking at this in a broader perspective, individuals' aging is experienced not just by them but by their families. Therefore, we wanted to link the supposedly private domain of the family to the public domain of domestic policy, and to show what happens in the sphere of the family is shaped by the public domain. Third, we wanted to explore how ideologies are reflected in the national agenda and how the latter shapes the kinds of policies and programs that are put into place, and thus effects the lives of families. Finally, while not an explicit focus, we hoped the chapters would provide a perspective for future exploration of differences between the United States and Canada.

The various contributors to this volume are in agreement, the United States places greater emphasis on both the ideology of individualism and of familism than is true in Canada, but that the difference is one of degree. Thus, despite some notable differences, there are many similarities in domestic policy directions in the two countries. Moreover, the potential results of current policy directions are indeed similar. Key among these is the shift toward greater reliance on family care of the elderly which, as

McDaniel (Chapter 5), Neysmith (Chapter 6) and other contributors emphasized, means primarily care by women. This shift is occurring despite the concerns of scholars that this is neither viable nor preferable, whether one argues from a feminist, humanitarian, or pragmatic position.

In many respects, the various authors feel the differences between the United States and Canada are differences in emphasis—with the United States being more "extreme" in a number of respects. The ideology of individualism is more fundamental and strongly supported; the ideology of familism plays a stronger role in public policy formation; class differences are somewhat more pronounced, and each is cast as an appropriate, indeed a valuable component of the complex of values upon which the country was founded.

This book has not examined or contrasted the impact of two very different health care systems at the level of individual experience. One cannot help but speculate that there must be substantial differences in the quality of life. For example, while Canadians do worry about their financial security in later life, they do not, in our experience, worry much about what the financial impact of a serious illness would be. They do perhaps worry about long-term institutional care, but this has to do more with the specter of having to enter an institution as opposed to remaining in the community. Canadians worry about the quality of institutional care but not about the cost of such care. The cost of obtaining higher quality long-term care than is covered by government support may be a concern to older Canadians, but it does not seem to be one that is paramount. In contrast, one would expect that in the United States concern over the financial effects of serious illness would be a much more common and serious concern. If, as Hendricks and Hatch pointed out, one third of the citizens of the United States do not have any form of health insurance, or the life-time savings of the typical couple in the United States is insufficient to provide for little more than three months of care on a long-term basis, then, to the extent that those most affected realize their plight, the prospects could well be unsettling. In other words, one could speculate that Canadian adults of all ages have greater feelings of security about the future than do their counterparts in the United States. The absence of such concerns is in itself, an important dimension of the quality of life and individual or his/her family experience. Future research exploring this speculation and its more specific relationship to the two different health care systems would be invaluable in understanding the links between public policy and individual experience.

Although the book represents an attempt to address later life issues in general, it must be acknowledged that throughout most of the book health care has tended to cast a shadow over other issues. Despite the fact that the scholars represented in this volume do not subscribe to the disease model of old age, this model exercises an almost inexorable pull because it drives so much of the current policy debate. Matthews' point (Chapter 4) bears repeating here. As she argues, within families, older members are not viewed in terms of the disease model of aging but rather as people—who may happen to have medical problems.

One of the novel aspects of this book has been the inclusion of chapters on health care decision making at the end of life. This issue is one of growing interest in both Canada and the United States. Public awareness of the negative aspects of prolonging life through life-sustaining technology has grown. The specter of spending one's last days maintained by machinery is a haunting one. Not surprisingly, then, both countries have seen a growth of interest in and legislation concerning advance directives, though this has been slower to develop in Canada than in the United States. Nonetheless, both countries are developing legal precedents and in both countries extensive media coverage has made a few of these precedent-setting cases familiar to millions of people. As High and Turner deftly pointed out, while advance directives may initially sound like a fine idea, they are not without pitfalls. Interestingly, the very notion of advance directives merges with the ethic of individualism so prominent in the United States. The sobering argument of High and Turner is that current directions are moving family members further from the center of decision making, in direct contradiction to what most older people seem to prefer. Moreover, they argue that the burden of proof is now on families to show good faith. While this may be quite consistent with legal practice and technicalities, what it implies to the public is that families cannot be trusted to act in the best interests of their elderly members. Fuelled as well by publicity on elder abuse, we may be witnessing the development of a new myth about the dangers of family care for the elderly. Evidence, however, supports the view that in the vast majority of cases children do act in the best interests of their parents, and certainly this is what older people, on the whole, seem to believe.

Finally, while there is a danger that any reference we make here to current political events will make this book seem outdated long before its time, we must choose to take this risk. As this book goes to press, both the United States and Canada are facing public decisions that may take each country in directions that will have a profound impact on future policy and

human experience in the domains of aging and family life. In the United
States, the presidential election will be held shortly after we go to press.
The campaign has been marked by unprecedented attention to the family as
a social institution. Ideological stances have been blatant. The term "family
values" has been widely bandied about but the reference seldom included
the elderly. Its usage has directly contradicted the assumptions underlying
this volume and for this reason we feel it is worth briefly exploring the
term. While the phrase "family values" and all its connotations may fade
after the 1992 Presidential election (depending, perhaps, on which party
gets elected), we may predict with some confidence that it will return in a
new guise in the future. We say this because "family values" is merely the
ideology of familism dressed in new clothes. As both Clark (Chapter 1) and
Hendricks and Hatch (Chapter 2) pointed out, this ideology has long
undergirded social policy in the United States. In its current political usage,
the term "family values" connotes a highly conservative, traditional view of
the family with respect to structure and roles. The family is assumed to
consist of an employed husband, a wife whose primary responsibility is
caring for family members, and their children. Responsibility for care is
seen as lodged firmly within the family. Government interference, for
example by providing day care for children, is viewed as not only
trespassing on what is rightly the responsibility of the family, but indeed as
weakening the fiber of the family. "Family values" operates at three levels.
At one level, it has is morally prescriptive: families should have a particular
structure, there should be a specific gendered division of labor, and families
should provide for their own. The term thus points to what constitutes a
"good family." At another level, the concept suggests that typical families
do indeed fit this ideal description, or at least that those which do not are
deviant. All social ills may be blamed on deviating from this depiction of
the ideal, traditional family. By extension, people who do not "fit" into this
ideal get blamed for current social problems no matter how removed. In this
perspective, while it may be necessary, unfortunately, to have some
domestic programs such as welfare to deal with these "deviants", it is seen
as a great mistake to have policies which might "encourage" alternative
family forms. At the third, level, then, upholding "family values" means
separating family and state, private and public. We hope the chapters in this
book have demonstrated the fallacies of this ideological stance.

In Canada, an imminent nation-wide referendum on a new
constitutional accord has created a climate of enormous uncertainty about
the future social, political and economic structure of the country. If the

accord is approved, one result would be a move toward giving increased power to the provinces. What effect would such a shift of power have on social programs? As Clark mentioned in Chapter 1, earlier changes in federal-provincial transfer payments have led to speculations that medical care may become increasingly "provincialized" into a number of systems, embodying the principles of the current system. This would seem even more likely, should the provinces be granted more power and autonomy. The obvious risks of decentralization and the potentials for "patchwork" policies are ever present.

Conservative forces have not been restricted to the United States, although their impact to date has been less visible in Canada. Such forces, combined with difficult economic times, create a situation of great vulnerability for social programs that benefit families. The dearly held principle of universality has been eroded in the old age pension and family allowance programs. The old age pension while paid to everyone is now "clawed back" from higher income persons through taxation. The "family allowance" used to be paid to parents on a monthly, per-child basis. This program has recently been terminated. In its place, additional funding has been allocated to places where it is "more needed," such as supporting mothers on social assistance. Our point here is not to argue the merits or faults of such thinking. Rather, it is to point to a trend in which universality of domestic programs is being eroded. Nor is the climate in Canada particularly favorable for initiating programs that would support families. As an example, the Canadian government recently announced that it was shelving plans for a national day care program. While it is true that the country is in the midst of a crippling recession, it must also be recognized that such a program was not a high priority in the best of economic times. With the economic currents mandating two wage-earner families, the burden for childcare has been shifted to those couples who have children, but it would be a mistake to think the problem has gone away.

The chapters in this book furnish different perspectives on the linkages between domestic policy, individual life worlds, and families. When rhetoric is put aside, and data from many sources examined, the so-called separation of public and private spheres is quite clear. We can only hope that the future in both countries will see efforts made in the public sector which will indeed strengthen the family to the benefit of members of all ages. to assume the one functions independently of the other would be a grievous error.

INDEX